THE GUN DIGEST® BOOK OF
TACTICAL GEAR

Dan Shideler & Derrek Sigler

©2008 Krause Publications

Published by

Gun Digest® Books

An imprint of F+W Media, Inc.
700 East State Street • Iola, WI 54990-0001
715-445-2214 • 888-457-2873
www.gundigestbooks.com

Our toll-free number to place an order or obtain
a free catalog is (800) 258-0929.

Library of Congress Control Number: 2008925110

ISBN-13: 978-0-89689-684-0
ISBN-10: 0-89689-684-6

Designed by Tom Nelsen
Edited by Dan Shideler & Derrek Sigler

Printed in the United States of America

OTHER GUN DIGEST® & KRAUSE TITLES

STANDARD CATALOG OF® FIREARMS

GUN DIGEST®

GUNS ILLUSTRATED

STANDARD CATALOG OF® MILITARY FIREARMS

STANDARD CATALOG OF® SMITH & WESSON

STANDARD CATALOG OF® COLT FIREARMS

STANDARD CATALOG OF® REMINGTON FIREARMS

STANDARD CATALOG OF® WINCHESTER FIREARMS

THE GUN DIGEST® BOOK OF THE
AR-15 VOLUME 1

THE GUN DIGEST® BOOK OF THE
AR-15 VOLUME 2

THE GUN DIGEST® BOOK OF RUGER
PISTOLS & REVOLVERS

THE GUN DIGEST® BOOK OF THE GLOCK

THE GUN DIGEST® BOOK OF RIMFIRE RIFLES
ASSEMBLY/DISASSEMBLY

THE GUN DIGEST® BOOK OF AUTOMATIC PISTOLS
ASSEMBLY/DISASSEMBLY

THE GUN DIGEST® BOOK OF TACTICAL WEAPONS
ASSEMBLY/DISASSEMBLY

FLAYDERMAN'S GUIDE TO ANTIQUE FIREARMS
AND THEIR VALUES

Contents

Introduction

Welcome to The Gun Digest® Book of Tactical Gear.

Without a doubt, tactical gear is the fastest-growing segment of the sporting goods market. But is it entirely accurate to call tactical gear a subset of sporting goods? Perhaps not.

Within what we might call the sporting goods market, tactical gear has traditionally been considered a red-haired stepchild; to mix metaphors, neither fish nor fowl. For years, tactical gear manufacturers were not allowed to exhibit their goods at the nation's largest shooting-oriented trade show, the Shooting, Hunting & Outdoor Trades (SHOT) Show. This has changed in recent years – changed so much, in fact, that tactical gear is now probably the single largest segment of the SHOT Show.

What contributed to this dramatic reversal? Without a doubt, the largest single contributing factor was the 9/11 attacks. On that cold, clear morning, America's awareness of tactical matters reached a new peak, one from which it has not even begun to retreat. With the subsequent founding of the Department of Homeland Security, and the grant money it distributed to law enforcement agencies large and small across the country, tactical was suddenly "in." This trend was reinforced even further by our military involvement in Iraq and Afghanistan, where the dividing line between "tactical" and "military" became blurred.

It's a truism in the outdoors industry that where the government and armed services go, the civilian market soon follows. In the firearms industry, for example, AR-15 style rifles became fashionable, even for purely sporting purposes. Tactical knives and optics experienced a huge surge in popularity, even among those who themselves never got closer to actual tactical situations than the nightly news broadcast.

Another truism of the outdoors industry, however, is that equipment manufacturers are no dummies, and they were quick to realize that most tactical gear is of a "crossover" nature that gives it legitimate sporting or civilian application. To cite a humble example, there is actually such a thing as tactical underwear. It wicks body moisture and provides comfort at extremely high and extremely low ambient temperatures. A police sniper would no doubt appreciate these qualities, but then again so would the November deer hunter. Thus these "crossover" tactical products find homes among the military, law enforcement, and civilian communities.

In this book, we have attempted to provide a sampling of the tactical gear that is available on today's market. We have not attempted to be complete because of the staggering amount of tactical products that are introduced literally every week. We have, however, provided manufacturer's suggested retail or street pricing where available, but please be aware that this information is provided for comparison purposes only. Note also that the prices cited herein were accurate at the time the data was collected but might not stay that way. The tactical gear market is a very dynamic one.

Note also that some of the items appearing in this book are not available for civilian sales, and for reasons that appear to us to be pretty good. Bulletproof body armor, for example, is generally not available for civilian purchase for reasons that we hope are apparent.

If this book gives the reader a new awareness of the breadth of the tactical gear market, then it wil have succeeded in its purpose. Enjoy!

Dan Shideler & Derrek Sigler,

Editors

INTRODUCTION TO
Tactical Knifes

BY JAMES MORGAN AYRES

Note: We are delighted to start off the Tactical Knives section of this book with an essay by Jim Ayres. Mr. Ayres's experience speaks for itself, and we think that his comments deserve consideration. We think you'll agree.

"What is a tactical knife?" A friend asked me that question the other day and I had a hard time answering him. I checked two dictionaries and found these definitions:

tac·ti·cal *adj*
1. relating to or involving tactics
2. done or made for the purpose of trying to achieve an immediate or short-term aim
3. showing skillful planning in order to accomplish something
4. used or made to support limited military operations
5. undertaken or for use in support of other military and naval operations

tactical:
Of, relating to, or using tactics
Of, relating to, used in, or involving military or naval operations that are smaller, closer to base, and of less long-term significance than strategic operations.
Carried out in support of military or naval operations: tactical bombing.
Characterized by adroitness, ingenuity, or skill.

So, are we talking about knives that are used in support of military operations, or those that can be characterized as having the qualities of adroitness, ingenuity, or at least having features that would support such qualities? Possibly. Maybe. Sort of.

I first heard the term some years ago and have given the matter considerable thought. Although in a pinch any knife can be used for anything (we've all seen broken tips, proof that sharp points don't make for good screwdrivers) I would say that in general what we today consider a tactical knife differs from ordinary knives in that it is designed to be used in extreme situations. For, say, wilderness survival or to rip through a locked fire door, or to cut your way out of a car sinking in a river, or as an emergency weapon, sort of a combination utility, survival and emergency weapon.

In some ways this is nothing new. For centuries there have been knives that served these functions. What differs somewhat today is that we have designs focused on better fulfilling all those functions in one package and that will fit into our daily lives more comfortably than, say, a Roman Gladius, or a machete, which is a multifunctional blade (maybe a little long to be called a knife) and certainly tactical.

If we go back to, say, the Paleolithic or even the Neolithic we can see... Uh, no that's too far back.

The Roman's had... hmm no, still too far back. OK let's start with the modern world, say, the early sixties, a period that served as the foundation and testing ground for the concepts behind the tactical knives of today.

The impetus for the development of the tactical knife concept came from the changing needs of the individual solider, particularly of the paratrooper, who by the nature of his mission started work surrounded by the enemy, and especially the unconventional soldier whose mission was to combat guerillas by in effect becoming a guerilla. This mission required him to work in small units, in some cases alone, with no support from the "tail" that provides the necessities of life and battle to line soldiers.

In both instances, the paratrooper and the unconventional soldier, the knife was seen as a weapon of last resort, a daily all purpose tool, and if totally cut off, a survival knife. In the past, infantrymen were in close contact with a long supply chain and war was fought according to "lines" of enemy or friendly occupation. That started to change in WWII, in small deadly and effective actions in the Pacific Theatre and in the European Theater. By Vietnam it was clear that unconventional warfare would be the most effective method of engaging a dispersed and elusive enemy.

All this meant that we were going to rely on small unit warfare, and that individual soldier had a higher likelihood of being separated from their units. In addition they would need to operate for extended periods in small groups with no support or contact with their supply chain. Therefore, the survival knife concept began to loom large. The idea behind the survival knife was that in one relatively compact tool/weapon, that could be carried at all times, the soldier would have a tool/weapon that would allow them to rip their way out of a downed helicopter, build shelters, make primitive (and silent) food getting tools, traps, bows, spears, etc, and serve as a silent emergency weapon. The knife had to be rea-

sonably compact or it would not be carried; troops will discard anything that's not useful. It had to have day-to-day utility for the same reason. Specialized edged weapons were seldom used and often discarded. It had to be sturdy. It had to be maintainable under field conditions.

The military supply chain gave little attention to knives for the troops; battles were not fought with edged weapons and hadn't been for over a century. This was true but failed to take into consideration the fact that individual soldiers are not as concerned about the big picture as they are their own survival. Every combat soldier can visualize a hand-to-hand fight to the death wherein an edged weapon might well save his or her life. The soldiers aren't wrong to do so. Even in today's high tech warfare with batteries for various electronic devices weighing down rucksacks, blades can and do save lives.

Back then the Marines had their KaBar and the Army had bayonets. But the issue bayonets were of soft steel to withstand impact and virtually useless as utility knives. A few soldiers got their hands on KaBars and that was fine as far as it went. But it didn't go far enough for the needs of a new kind of solider. What was a paratrooper or an unconventional soldier to do? We bought our own knives.

I was at Smoke Bomb Hill (the home of Special Forces, the Green Berets) in the early sixties when these requirements were being defined. I also served with the 82nd Airborne Division during the same period. In our group we bought virtually every commercial knife available. All fell short on one way or another. We learned that there was nothing being currently manufactured commercially that met all of our needs in one package. Machetes were terrific tools for the tropics (awesomely destructive weapons also) but too large to carry at all times. The Scandinavian knives were good cutters but too weak to pry with and lacked hand guards, which are needed if the knife is to used as a weapon.

The KaBar was a pretty good utility knife and not a bad weapon, but the ones we used bent easily and had a tendency to break at the tang-blade intersection. Buck knives of that era were tempered very hard and would hold an edge. But they broke with very little sideways pressure. Gerber got a horse in

the race with its wasp waisted dagger, but that knife was modeled on the Sykes-Fairbarin dagger, a killing knife but not a utility or survival knife and so it had few takers, except among those who were impressed by it's looks. The general run of commercial hunting knives failed in one respect or another: they broke too easily, or didn't take or hold a good edge, or the designs were for skinning with upswept trailing points, in some cases all of the above.

During this period of relentless testing the Randall emerged as the knife. Randall knives were made in a semi-custom shop with a few highly skilled workers and operated by one man, W.D. "Bo" Randall. Randall's knives had gained acclaim during WWII and virtually every experienced NCO (Non-Commissioned Officer, i.e., sergeant) at SBH carried a leather sheathed Randall on his pants belt, not his equipment harness, so that the knife would stay with him if he became separated from his gear, the idea being was that habits developed in training stay with you in your AO (Area of Operations). The Model 14, Attack, was the choice of many; with its seven and a half inch Bowie style blade of quarter inch tool steel, overall sturdy construction and well thought out design it was a knife user's knife. So too was the Model 1, All Purpose Fighting Knife, a slimmer Bowie style blade with antecedents going back to World War II.

Both were used for making shelters, traps, bows, spears and other primitive weapons and tools, and in training for knife fighting and killing with the knife. In this combination of use they had no equals. The Model 14 was the stronger of the two, easily capable of slashing through helicopter skin or ripping a man sized hole completely through a barracks wall in under five minutes, as a certain fellow did one might after a sufficiency of whiskey and during a discussion of E&E (Escape & Evasion) methods. But we didn't manage to break a Model 1 either, and not for want of effort.

The Randalls were unique in their day. The designs were almost perfect. Forged of tool steel and tempered fairly soft, they were virtually unbreakable. The soft temper required them to be sharpened more often than some of the knives with a harder temper, but that was no problem because they were easy to sharpen, even under field conditions with a small stone. The Randalls hit the sweet spot, light enough to carry at all times in the AO, strong enough to withstand extreme use, capable of taking a razor edge, and highly functional as a utility knife or a killing weapon. We didn't call them tactical knives, never heard the term, but that's what they were. This nexus of need still today defines the fixed blade tactical knife of today.

One thing that became crystal clear (clichés, after all, have a reason for being) and remains true today: if a knife was not useful for everyday tasks it would be left behind. If it was too big or heavy it got left behind. Even then soldiers were burdened with massive amounts of ammunition, weapons, radios, personal items, sometimes amounting to over a hundred pounds Today's soldiers even more so with all the electronics and batteries to run them. Sometimes I think our troops might be more effective if we could get the Pentagon planners and contractors out of the game and let the guys in the field go back to a rifle, ammo, and a little food. And a good knife. Lighten their load and ease the mission. OK, sorry about the rant, back to tactical knives.

At that time folding knives were also important, but were not seen as being mission critical as was the fixed blade embodied in the Randall. There was an Army issue Shrade switchblade that had been in use since World War II, but they were in short supply and no new requisitions were being made. The Shrade had the virtue of opening with one hand, vital for a paratrooper entangled in his lines, equally so for countless other uses, but was not very strong and saw little use as a utility knife.

I carried mine secured by a lanyard in my left flapped and buttoned shirt pocket, where I could reach it with either hand while rigged in full jump gear. I had also found the "Black Cat" folder, one of the first, if not the first, front locking lockbacks. Made by Linder in Germany, the Black Cat was inexpensive, had decent steel in the blade, and was very thin. With a little practice I could get it open with one hand. I had flat slip sheaths sewn into the tops of my Corcoran jump boots and carried one in each boot, reasoning that if I were to break one arm in, say, a bad tree landing I could reach the other one. Later on I did the same with my jungle boots. The Black Cats were so light as to be unnoticeable. Linder still makes the Black Cat and you can buy them for about twenty bucks, a bargain in today's world.

With the Shrade I now had three small folders, none of which weighed more than a couple

able and quick to hand so they could be deployed in an emergency where an operative might have to "cut and run." Some carried single edged razor blades for the same purpose, a trick learned from criminals. There were also some "sleeve daggers" and a variety of small edged weapons in use with certain civilian clandestine operatives, all of which could be deemed tactical. Personally, I never carried any such knives while in civilian service. A stag handled folder was something anyone might have in his pocket and thus aroused no suspicion with border guards and foreign custom agents.

During that same period the Buck 110 was released and with its sturdy construction and needle sharp clip point became popular with about a million civilians and quite a few troopers in the 82nd. It never gained much of a following with Special Forces. SF soldiers work their blades hard, and the 110, at least the ones I worked with, still had the Buck flaw of being too brittle. And, for all its weight, it was not in practical use any stronger than the much lighter weight German lockbacks. Actually, the 110 was much too heavy to carry in a pants pocket, thus requiring a belt sheath, which then came into common usage across the country among military and civilians alike. But the folding knife in a belt sheath had no traction in my (admittedly small) crowd. The reasoning was: if you're going to have a belt sheath you might as well have a fixed blade which offered more utility by an order of magnitude. Also, in civilian service there were many reasons to not to be seen to have a knife and none to be so seen.

And there the matter of tactical knives stood for about a decade. Fast forward to the late seventies. Al Mar, a former paratrooper and SF soldier and a brilliant knife designer, started his own company. One of his first designs was called the Eagle, a handsome lockback, graceful, incredibly strong for its size and construction. Two of those replaced my stag handled lockbacks. Later I gave one away and the other just plain wore out after a decade of constant use. They were fine knives, and I'd love to have another of the out of production beauties, but essentially they were the same technology as the German lockbacks.

In the early eighties Al Mar (he was the artist of knife design of his era) worked with Colonel James "Nick" Rowe to create the first purpose designed Survival Escape Rescue & Evasion folding knife. Colonel Rowe was, and is, famous in the SF community, a true hero who survived five years of captivity during the war in Vietnam, and who escaped his captors on his own and was later picked up by a rescue chopper. Colonel Rowe was looking for something smaller and more carryable than any fixed blade. The result of their collaboration was the SERE, a heavily constructed folder that was meant to serve the cut off or isolated solider as his last ditch and only tool/weapon.

The SERE was a thing of beauty, as were all of Al's knives. In one of our conversations Al told me of his design education and how his artistic skills and vision were combined with his military experience in each of his knives. Al's company, Al Mar knives continues, but Al passed on some years ago, still a young man, and still unsurpassed as a knife designer. While the SERE was a leap forward it did not break new ground technologically speaking. In some ways the most important thing the SERE accomplished was to ignite a revolution in thinking with one simple question: can a folder replace a fixed blade? That question and concept drove the development and design of an entirely new class of knives: the tactical folder.

During the following decade folding knife design exploded. Dozens of variations on the theme were tried; many were discarded. One that was not, the liner lock, was reintroduced and repurposed by a custom knife maker, Michael Walker, and became a stand locking mechanism. Many believed the liner lock to be intrinsically stronger than the lockbacks. Others did not. The discussion continues today.

I first met Sal Glesser, the founder and CEO of Spyderco, at a gun show where he showed me three of his innovations in one small knife: the pocket clip, the opening hole in the blade and the serrated edge, all of which have become standards of the tactical folder.

Much creative energy came together during this period. Unless my memory fails me Bob Terzuloa was the first to bring together some of these elements in a folding knife that broke new ground. I bought one of Bob's first prototypes at a custom knife show, a titanium handled liner lock with a thumb stud and a blade of some high tech steel. It locked up more solidly than any folder I had ever seen. For the first time I thought that, maybe, the answer to the question, "Can a folder replace a fixed blade?" might be yes.

The explosion of creative energy through the custom knife community quickly spread to knife manufacturers and is still expanding today. We now have the strongest, most innovative folding knives the world has yet seen. Tactical folders in some ways now define the tactical knife both for military and civilians. Folders are purchased twenty to one to fixed blades. This is understandable. Few civilians will carry a fixed blade in their daily rounds. Most military people also elect the folder. This is due to the nature of the conflict zone, current strategy and tactics, changes in logistics and communications, and to the fact that today's folders can stand in for many functions formerly limited to fixed blades.

Over the past decade or so I have used and tested dozens, perhaps hundreds of what we now call tactical folders. Often testing included use by my students, including some teenagers who could break a bowling ball in a padded room. I have provided survival training free of change to many young people who pursue outdoor recreation. Most of them are city kids who have no idea how quickly things can go wrong in the wilderness. These kids have shown the value of the tactical folder by a number of means.

Influenced by fashion and social pressures as much as practicality, these kids totally refuse to carry a fixed blade while skiing, snowboarding, backpacking, white water rafting, hunting, fishing, or a dozen other outdoor activities that have the potential for disaster. They will, and do, carry a folder. With proper technique and training, and a good folder, these kids have built "One Hour Shelters" good enough to protect them, and me, from a winter storm in the Northwest. They've made rabbit sticks and fish traps and started fires with their folders and sparking rods. They have learned to survive and their tactical folders worked for them.

A Marine I correspond with used a CRK&T M16 folder to dispatch an enemy in the canals of Iraq. He said, "It was the only weapon I had and fast to get to." I have heard similar stories from other currently serving soldiers, Marines and covert opera-

development of the frame lock, an integral component of one of today's best known and highly regarded folders, the Sebenza. The Sebenza embodies minimalist industrial chic and is as much a work of modern art as a functional knife. Nothing needs to be added. Nothing can be taken away. I get the feeling that Mr. Reeve read the story about Michelangelo who when asked how he visualized a statue in a block of marble said that he just took away everything that wasn't the statue. The Sebenza is nothing but knife, one of the best.

Spyderco has kept to the forefront of the revolution they helped ignite. They have a number of excellent tactical designs, but the one that catches my fancy is their Military model. The Military is so slender it appears delicate. It is not. With its nested liner lock and attention to geometry the Military belies its appearance. I've loaned Militaries to my survival students and watched them baton their way through dozens of wrist thick saplings to make shelters with no damage to the knife. In some ways I think of the Military as today's Black Cat. Although the Military has a level of quality and strength I never dreamed of with the Black Cat, it has a similar slim profile and is a featherweight, lending itself to effortless carry in boot tops and certain unlikely places. It's also black.

Benchmade made its name with the Balisong, a high quality butterfly knife, something I saw quite a bit of when I was knocking around Southeast Asia and the Philippines. Les De Asis, the founder, established Benchmade as an industry leader, well know for innovation and quality. One of its newer models, the Ruckus, employs their AXIS lock and good blade geometry to make an exceptionally strong and useful tactical folder. Benchmade's range includes many good tactical folders.

The Zero Tolerance 0301 is not the knife with which to spread your Camembert at the wine tasting, unless shock and awe is your goal. The 0301 has all the subtlety of an Abrams tank crashing through your wall, and much of the strength, relative to folding knives. The other day I was at a film production company office and thought I'd have some fun. I took out the monster folder and said, "Hey guys check this out." As I did so I flicked the

tors. Their tactical folders work for them also.

Below I'll briefly comment of a few tactical folders and fixed blades. This small selection is in no way a complete overview of tactical knives today. For that you'll need to go to our sister publication, *Knives Annual*.

To evaluate this small selection we chopped up some 2x4s, cut stacks of cardboard (which dulls knives very quickly) made a hobo stove and in general put them through their paces. Every knife in the photos performed like the champs they are.

FOLDERS

Chris Reeve upped the strength ante with his

opener and the blade flashed open with an audible SNAP. One of the editors leaped out of her chair and shouted, "What the f*** is that?" You gotta love a knife that will produce that reaction in a seen-everything twenty-something blonde. The ZT also works. You could field-dress a Honda with it. Having field-dressed more than one Honda, and Subaru, in the pursuit of knife knowledge I know whereof I write. ZT has fielded a full range of folders and fixed blades all with the same consciousness and high degree of utility.

Columbia River Knife & Tool produces some of the best values in tactical folders today. Their M16, designed by former paratrooper Kit Carson (yes, that's his real name) is famous among the troops and is one of the most popular knives sold at the PX, and for good reason. Well designed and well executed, this model was the one used by the Marine I wrote of above.

Lone Wolf makes some excellent tactical folders. Unfortunately, the new models did not arrive in time for photos but I'm sure they have the same level of quality that last year's models did. One of my correspondents (a young Ranger newly home from the war) used his Lone Wolf to pry open file drawers in search of info on weapons of mass destruction. He did so because he didn't have a pry bar at the time and he was under fire from Jihadis in the next building. His unit had to get the files and get out before being overrun, which they did. The Lone Wolf suffered no damage. He still carries it today. (As a footnote, the files revealed much about Iraqi army field rations but nothing about WMD.)

Victornox, the world famous maker of Swiss Army Knives, now makes a number of models with locking blades, some of them with one handed openers, thereby qualifying them as tactical. While built too lightly for extreme use their newer models are in the pockets of almost every survival teacher I know, which is about the best recommendation I can offer. The photos show their new Rescue Tool complete with glass breaker and seat belt cutter, which cuts through seat belt webbing like it's thread.

What about today's fixed blades? Has the folder entirely replaced them? No.

However undeniable the virtue of today's folders, the very thing that makes them convenient to carry is also their greatest weakness: they fold. No folder can be made as strong as a fixed blade. It's a matter of physics. No matter how strong today's locks, and some of them are extremely strong, none can match the strength of a straight slab of well-tempered steel. Fixed blades can pry open doors and rip through materials that would cause the strongest folders to fold.

While all this development has been going on with folders fixed blades have also developed, not so much in basic design concepts as in formulations of steel and refinements of proven designs. In folders it's a different order of reality, as if the mothership landed and emissaries from another planet said," You need new folding knives." In fixed blades the changes have been evolutionary rather than revolutionary

Boker's Chad los Banos line is designed with defense in mind, but the little fixed blade did well being batoned through lumber and cutting its way through a couple of cans to make a hobo stove. As a defense blade, I like it. The handle is comfortable and snugs tight and secure in your hand. The recurved blade gets a lot of edge into not much room.

Chris Reeve makes bulletproof hollow handled fixed blades in a range from very large to fairly pe-

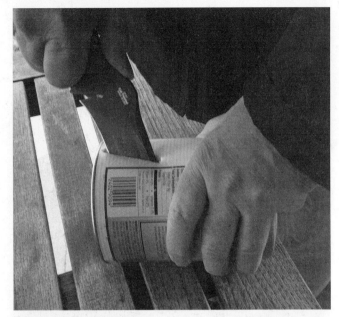

tite. He also makes the official knife awarded to those who graduate today's Q Course at the Special Warfare Center. It's known to the U.S. Army Special Forces as "The Yarborough" and to everyone else as "The Green Beret Knife." It is a no-nonsense, hardworking tool, designed by renowned knife maker and designer Bill Harsey, with function and manufacturing input from Chris Reeve.

Columbia River Knife & Tool also make good solid fixed blades at a price our guys in uniform can afford. Take a look at the photos to see their Dragon model in action. CRKT is also now making the Sting, a model designed by A.G. Russell some years ago, and named for Frodo's famous blade. The Sting is a dandy little dagger and comes with a forearm sheath secured with Velcro.

Fallkniven makes some of the best factory made survival knives now extant. I haven't seen a new model Fallkniven in some years, but for this article I dug out an old F1 from the bottom of my knife bag. The F1 is billed as a survival knife and fits the bill quite well; today we used it to make a hobo stove and batoned it though a pile of lumber. Yep. It's still good to go. Other makers could benefit from following Fallkniven's lead: clean design, convex grind, nothing to stop the knife getting through a cut.

Spyderco has quite a few fixed blades that fit into the tactical category; all of them are good knives, especially including the old Morans. But my favorite is the Fred Perrin, a small knife designed by the well-known French designer, martial artist and veteran of Special Operations: good flat grind, clean design, excellent quality.

The Perrin is almost the perfect covert operatives fixed blade: functional and efficient for everyday use, strong enough to punch through a plaster wall (I tried it) with no damage, light enough to carry anywhere – tucked in a sock, up a sleeve, on a cord around the neck, even in a pocket, and with the ability to take, and hold, an edge that will cut through denim like gauze.

Also, of critical importance, it is not black, which is a major plus. It is disarmingly pretty, which is a Good Thing. A fierce looking black knife with teeth and barbs will not get a cutting job done any better than a nicely finished knife such as the Perrin, and those teeth will likely hang up on clothing. What your black knife will do is attract the alarmed attention of anyone who sees it: passersby, customs officials, cops, dog walkers and bad guys. The Perrin looks like a polite picnic knife you can use to slice your baguette and spread your Brie without anyone raising an eyebrow. It will also do whatever needs to be done to help you escape those bad guys, or otherwise deal with them according to your mission and disposition.

Zero Tolerance fixed blades are solid, sophisticated designs, well made of high tech steel. The 0100 is quite swoopy in appearance. Its reverse curved blade cuts soft materials quite well but the thick bevels tend to hang up in wood. Still, it will do the job. The ZT 0121 is a sturdy bulldog of a fixed blade, with a very well shaped handle and the ability to pry open a locked steel gate, couldn't resist trying it, worked fine, no damage – to the knife. There's a nasty little hook at the choil. According to the factory literature it's a cord cutter designed to rip through 550-cord or wire insulation. What I know for sure is that it will rip through any loose clothing in its area, and the heel of your hand if you use a reverse grip. That said I like the handle design very much. Many knife designers seem to have the notion that longer is always is better in handles. But not so. If ZT ever decides to get rid of that wire/hand ripper and smooth out the design a little they will have a terrific covert knife, one handy enough for the civilian operative and strong enough to punch through walls and so fourth.

Clearly the new folders are an improvement over the old. How do the old fixed blade standards stack up against the newer designs, most of which utilize high tech steel and heat treat?

Well, if you look at the accompanying photos you'll see a rather plain looking fixed blade

with a wooden handle, nothing much new in the design, which is a variation on a very old design. The steel was taken from an industrial saw blade used for timber cutting, and then forged and tempered by Master Bladesmith Wayne Goddard, who has taught me more about sharp than anyone I've ever known. The genius is in the execution of the entire package: heat treat, convex grind, the subtlety of the curved blade.

This simple blade has outperformed every fixed blade that has been measured against it since I first got the knife in 1992. With proper technique it will slash though a three-inch standing sapling in two strokes. It slices meat like the best butcher knife, cuts through denim and rope like they were paper and will slice through a falling silk scarf when the edge is tuned up a little. It stays sharp for a looooong time and is easy to sharpen when the time comes. I've bent the blade to thirty degrees and it sprang back to true with no deformation. It cuts everything with ease. Isn't that a knife's primary purpose, to cut things? Around camp when there's job of tough cutting to do everyone who has once used it asks me for the loan of "Wayne's Knife."

In all fairness I'm writing about a custom knife made by one of the most respected Master Bla-

desmiths in the country today. It's not really fair to compare this kind of knife to a factory knife. I do so only to point out two things: there's little that's new under the sun in the design of fixed blades, and that there are today many smiths capable of making such a knife, and often at a cost similar to the best factory knives.

Gary Randall has taken over for his father, W.D. "Bo" Randall, and is carrying on the traditions. Unfortunately, Randall knives have become collector's knives today and are much prized by devotees of various cargo cults, which makes them hard to come by. I guess it's understandable, given all the mojo the Randall name conjures up. Collector's mania aside, Randalls are still made with good honest tool steel to time proven designs by men who care about their work and take pride in producing one of the most famous knives in the world. And they still work as well as they did forty years ago when I was a skinny kid at SBH.

A few years ago my middle son went off to a very advanced three month long survival school where he had to make his own shelter on arrival and had nothing to eat he didn't kill, catch, dig up or scrounge, except for a small sack of cornmeal and a few ounces of nuts given to him the first day. No guns allowed, not even when Brother Bear comes snooping around at night. He lost a few pounds but learned to kill, cook and eat everything from deer to tadpoles, cattails, possums and grubs. The graduation exercise was a weeklong float trip down the Green River - without the luxury of a canoe or a raft or a boat of any kind. My son tells me he became quite fond of his log during that week, and of the fish he caught on the line he trailed behind his log.

My 17-year-old son departed for this survival school with a leather hunting pouch over his shoulder containing some line and hooks, snare wire, flint and steel, a flat 3x5 inch aluminum box to be used as a cook pot and a few other odds and ends. The day before he left I gave him an old Randall Model One that I had modified and that the Randall shop had refurbished for me. That might give you some idea of how I feel about Randalls. If you buy a Randall, then for the sake of all the men who have carried them in harm's way, don't behave like a squirrel gathering nuts for the winter. Use the knife. Don't let it lay around gathering dust. Good knives want to be used. Failing to do so might cause them to get irritable and bite you the next time you pick them up.

Yeah, the old fixed blades are, in my not-so-humble opinion, as good as the new ones, but not the folders. Never would the old folders have done half what the new ones can do. The revolution in folders is a Good Thing because there are much betters odds that a person will have a folder than a fixed blade when fate come knocking.

There are dozens of other makers, both custom and factory, I haven't been able to mention due to lack of space, all worthy of mention. Bud Nealy, for example, makes terrific small fixed blades that meet every definition of tactical. We hammered one of his pretty little knives though the roof of a Honda and batoned it with a Maglight, cutting a hole you could crawl through with no blade damage whatever. And then there's… I could go one for another few hundred pages, but I have to stop now.

I have been privileged to witness the development of tactical knives over the past forty years. Many good men have come and gone during that time and this brief article doesn't begin to tell the whole story. There's a book here waiting to be written and maybe one day I'll write it.

Columbia River Knife & Tool

MAK 1 Knife and Extrik 8 R System: Realistic Tools for the SWAT Mission

BY SCOTT W. WAGNER

Boy do I hate reality checks! You've got a perfectly good fantasy about something going then WHAM! Someone dumps a reality check on you and then that perfectly good fantasy is ruined. I remember my very first law enforcement reality check. I was seated in my first police academy class in (I hate to admit it) 1980, and one of my favorite, highly respected instructors, a Vietnam combat veteran, was explaining actions to be taken when off duty. Pumped with excitement, I raptly listened, anticipating how I was told I would be jumping into the middle of the armed robbery we were discussing with my 5 shot .38 in hand and save the day. The fantasy was in high gear when the aforementioned WHAM! was delivered. The Sergeant said that often our best action was to stay outside and be a

good witness while trying to get someone to call for assistance from a payphone (uh, no cell phones in 1980). I was crushed as the bubble burst around me. Then something happened, a couple of hours, maybe days later I realized that the Sergeant was right (which is why I respected him in the first place) and that being a good witness WAS indeed the best course of action to take in that situation where no ones life was in immediate danger. Since that time I have probably broken just as many bubbles in the academy classes that I teach when the same topic comes up.

I say all that because I may be bursting some bubbles when I announce that I have found what I think to be the best SWAT knife ever designed (and it didn't start out as a SWAT knife), the Columbia River Knife and Tool MAK-1 (Multiple Access Knife) and Extrik-8-R Tool system. Before I talk about the knife let me go ahead burst this particular bubble. Everyone take a deep breath because here we go. What is the mission of the SWAT fixed-blade knife for American Law Enforce-

MAK-1 with sheath and Extrik-8-R. The sheath needs improvement, and paracord should be black, but the orange cord on the Extrik-8-R tucks into the pouch.

ment? Is it to allow us to silently eliminate posted sentries by cutting their throats for a quick bleed out? Is it to serve as a last-ditch weapon when our M4's and pistols both fail in extended firing, allowing us to continue the fight and to engage the terrorist hordes at bad-breath distance-or better yet knife-throwing distance? If you answered "yes" to either of the last two questions, you may be thinking of the military-type combat knife or current-issue bayonets for the M-4 weapon system, and you would be thinking wrong. So go ahead, recover and read on.

A SWAT knife is or should be a rescue tool, one designed to cut, to pry, to help force entry, to break out glass, to disable equipment that poses a hazard to us or others. I am embarrassed to say that it took a firefighter (James McGowan of Toronto, Canada) to figure out our mission for us, because he designed the knife as a firefighter rescue tool, but CRKT is discovering that the same tool has SWAT applications perhaps beyond the initial fire/ rescue applications originally envisioned.

Well, all this sounds great, but where is that bubble bursting WHAM! thing? Here it is, the MAK-1 does not have a pointy end, rather, it comes with a chisel wedge tip that is not as sharp as the blade's cutting surface. That's the first thing that makes this blade distinctively different. The 3Cr13 stainless steel blade is designed to do one of the things we use our fixed and folding blades for the most, to pry stuff open, like windows, doors etc. And when we do those things with our standard blades, what happens? We break the tip because we are using a fighting knife to do hand tool work, not the killing or even animal skinning work that it was designed for. And now reality sets in. How often do you really need that tip on your fixed blade for a SWAT mission? With the MAK-1, if you do need a pointy end, the top edge of the blade ends in a 90 degree point as it meets the front edge of the chisel. That front edge could be sharpened in to a more significant cutting surface while still being useful for prying.

Speaking of prying, the next quality of the MAK-1, one which makes it ideal for this task is the thickness of the blade, which for most is the second thing you notice after the chisel tip. The blade thickness from the spine of the knife to where the bevels for the cutting or prying surfaces begin is almost ¼ inch. By comparison, the Smith & Wes-

Smith and Wesson Search and Rescue Knife alongside the MAK-1. The sheath on Smith and Wesson is polymer and locks the knife firmly in place, plus contains slot for thigh tie down.

son Search and Rescue Knife, a takeoff on the original Ka-Bar WWII design measures 1/8 th of an inch think and it is a pretty stout knife.

As we move down the MAK-1 we see that there is a rounded ridge finger choil at the bottom of the blade and a rounded ridge surface on the spine. There is no hilt-type guard. These areas allow for different hand positioning on the grip depending on the task you are performing. The cutting edge is plain, not serrated, for easy sharpening and measures 3 inches in length, while the overall blade length is 5 inches. In contrast the Smith & Wesson SAR knife has a 6-inch blade.

At the far end of the knife, beyond the grooved G10 grip scales (which have large screws holding them in place to allow for easy removal of the scales for cleaning the blade surface) is the uniquely shaped pommel end. This end is notched to allow for use as a wrench to undo automotive battery cables (firefighter thing) or to put over the top of a partially open automobile side window, and with a push, break the window (firefighter or police thing). Break car windows, you say? To really facilitate that there is a carbide window breaker tip at the end that might come in very handy on a hostage rescue or a suspect that has barricaded himself in a car, or when rescuing someone actually trapped in a car. Completing the MAK-1 is a lanyard hole at the end wherein there WAS a rescue orange paracord lanyard that was removed before carrying the MAK-1 for SWAT duty. The rescue mission is so enhanced by this knife system that the Columbus Police Department Rescue Dive Team ordered MAK-1's as soon as they saw them. The team views the knife as much more useful than the standard dive knives that they were using, even though the MAK-1 wasn't originally designed as a diving knife.

Let me tell you that if you accept what the mission of the fixed blade SWAT knife really is, this is just the tool for the job! But there is more.

I mentioned the Extrik-8-R tool. The Extrik-8-R is a stainless steel unit that serves primarily as a

Standard Bowie type point vs. MAK-1 Chisel. For the Law Enforcement SWAT mission, the MAK-1 is far more useful.

safety seat belt cutter. It has a sharp, recessed curved cutting surface that makes it darn near impossible to injure those being rescued, something entirely possible when the tension is high and time is tight and you are using a standard cutting blade. The Extrik-8-R completes the tool kit by also having an emergency Phillips screwdriver tip on one end (flat and angled inward to fit a variety of sizes) and a flat blade tip at the lanyard end. It also has a built in wrench for turning standard oxygen bottles off and on. The Extrik-8-R conceals neatly in a pocket on the front of the Cordura nylon sheath supplied with the MAK-1. The MAK-1 can be purchased without the Extrik-8-R, but I would recommend having both.

The 727 Counter Terror Training Unit at Columbus State has adopted the MAK-1 and Extrik-8-R as its standard rescue knife and tool. We felt it was ideal to fulfill mission requirements that SWAT teams might encounter while assaulting buses, trains and aircraft, needing to gain access without having room for cumbersome breaching equipment. This is especially true because the areas where a tool like the MAK-1 might be needed tend to be relatively thin-skinned. Also having a tool

The MAK-1 is SWAT mission capable.

with an oxygen wrench on it seemed like a handy thing to have around aircraft oxygen bottles, and the window punch would certainly be helpful on bus or automobile assaults.

Is there anything I would change about the MAK-1? Yes a few things that have been mentioned to CRKT. First, I think the sheath should be upgraded to Kydex from nylon and be MOLLE capable, with extensions for thigh carry. Second, there needs to be a protective cap on the carbide tip as it is possible to get poked with it on a standard belt carry position (not badly poked mind you, just enough to notice, and only when seated) unless you get a leg-drop extender. Third, for SWAT use, the blade could be black coated, (although I will use mine as is), and finally for the SWAT version, include black paracord. Other versions could be done in Desert

or OD (I am sure these will come down the pike), with maybe orange G3 handles for the rescue and dive version. If dropped while diving, that would make it a lot easier to find.

The MAK-1 is, in my opinion, one of the greatest LE knives to hit the market in a long time, although it wasn't aimed at the tactical market initially. It also shows that we can take some lessons from our brothers and sisters in the fire/rescue services since our missions really do overlap. Will the MAK-1 replace my Smith and Wesson for Tactical use? Yes, it already has. But the Smith and Wesson still makes an outstanding outdoors survival knife (different mission than rescue) and will still find plenty of use outside. The MAK-1 from Columbia River Knife and Tool retails at $79.99, the Extrik-8-R retails at $29.99.

KNIVES

Blackhawk/Nightedge

Blackhawk/Silent Partner

Boker/Subcom FB

NIGHTEDGE BY BLACKHAWK

Designed by renowned custom knifemaker Allen Elishewitz, the Nightedge is a full-sized fixed-blade knife inspired by the popular MOD Nightwing. Its serrated back edge optimizes the knife's utility and combat potential by providing a secondary edge suitable for heavy cutting, back cuts, and draw cuts. This unique grind also produces a reinforced point for extreme tip strength and penetration. To make this dramatic design more affordable to field soldiers on a budget, the Nightedge is ground from tough 1085C high-carbon tool steel and coated with a non-reflective, corrosion-resistant black epoxy coating. Each Nightedge comes equipped with a plastic-lined ballistic nylon sheath.

Specifications:
- **Blade Length:** 5.900"
- **Overall Length:** 10.900"
- **Blade Material:** 1085C high-carbon tool steel
- **Blade Finish:** Black epoxy coating
- **Edge type:** Partially serrated
- **Handle Material:** Thermoplastic rubber with textured panels
- **Sheath:** Plastic-lined foliage green ballistic nylon

Price: $149.99

SILENT PARTNER BY BLACKHAWK

Designed by noted custom knife maker Howard Viele, the Silent Partner combines the compactness of a gentleman's pocketknife with the strength and reliability of a purpose-designed tactical tool. Built on a framework of solid stainless steel handles and textured G-10 handle slabs, its blade locks open via a rugged integral frame-lock mechanism. Its hollow-ground drop-point blade is precision machined from tough 440C stainless steel and features both an ambidextrous thumb stud and an index finger "flipper" to ensure rapid and reliable one-handed openings.

Specifications:
- **Blade Length:** 3.200"
- **Overall Length:** 7.750"
- **Blade Material:** 440C stainless steel
- **Blade Finish:** Bead-blasted matte finish
- **Edge type:** Plain or partially serrated
- **Handle Material:** Stainless steel with textured G-10 scales
- **Pocket Clip:** Right side tip-down carry

Price: $59.99

BOKER BO012 BOKERPLUS FIXED BLADE SUBCOM FB

The Subcom FB fixed blade will stand up to any and all of the competition. This formidable workhorse has a blade

**Boker/Armed Forces
Tactical Tanto Fixed Blade**

**Boker/U.S. Army
Ranger Folder**

Boker/Tactical Camo II

length of 2 3/8" and an overall length of 5 1/2". Made of bead-blasted 440C stainless steel, this Boker USA production piece sports index ramps for secure grip. Kydex sheath is adaptable to a number of carry positions. At a little over 3 ounces, this compact and beefy fixed blade is the only security that you will need.

Everyone knows the so-called PX Shops that you can find on U.S. military bases all over the world. U.S. soldiers can buy additional equipment, like knives, privately. Aside from the regular manufactured brand knives, the ARMED FORCES develops some special models that perfectly fit the needs and requirements of the fighting soldiers. Titanium nitride coated 440C stainless steel blades provide the best edge-holding ability, ideal for rugged field use. The handles are made of solid G-10, which will hold up even under rigorous field use. A deep checkering prevents slipping of the handles.

Price: $69.95

BOKER BO216 BOKERPLUS ARMED FORCES TACTICAL TANTO FIXED BLADE

The first time you grab the handle of this knife, you will know that it will withstand harsh field use. The 7 1/3" tanto blade has a chisel grind and is partially serrated. Sturdy Cordura sheath included. Overall length: 13". Weight: 12 2/5 oz.

Price: $69.95

BOKER 01RY1444B U.S. ARMY RANGER FOLDER

The Rangers are the elite warriors of the U.S. Army. This knife was made to honor these special troops. The rust resistant 440 stainless steel blade features a partial serration, and the black titanium coating gives the knife a perfect camo finish. Includes pocket clip. Blade length: 3 5/8". Overall length: 8 5/8". Weight: 4.8 oz.

Price: $24.95

BOKER 01YA119 TACTICAL CAMO II

The popular camo pattern for urban areas. Modified Bowie blade made of 440 stainless steel and a metal handle with camo finish. Liner locking mechanism. Includes pocket clip. Blade length: 3 7/8". Overall length: 8 7/8". Weight: 5.3 oz.

Price: $19.95

BOKER MAGNUM TI-MARINER DIVING KNIFE

The Boker Magnum Ti-Mariner Diving Knife was developed by knife designer Dietmar Pohl and German deep sea diving champion Jens Honer. Several design revisions and steel and titanium prototypes have been produced to create the ultimate rustproof cutting tools for divers. The Ti-Mariner diving knife is made of a single piece of Grade 5 Alpha-beta-titanium that inhibits the formation of salt crystals on the handle. This Boker Magnum diving knife

Boker/Chad Los Banos Trance Black

Boker/Throwing Knife

Boker/RBB Tanto

is compact and lightweight enough to be attached to the forearm, with a handle large enough to fit a neoprene gloved hand comfortably.

The Boker Magnum Ti-Mariner diving knife has a 4" part serrated double edge blade made of rustproof Grade 5 Alpha-beta-titanium, with micro-serrations to the tip. The handle, drilled to lessen weight, has texture notches for secure grip, and an integral cross guard. A multifunctional Kydex sheath with leg/arm straps is included. The Ti-Mariner diving knife has an overall length of 8", and weighs 2.8 ounces.

Price: .... N/A

BOKER 01BO592 CHAD LOS BANOS TRANCE BLACK

This Chad Los Banos design fashionably combines a functionally powerful AUS-8 blade with an ergonomically shaped handle made of fi ber reinforced nylon. Features a tactical black coated blade, stainless steel frame lock and pocket clip. Blade length: 2 3/4". Overall length: 6 1/4". Weight: 3.2 oz.

Price: $44.95

BOKER MB125 THROWING KNIFE

8 3/8" overall length, made of tough 420J2 stainless steel, this thrower will provide many years of service at a terrific price. Includes black nylon belt sheath. Knife alone weighs 3.9 ounces.

Price: $8.95

BOKER RBB TANTO, BK-BO54

The Reality Based Blade was designed by world famous knife fighting expert Jim Wagner. The illustrated Boker Knife is the Boker RBB Tanto Knife that features a 3 1/4" serrated tanto blade made of 440C stainless steel. The blade of this Boker knife has a non reflective black coat and a notched spine. The black coated aluminum handle, 4 1/4" closed, has textured finger grooves and a notched spine for secure grip, a push button lock and a lanyard hole. A clip kit with glass breaker clip and false writing pen clip for mounting at the butt end is included with this Boker knife. The Boker RBB Tanto Knife has an overall length of 7 1/2" when open, and weighs 3.5 ounces.

Please note: the slider lock on the back of the handle has no function, and this knife is manual action, not a switch blade.

Price: $56.97

BUCK 151 MAYO KAALA

Lightweight, convenient and easily accessible. This ultra-smooth, slim profile, fixed-blade knife is designed to be light, fast and agile. It features top quality S30V stainless steel with lightening holes and a fitted sheath to wear around the neck. Made in USA.

Price: $105.00

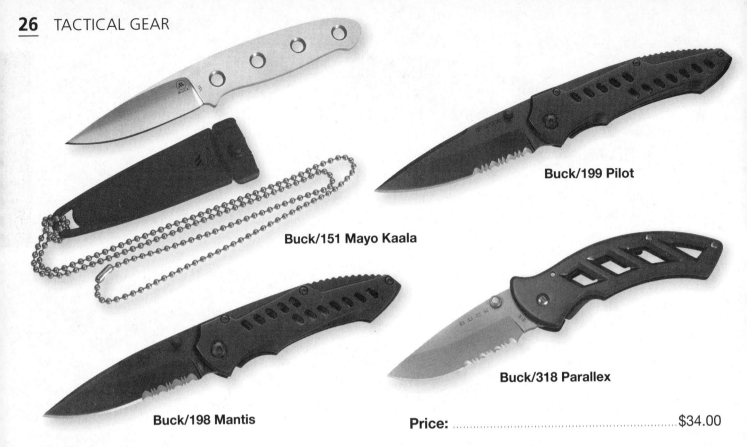

Buck/199 Pilot

Buck/151 Mayo Kaala

Buck/318 Parallex

Buck/198 Mantis

Price: $34.00

BUCK 198 MANTIS

Lightweight, compact and one-hand opening. A fully cloaked folder with frame-lock design, lightening holes and grip ridges.

Price: .... $ 39.00

BUCK 199 PILOT

Lightweight, reliable and one-hand deployment. A full-sized, fully cloaked folder with frame-lock design, lightening holes and grip ridges for easy handling.

- **Blade Length:** 3 3/4" (9.5 cm)
- **Blade Material:** 420HC Stainless Steel
- **Blade Serrated:** Yes
- **Coated:** Yes
- **Handle Material:** Stainless steel with lightening holes and grip ridges, Black Oxide coated
- **Length Closed:** 4 1/2" (11.4 cm)
- **Locking:** Yes
- **One Hand:** Yes
- **Weight:** 4.2 oz. (119.6 g)

Price: $45.00

BUCK 318 PARALLEX

Strong, versatile and heavy-duty. Slightly larger than the 316, the 318 Parallex® comes with a partially serrated blade for more aggressive cutting needs.

BUCK 650 NIGHTHAWK

Rugged, reliable and durable. A full-sized, fixed blade knife with dramatic, ergonomically designed two-tone non-slip grip handle. Made in USA.

- **Blade Length:** 6 1/2" (16.5 cm)
- **Blade Material:** 420HC Stainless Steel, Black Oxide coated
- **Fixed Blade:** Yes
- **Handle Material:** Reinforced molded nylon, rubberized grip
- **Weight:** 10 oz. (284.7 g)

Price: $80.00

BUCK 655 SHORT NIGHTHAWK

Rugged, reliable and durable. A compact, fixed blade knife with dramatic, two-tone non-slip grip handle. Made in USA.

- **Blade Length:** 4 7/8" (12.4 cm)
- **Blade Material:** 420HC Stainless Steel, Black Oxide coated
- **Blade Serrated:** Yes
- **Fixed Blade:** Yes
- **Handle Material:** Black/Olive, reinforced molded nylon, rubberized grip
- **Weight:** 9.4 oz. (267.6 g)

Price: .... $ 74.00

Buck/655 Short Nighthawk

Buck/870CM Bones

Buck/860 BK Hartsook Ultralight

BUCK 870CM BONES

Lightweight, reliable and dual deployment options. This hightech frame-lock knife has a skeleton frame, a Tiger Stripe camo blade with a 2-hand deployment groove and a handle with lightening holes and grip orientation points. Lanyard hole for easy attachment.

- **Blade Length:** 3" (7.6 cm)
- **Blade Material:** 420HC Stainless Steel
- **Blade Serrated:** Yes
- **Handle Material:** Stainless steel with Tiger Stripe camo
- **Length Closed:** 4 1/2" (11.4 cm)
- **Locking:** Yes
- **One Hand:** Yes
- **Weight:** 4.4 oz. (125.3 g)

Price: $34.00

BUCK 860 BK HARTSOOK ULTRALIGHT

Extremely lightweight, compact and easily accessible. This ultra-slim, compact, fixed-blade knife features top quality S30V stainless steel in low-profile Black Oxide. It is designed for wearing primarily around the neck for easy access.

- **Blade Length:** 1 7/8" (4.8 cm)
- **Blade Material:** Black oxide S30V
- **Fixed Blade:** Yes
- **Handle Material:** S30V skeleton with

black oxide coating and lanyard hole
- **Quantity:** Yes
- **Upgraded Steel:** Yes
- **Weight:** 0.5 oz. (14.2 g)

Price: $37.00

BUCK 871 GHOST RIDER

Strong, reliable and dual deployment options. This hightech tactical folder with liner lock has a durable and nearly indestructible G10 handle. The Tiger Stripe camo blade has a 2-hand deployment groove and angled handle with finger groove and grip orientation points for easy handling. Lanyard hole on knife for easy attachment.

- **Blade Length:** 3" (7.6 cm)
- **Blade Material:** 420HC stainless steel, tiger stripe camo
- **Blade Serrated:** Yes
- **Handle Material:** Textured G10
- **Length Closed:** 4 3/4" (12 cm)
- **Locking:** Yes
- **Weight:** 5 oz. (146.7 g)

Price: $44.00

BUCK 872 BK/872 CM SANDMAN

Strong, reliable and dual deployment options. This military style tactical folder has a 2-hand deployment groove on the blade and a liner lock with a curved handle with

Buck/871 Ghost Rider

Buck/873BK Iceman

Buck/872 BK/872 CM Sandman

Buck/759RD Metro

finger groove and grip orientation points for easy handling. Lanyard hole on knife for easy attachment.

- **Blade Length:** 3 3/4" (9.5 cm)
- **Blade Material:** 420HC Stainless Steel, Black Oxide coated
- **Blade Serrated:** Yes
- **Handle Material:** Anodized aluminum, Black
- **Length Closed:** 5" (12.7 cm)
- **Locking:** Yes
- **One Hand:** Yes
- **Weight:** 4.7 oz. (133.8 g)
- **Price:** $38.00

BUCK 873BK ICEMAN

Strong and reliable with dual deployment options. This folder has a liner lock with a curved handle featuring grip orientation points for easy handling. Lanyard hole for easy attachment.

- **Blade Length:** 3 1/2" (8.9 cm)
- **Blade Material:** 420HC Stainless Steel, Black Oxide coated
- **Blade Serrated:** Yes
- **Handle Material:** Black anodized aluminum, inlayed textured rubberized grip
- **Length Closed:** 5" (12.7 cm)
- **Locking:** Yes
- **One Hand:** Yes

- **Weight:** 6.3 oz. (179.4 g)
- **Price:** $40.00

BUCK 759RD METRO

Small, convenient and multi-purpose. This compact knife has numerous features including a small blade, a bottle and soda can opener and can be easily attached to a key ring.

- **Blade Length:** 1 1/8"(2.9 cm)
- **Blade Material:** 420J2 Stainless Steel
- **Handle Material:** Anodized Aluminum, Red
- **Length Closed:** 2 3/8" (6 cm)
- **Locking:** Yes
- **One Hand:** Yes
- **Weight:** 1.5 oz. (42.7 g)
- **Price:** $23.00

BUCK 297BK SIRUS

Quick, easy, one-hand deployment. An assisted-opening knife with patented ASAP Technology® and unique designs for a variety of personalities. Convenient belt clip for easy carry and a safety lock prevents the blade from accidentally opening. Made in USA.

- **Assisted Opening:** Yes
- **Blade Length:** 3 1/4" (8.3 cm)
- **Blade Material:** 420HC Stainless Steel
- **Handle Material:** Anodized Aluminum in Black with machined handle grooves

Buck/297BK Sirus

KA-BAR/5552 Fin Folding Hawkbill Tanto

KA-BAR/1219 Full-Size USMC

- Length Closed: 4 1/2" (11.4 cm)
- Locking: Yes
- Weight: 3.9 oz. (111 g)

Price: $98.00

KA-BAR 5552, 5553 (SERRATED), AND 5554 FIN FOLDING HAWKBILL TANTO

Designed by Peter Janda, the FIN Folders are stout while maintaining a thin profile. The frame lock design ensures the blade will stay locked in open position even when gripped in a fist.

- Weight: 0.35 lb.
- Lock Style: Frame lock
- Blade length: 2-3/4", Overall length 6-7/8"
- Grind: Hollow
- Shape: Hawkbill Tanto
- Handle Material: Stainless Steel
- HRC: 57-59 CR
- Edge Angle: 15 Degrees
- Steel: AUS 8A SS
- Country Manufactured: Made in Taiwan
- Pocket Clip: Yes

Price: $84.09

KA-BAR 1214 FULL-SIZE BLACK KA-BAR, SERRATED EDGE

A partially serrated edge makes cutting looped and synthetic materials a breeze. Blade marked 1211.

- Weight: 0.66 lbs.
- Blade length: 7", Overall length 11 3/4"
- Grind: Flat
- Shape: Clip
- Handle Material: Kraton G
- HRC: 56-58
- Edge Angle: 20 Degrees
- Butt Cap /Guard: Metal/1095 Carbon
- Steel: 1095 Carbon
- Country Manufactured: Knife Made in USA, Leather Sheath Made in Mexico

Price: $92.17

KA-BAR 1219 FULL-SIZE USMC KA-BAR, SERRATED EDGE

The most famous knife in the World gets updated with a serrated edge to better cut synthetic and looped materials.

- Weight: 0.68 lbs.
- Blade length: 7", Overall length 11 7/8"
- Grind: Flat
- Shape: Clip
- Handle Material: Leather
- HRC: 56-58
- Edge Angle: 20 Degrees
- Butt Cap /Guard: Metal/1095 Carbon
- Steel: 1095 Carbon
- Country Manufactured: Knife Made in USA, Leather Sheath Made in Mexico

Price: $79.46

BLACK KA-BAR 1249 KUKRI MACHETE

Surviving the toughest field testing, the Kukri boasts excellent test results in chopping and basic field use.

KA-BAR/1276 Heavy Bowie

KA-BAR/1477 TDI Law Enforcement Knife

- **Weight:** 1.26 lbs.
- **Blade length:** 11 1/2", Overall length 17"
- **Grind:** Hollow
- **Shape:** Kukri
- **Handle Material:** Kraton G
- **HRC:** 52-54
- **Edge Angle:** 20 Degrees
- **Steel:** 1085 Carbon
- **Country Manufactured:** Made in Taiwan

Price: $66.08

KA-BAR 1276 - 12-5/8" HEAVY BOWIE AND 1277 - 14-1/4" HEAVY BOWIE

Extra-thick blades measuring .236" (6mm) make these knives almost as rugged as pry bars. The Heavy Bowies will perform well at chopping, digging, cutting, and in other tough applications.

- **Weight:** 0.8 lbs.
- **Blade length:** 7-3/8", Overall Length 12-5/8"
- **Grind:** Flat
- **Shape:** Bowie
- **Handle Material:** Kraton G
- **HRC:** 55-57
- **Edge Angle:** 20 Degrees
- **Steel:** 1085 Carbon
- **Country Manufactured:** Made in Taiwan

Price 1276: $66.08

Price 1277: $69.57

KA-BAR 1477 & 1480 TDI LAW ENFORCEMENT KNIFE

In extreme close quarters encounters where a suspect is attempting to take an officer's handgun, or an officer can-

not access his handgun, the TDI knife is available as a "last option" knife. When worn on the pant belt the entire unit - knife and sheath - is well concealed. Designed by John Benner, founder and owner of Tactical Defense Institute.

- **Weight:** .18 lb.
- **Blade length:** 2-15/16", Overall length 5-5/8"
- **Grind:** Hollow
- **Shape:** Drop Point
- **Handle Material:** Zytel
- **HRC:** 57-59 CR
- **Edge Angle:** 15 Degrees
- **Steel:** AUS 8A SS
- **Country Manufactured:** Made in Taiwan

Price: $51.30

KA-BAR 1478 - TDI LDK (LAST DITCH KNIFE)

With an overall profile about the size of a credit card, this knife can be concealed just about anywhere. Pin it under a tactical vest strap, hang it around your neck, or carry it in your wallet. This backup knife is intended to be readily available as your "Last Ditch" attempt at defense when all other weapons have been removed. Sold with a hard plastic friction sheath and black cord.

- **Weight:** 0.05 lb
- **Blade length:** 1-5/8", Overall length 3-5/8"
- **Grind:** Flat
- **Shape:** Drop Point
- **HRC:** 58-59 CR
- **Edge Angle:** 15 Degrees
- **Steel:** 9Cr18 ss
- **Country Manufactured:** Made in China

Price:...$20.94

KA-BAR 3070, 3071, 3074, 3075 – WARTHOG FOLDERS

Straight blade, serrated, tanto, and serrated tanto Modestly sized folder that fits well into a pocket.

KA-BAR/1478 TDI LDK (LAST DITCH KNIFE)

KA-BAR/3070 Warthog Folder

KA-BAR/6002 K2 Tactical Folder

Kai/ZT Knives/0100

- **Weight:** 0.25 lbs.
- **Lock Style:** Liner lock
- **Blade length:** 3-1/16", Overall length 7-1/2"
- **Grind:** Hollow
- **Shape:** Warthog
- **Handle Material:** G10
- **HRC:** 56-58 CR
- **Edge Angle:** 15 Degrees
- **Steel:** DIN 1.4116 ss
- **Country Manufactured:** Made in China
- **Pocket Clip:** Yes

Price: $16.94

KA-BAR 6002, 6003 – K2 TACTICAL FOLDER

Affordably priced liner locking folders are made with Teflon coated stainless steel blades, G10 handles, and pocket clips.

- **Weight:** 0.3 lb
- **Lock Style:** Liner lock
- **Blade length:** 3-1/2", Open length 8-3/8"
- **Grind:** Hollow
- **Shape:** Warthog
- **Handle Material:** G10
- **HRC:** 50-52
- **Edge Angle:** 20 Degrees
- **Steel:** 3Cr13 ss
- **Country Manufactured:** Made in China
- **Pocket Clip:** Yes

Price: $18.62

KAI/ZT KNIVES 0100

Fixed blade military knife designed by KAI's Ken Onion. Unique blade style is designed for multi-tasking, minimal mass, and maximum performance. Offers ideal leverage for tough cutting situations and precisely centered point for piercing tasks.

- **Steel:** CPM3V tool-steel with Tungsten DLC coating
- **Handle:** 3D machined, G-10 in matte black
- **Blade Length:** 5-3/4 in. (13.6 cm), .190 in. thick
- **Closed Length:** N/A
- **Overall Length:** 10-1/2 in. (26.7 cm)
- **Weight:** 11.4 oz.

Price: $295.00

KAI/ZT KNIVES 0121

Fixed blade military knife designed by Strider. The Tungsten DLC coated laser machined blade features full-tang construction and the Ranger Green G-10 handles are 3-D machined for a superior grip in all weather conditions. Includes a cord cutter located on the choil of the blade.

- **Steel:** S30V stainless-steel with Tungsten DLC coating
- **Handle:** Handle information not available for this product.
- **Blade Length:** 4-1/4 in. (10.8 cm)
- **Closed Length:** N/A
- **Overall Length:** 8 in. (20.3 cm)

KAI/ZT Knives 0150

KAI/ZT Knives 0200ST

KAI/ZT Knives 0200

- **Weight:** 9.1 oz.
- **Price:** $235.00

KAI/ZT KNIVES 0150

Fixed blade military boot knife designed by Tim Galyean. The PVD coated laser machined blade features full-tang construction, a blood groove and the matte black G-10 handles are 3-D machined for contour and a superior grip in all weather conditions. Finger groove notches on the tang provide an excellent purchase. Includes a MOLLE compatible multi-position Kydex® sheath for belt, boot or tactical vest.

- **Steel:** S30V stainless-steel with PVD coating
- **Handle:** Handle information not available for this product.
- **Blade Length:** 3-5/8 in. (9.2 cm)
- **Closed Length:** N/A
- **Overall Length:** 7.5 in. (19.0 cm)
- **Weight:** 3.6 oz.
- **Price:** $150.00

KAI/ZT KNIVES 0200

Same multi-task Ken Onion design as the 0100, but in a compact folding knife. 3/8-in. hex head pivot shaft nut makes field adjustments possible with minimal tools. Ambidextrous thumb stud or index-finger protrusion for one-handed opening.

- **Steel:** 154CM stainless-steel with Tungsten DLC coating

- **Handle:** 3D machined, G-10 in matte black
- **Blade Length:** 3-7/8 in. (9.8 cm)
- **Closed Length:** 5-1/4 in. (13.3 cm)
- **Overall Length:** N/A
- **Weight:** 7.7 oz.
- **Ambidextrous Opening**
- **Locking Liner**
- **Coating**
- **Thumb Stud**
- **Pocket Clip**
- **Price:** $160.00

KAI/ZT KNIVES 0200ST

Same multi-task ken Onion design as the 0100, but in a compact folding knife. 3/8-in. hex head pivot shaft nut makes field adjustments possible with minimal tools. Ambidextrous thumb stud or index-finger protrusion for one-handed opening.

- **Steel:** 154CM stainless-steel with Tungsten DLC coating
- **Handle:** 3D machined, G-10 in matte black
- **Blade Length:** 3-7/8 in. (9.8 cm)
- **Closed Length:** 5-1/4 in. (13.3 cm)
- **Overall Length:** N/A
- **Weight:** 7.7 oz.
- **Ambidextrous Opening**
- **Locking Liner**
- **Serrated**
- **Thumb Stud**
- **Pocket Clip**
- **Price:** $160.00

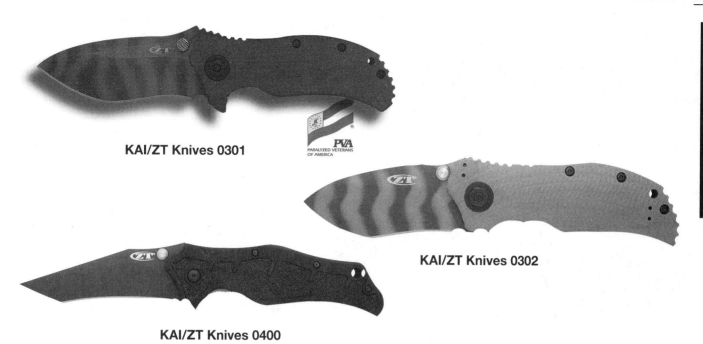

KAI/ZT Knives 0301

KAI/ZT Knives 0302

KAI/ZT Knives 0400

KAI/ZT KNIVES 0301

Folding knife co-designed by KAI's Ken Onion and Strider. Features SpeedSafe® assisted opening system. 3/8-in. hex head pivot shaft nut makes field adjustments possible with minimal tools. Ambidextrous thumb stud or index-finger protrusion for one-handed opening.

- **Steel:** S30V stainless-steel with Tungsten DLC coating with Tiger Stripes
- **Handle:** 3D machined, G-10 and Titanium
- **Blade Length:** 3 3/4 in. (9.5 cm)
- **Closed Length:** 5 1/4 in. (13.3 cm)
- **Overall Length:** N/A
- **Weight:** 8.6 oz.
- SpeedSafe
- Ambidextrous Opening
- Frame Lock
- Coating
- Titanium
- Thumb Stud
- Pocket Clip

Price: $295.00

KAI/ZT KNIVES 0302

Folding knife co-designed by KAI's Ken Onion and Strider. Features SpeedSafe® assisted opening system. 3/8-in. hex head pivot shaft nut makes field adjustments possible with minimal tools. Ambidextrous thumb stud or index-finger protrusion for one-handed opening.

- **Steel:** S30V stainless-steel with Tungsten DLC coating with Tiger Stripes
- **Handle:** 3D machined, G-10 and Titanium
- **Blade Length:** 3 3/4 in. (9.5 cm)
- **Closed Length:** 5 1/4 in. (13.3 cm)
- **Overall Length:** N/A
- **Weight:** 8.6 oz.
- SpeedSafe
- Ambidextrous Opening Frame Lock
- Titanium Coating
- Thumb Stud
- Pocket Clip

Price: $295.00

KAI/ZT KNIVES 0400

Folding blade knife designed by Kershaw's Ken Onion. Features SpeedSafe® assisted opening system, Trac-Tec handle inserts for sure grip, and modified Tanto blade. 5/16-in. pivot shaft adjustment enables tighter or looser blade deployment. Ambidextrous thumb stud or index-finger protrusion for one-handed opening.

- **Steel:** S30V stainless-steel with Tungsten DLC coating
- **Handle:** Machined, aircraft aluminum, black anodized
- **Blade Length:** 3 5/8 in. (9.2 cm)
- **Closed Length:** 5 in. (12.6 cm)
- **Overall Length:** N/A
- **Weight:** 5.3 oz.
- SpeedSafe
- Ambidextrous Opening
- Locking Liner
- Thumb Stud

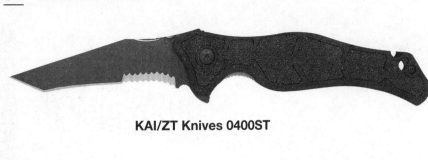

KAI/ZT Knives 0400ST

- Pocket Clip

Price: $150.00

KAI/ZT KNIVES 0400ST

Folding blade knife designed by Kershaw's Ken Onion. Features SpeedSafe® assisted opening system, Trac-Tec handle inserts for sure grip, and modified Tanto blade. 5/16-in. pivot shaft adjustment enables tighter or looser blade deployment. Ambidextrous thumb stud or index-finger protrusion for one-handed opening.

- **Steel:** S30V stainless-steel with Tungsten DLC coating
- **Handle:** Machined, aircraft aluminum, black anodized
- **Blade Length:** 3 5/8 in. (9.2 cm)
- **Closed Length:** 5 in. (12.6 cm)
- **Overall Length:** N/A
- **Weight:** 5.3 oz.
- **SpeedSafe**
- **Ambidextrous Opening**
- **Locking Liner**
- **Thumb Stud**
- **Pocket Clip**

Price: $150.00

ONTARIO KNIFE SPEC PLUS

Ontario Knife is a major supplier of Military Knives. Spec Plus® represents our original vision of the next generation of military/sporting knives. Features include comfortable handles manufactured with a Kraton® polymer or Gnvory®, 1095 epoxy powder-coated carbon steel blades, full tang construction, wide, razor sharp edges, combination leather/cordura sheaths. Made in the USA.

SP2 - Air Force Survival
- 5 1/2" Blade, 10 5/8" Overall
- 3/16" Blade Thickness

Price: $39.99

SP4 – Navy
- 6" Blade, 11 1/8" Overall
- 3/16" Blade Thickness

**ONTARIO KNIFE
ASEK™ Survival Knife**

Price: $40.99

SP 6 – Fighter
- 8" Blade, 13 1/8" Overall
- 3/16" Blade Thickness

Price: .... $ 44.99

SP8 – Machete
- 10" Blade, 15 1/8" Overall
- 1/4" Blade Thickness

Price: $55.99

SP17 – Quartermaster
- 6" Blade, 11" Overall
- 3/16" Blade Thickness

Price: $54.99

SP19 – Taskforce
- 7 3/8" Blade, 12 3/8" Overall
- 1/4" Blade Thickness

Price: $56.99

SP25 USN-2
- 5" Blade, 9 1/2" Overall
- .187" Blade Thickness

Price: $44.99

SP26 USN-3
- 5" Blade, 9 1/2" Overall
- .187" Blade Thickness

Price: $45.99

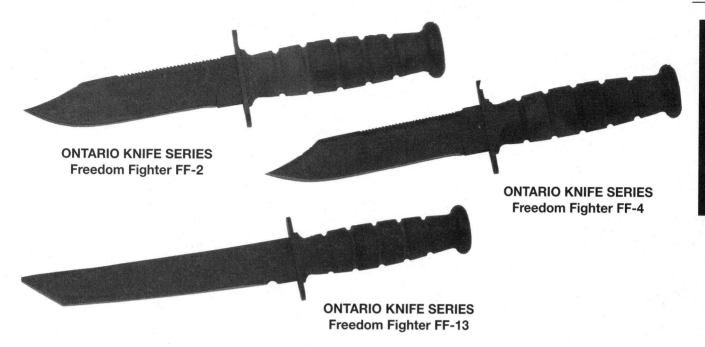

ONTARIO KNIFE SERIES
Freedom Fighter FF-2

ONTARIO KNIFE SERIES
Freedom Fighter FF-4

ONTARIO KNIFE SERIES
Freedom Fighter FF-13

ONTARIO KNIFE ASEK™ SURVIVAL KNIFE

The ASEK™ Survival Knife System designed and manufactured by The Ontario Knife Company is the one and only Survival/Egress knife chosen by the Untied States Army to be included in its Air Warrior Equipment System. Don't be fooled by imitations - This is the only ASEK™ Survival Knife Systems tested and approved by PM Soldier and Natick Research Labs to meet the criteria defined by the US Army. This system is a Survival/Egress Knife with Plexiglas Breaker, Hammer, Saw teeth, serrations, spear holes, lanyard hole and insulated guard. It comes with an anodized aluminum strap cutter to cut webbings, cord, cloth, etc. It has a screwdriver and a honing rod to keep your knife field sharp. The fire retardant scabbard fits on the pilot's vests, load bearing equipment, web belt, belt or can be worn on the calf as designed for Air Warrior. The strap cutter fits in the left leg pocket on flight suits and is a must for medical crews. Each part of the system can be ordered individually.

- 1095 carbon steel blade
- .1875" thick; 5" blade; 10 1/4" overall length
- Hardness Rc 50-54
- Zinc phosphate finish to inhibit rust

Price: $182.10

ONTARIO KNIFE FREEDOM FIGHTER SERIES

The features of this new series include: Comfortable handles made with Kraton®; 1095 texture epoxy powder-coated carbon steel blades; texture-coated steel safety guard & threaded butt cap; combination leather/Cordura® sheath. Made in USA.

FF2 - Freedom Fighter Survival
- 5 1/2" Blade
- 10 5/8" Overall

Price: $78.60

FF4 - Freedom Fighter Navy
- 6" Blade
- 11 1/8" Overall

Price: $78.60

FF12 - Freedom Fighter Tanto 6
- 6" Blade
- 11 3/8" Overall

Price: $78.60

FF13 - Freedom Fighter Tanto 8
- 8" Blade
- 13 1/8" Overall

Price: $78.60

ONTARIO KNIFE RTAK-II

In 2002, Ontario Knife Company entered into an exclusive collaboration with the professional survival training team Randall's Adventure & Training (RTAK).

The Randall's Adventure & Training knives have a full flat grind and 57-58 Rc hardness. The handles feature Micarta ergonomic handle slabs for increased grip when wet. The handle slabs are attached to a full tang and secured with stainless steel screws. Each knife also features an extended pommel with lanyard hole.

ONTARIO KNIFE /RAT Folder
Satin Black/Plain Edge

ONTARIO KNIFE /RAT Folder
Satin Black/Serrated Edge

ONTARIO KNIFE /RAT Folder
Black Blade/Plain Edge

RTAK-II
- 1095 Carbon Steel Blade
- Zinc Phosphate Finish
- 10" Blade
- 17 1/8" Overall
- Blade-.1875" Thick
- Black Linen Micarta Handle
- Ambidextrous sheath with gear pocket and lashing holes

Price: $164.20

ONTARIO KNIFE RAT-7 AND RAT-7 SERRATED

The RAT-7 knife was developed by the Ontario Knife Company in collaboration with its designer, Randall's Adventure and Training, a professional survival team, and is not associated with any other knife manufacturer.

NSN: 1095-01-523-1972
- 1095 Carbon Steel Blade
- Zinc Phosphate Finish
- 12" overall length
- 6.5" cutting edge length
- Blade: .1875" thick
- Thumb grooves in spine
- Green Canvas Micarta Handle
- Cordura® Sheath with gear pocket and Kydex® blade liner

Price: $165.74

ONTARIO KNIFE RAT™ MODEL 1

Built for the field, the RAT is carried by US forces in Iraq and Afghanistan. Now it's a folder for everyday carry!

- Blade length: 3.25"
- Overall length: 8.6"
- Closed length: 5.0"
- Blade material: AUS8
- Blade Hardness: 57–59Rc
- 4-Position Pocket Clip
- Reversible thumb stud
- Open-Post construction
- Hardened stainless steel liners
- Heavy-duty liner lock
- Weight. 5 oz.
- Shipping Weight: 0.37 lb / 0.17 kg

Price: .... $41.72-$46.76

ONTARIO KNIFE RAT-3 KNIFE D2 STEEL

The RAT-3 D2 tool steel knife is a fully concealable sheath knife designed for law enforcement, military and outdoorsmen. A compact full flat grind 3.3" blade for excellent slicing and cutting efficiency. Grooves along the spine offer a secure grip. The full tang extends into ergonomic black linen Micarta® handle slabs.

- Blade length: 3.3"
- Overall length: 7.8"
- Blade material: D2 Tool Steel
- Blade Hardness: 58–60Rc
- Thickness: .125"
- Handle: Black linen Micarta®
- Textured gray finish.
- Handle hardware: Stainless Steel
- Molded Blade:Tech sheath easily adapts to rigs commonly used by military and law enforcement.

ONTARIO KNIFE /RAT-5
Plain Edge

ONTARIO KNIFE /RAT-5
Serrated Edge

- Sheath: Molded Blade-Tech
- Sheath available in three colors
- Multiple lashing holes allow additional carry options
- Wearable as a neck knife
- Made in USA.
- Shipping Weight: 0.62 lb / 0.28 kg

Price: $106.18

ONTARIO KNIFE RAT-5™ BUSH/SURVIVAL KNIFE

Designed by Randall's Adventure and Training, the RAT-5 is a midrange knife of choice for outdoorsmen and military professionals worldwide!

- Blade: 5"
- Overall 10.75"
- Thickness: .1875"
- Metal: 1095c Steel
- Hardness: 57-58 Rc
- Flat Ground
- Black Zinc Phosphate Finish
- Thumb Grippers On Spine
- Generous Choil
- Plain Edge
- Handle: Canvas Micarta
- Skull-crusher Pommel
- Lanyard Hole
- Sheath: Molle-compatible Cordura® With Kydex® Blade Liner
- Accessory Pouch
- Made In USA
- Shipping Weight: 0.37 Lb / 0.17 Kg

Price: $145.88

ONTARIO KNIFE U.S. MILITARY ISSUE KNIVES

These rugged military issue knives have been serving our U. S. Military soldiers for over 50 years. Each knife is manufactured in accordance with U.S. Government specifications.

M-9 Bayonet with Scabbard; NSN: 1095-01-277-1739

- **Blade length:** 7" Blade
- **Overall length:** 12 1/8"
- **Thickness:** Blade-.235"
- **Blade material:** 420 Modified Stainless
- **Milled Saw-teeth on Back**
- **Black Oxide non-reflective finish**
- **Fits M16 Rifle**
- **Textured Thermoplastic Nylon Handle**
- **Scabbard**
- **Thermoplastic Nylon**
- **Wire Cutter & Screwdriver**
- **Equipped with a quick release Military-style Holster**

Price: $182.10

ONTARIO KNIFE M10™ BAYONET WITH SCABBARD

It's mighty convincing when viewed from the pointy end—and it never runs out of ammo! World War II, Korea, Vietnam, the Falklands, Somalia, Iraq…the bayonet has "Been There, Done That." This new design, made with quality materials and attention to detail in its construction. Made for M-16, M-4, and AR-15 rifles, and doubles as a utility knife.

- Blade length: 7"
- Overall length: 12.125"
- Blade thickness: .235"

SOG/Bi-Polar BP-1

SOG/Flash II Camouflage Handle

- **Blade Material:** 1095 carbon steel with a black zinc phosphate finish
- **Milled saw teeth on blade spine**
- **Handles:** Brown ergonomically designed grooved handles of glass-reinforced nylon
- **MOLLE-compatible Slim Line hard sheath included**
- **Hole in the blade works with scabbard as a wire cutter**
- **Made in USA**
- **Weight:** 10 oz.
- **Shipping Weight:** 1.62 lb / 0.73 kg

Price: $163.38

SOG BI-POLAR BP-1

The Bi-Polar is very capable. It's the first dual assisted knife with twin blades. Using patented SOG Assisted Technology™, each blade is propelled out once the operator has initiated the blade opening action. It might be the perfect rescue knife, whether used by law enforcement, emergency medical personal or in your garden releasing the grip of a tenacious vine. The Bi-Polar is the perfect combination of might and right with main blade, patent pending V-Cutter, and glass breaker. The V-Cutter will easily cut seatbelt material, paracord, fishing line, strip most types of wire, zip electrical cable sheathing, open packages, cut nylon banding straps, etc. Dual blades, double lockbars and twin safeties all work to lock the blades closed or double lock the blades open.

Price: $145.00

SOG FLASH II (CAMOUFLAGE HANDLE) CFSA-98; CTFSA-98; FLASH II (DIGI CAMO 1/2 SERR - BLACK TINI); DFSA-98

The Flash family of knives features SOG Assisted Technology™ (S.A.T.), which employs a powerful piston lock that is easily released with a sliding button.

The Flash II (Camouflage Handle) comes standard with camouflage Zytel™ handle and 1/2 serrated, Satin finish blade. The Flash II (Digi Camo - Black TiNi) comes standard with ACU camouflage Zytel™ handle and black TiNi 1/2 serrated blade/clip/pivot. All Flash knives come standard with SOG's patent pending, reversible bayonet mounted clip that ensures the lowest, most discreet carry possible. We also had the foresight to incorporate an additional safety lock that gives added security when the blade is closed.

Price: .... $78.00 - $94.00

SOG DAGGERT 1 (BEAD BLASTED) D25B; DAGGERT 2 (BLACK TINI); D26T

The challenge was to create a new breed of extreme fixed blades... suitable for today's modern military, capable night and day, wet or dry, and able to be carried in a variety of ways. The Daggerts easily answer this call with contemporary solutions and have been tuned and tweaked for performance at every level.

Price: .... $130.00 - $175.00

SOG SEAL PUP ELITE (STRAIGHT EDGE BLACK TINI) E37S

The SEAL Pup Elite is SOG's high performance edition to the SEAL family of products. Sometimes... we just "have to have" more horsepower, the racing suspension, and every available option including sunroof. All kidding aside – the SEAL Pup Elite is serious business and carries on the tradition of supplying the world's elite military forces.

Features include:
- **Thicker steel stock (.185)**
- **Hardcase Black TiNi blade**
- **Newly designed longer ergonomic handle with deeper finger grooves**

SOG/SEAL Pup Elite Straight Edge Black TiNi

SOG/Fusion Battle Ax

- New blade shape with longer cutting edge
- Added blade spine rasp for notching, filing, and thumb placement
- Injection molded glass reinforced handle scored with grip lines

Price: $120.00

SOG FUSION BATTLE AX F02T

SOG's modern battle/throwing ax evokes its origins from medieval times, which some might consider to be the present. Whether used as a target ax, SWAT tool, universal back up, or hung above the fireplace, it is very effective. The pike in the back is upswept for better target penetration. Size and heft are balanced for optimum swing control. The handle is sculpted from heavy duty black Pakka wood and the entire solid blade is protected with SOG's Hardcased coating. Nylon sheath included

Price: $55.00

SOG FUSION JUNGLE PRIMITIVE (BLACK) F03T

For the primitive in all of us. When the only thing that separates you from them is your equipment, it better be good. Using SOG's Hardcased black coating, the Jungle Primitive is durable and comfortable with a molded Kraton handle that features Digi-Grip™, a way to guarantee gripping power where you need it. One can instantly turn the Primitive into a small machete, limb saw, or hammer. Includes a Nylon sheath with utility pouch.

Price: $62.00

SOG FUSION THROWING KNIVES F04T

These stylized knives are not only fun to sail through the air, they are practical as well. Completely protected by SOG's Hardcased black coating, they are extremely scratch resistant. Their balance, aerodynamics, and proportions make them great throwing knives. For the same reasons they also make great back-up field knives. Wrap the handles with paracord or use as is and you have three knives for the price of one! Includes nylon sheath that safely carries all three.

Price: $55.00

SOG FUSION SALUTE (BLACK OXIDE) FF-11

Take the machined G10 handles in combination with scalloped full-length steel liners for a whole new look. Add a big lockback, smooth as silk operation, and a proven Bowie style blade. For good measure, throw in our new invention- a movable thumb stud so you can tailor the position to your own hands. SOG didn't forget to incorporate their trademark low carry bayonet clip either.

Price: $50.00

SOG FUSION FULCRUM I FL-10

This new concept in throwing knives allows precise adjustment of the balance point for more accuracy and helps improve your technique! The Fulcrum knives are styled after traditional throwing knives and perfect for backyard competitions. Available in two sizes with black oxide coating.

Price: $32.00

SOG FUSION FIXATION BOWIE FX-01

Among other things, SOG has a reputation for produc-

SOG/Meridian - Topo M46

SOG/Fusion Micron

SOG/Fusion Fixation Bowie FX-01

ing some of the finest production fixed blades in the world. Now they have developed along with military consultants an even more economical choice with the Fixation series. Seamless fits between blade and cross guard, wrap-around checkered handles, blade grooves, thumb notches, spanner nuts, and crossguard cutouts all say this knife is as distinctive as you are. Great balance and proportion make these knives very agile.

Price: $50.00

SOG MERIDIAN - TOPO M46 AND M46T

SOG continues to delight with innovation and forward thinking to bring you products that make you stand out, products that are as individual as you are.

Features include:
- Patented SOG Assisted Technology™
- Pass through lock bar
- Safety locks open & closed
- Satin finished blade
- Upswept blade design
- Wave-like grip surface
- Ambidextrous design
- Also available in Black TiNi finish.

Price: ....$100.00; TiNi finish for $125.00

SOG FUSION MICRON

This tiny beauty is crafted from high quality stainless steel and designed to be carried on a key ring or stashed in your pocket. It's a SOG so you know the Micron is built to last and is going to be there when you need it.

Price: $18.00

SOG GOV-TAC (BLACK TINI) S21T

The Gov-Tac transcends the competition with double precision ground grooves, thumb control ridges, and an extremely thick blade. Other features include:
- An instinctual new handle shape with bold diamond checkering and scored with grip lines
- Signature washer construction that has never before been accomplished with a molded Kraton rubber grip handle
- SOG's low-reflexive Hardcased™ TiAlN coating on blade, pommel, and crossguard
- A proven blade style that is robust with flat ground bevels and precision ground grooves
- Stainless steel sculpted crossguard and pommel (capable of being used as a field hammer)
- Weighted and balanced for perfect control
- Also available in a Bead Blasted finish- SOG Gov-Tac (Bead Blasted)

Price: $175.00

SOG ACCESS CARD SOGAC75

Now you can carry a SOG knife in your wallet, as a money clip, in your pocket or virtually anywhere. The new SOG Access Card lives up to its name as it is slim enough to carry among your credit cards and provides easy Access to an array of everyday essentials.

The SOG Access Card is crafted with elegant slim-line stainless steel which is not only aesthetically appealing, but also exceptionally durable. So light and sleek, it is both comfortable to hold and carry. The uniquely sculpted 2.7"

**SOG/Access Card
SOGAC75**

SOG/TAC-ST-02 Automatic

SOG/TAC-ST-03 Automatic

blade opens swiftly and smoothly with one-hand and is securely locked into place with SOG's revolutionary Arc-Lock. Its stout clip provides multiple attachment options or will securely hold your bills! This futuristic knife is further distinguished for its secret Access to a handy tweezers, small screwdriver and pick that are hidden within the handle. With so many advantages, this is definitely an accessory you won't want to be without!

Price: $65.00

SOG SOG-TAC AUTOMATIC (BLACK TINI) ST-02; (HALF SERRATED) ST-03; SOG-TAC AUTO (TANTO BLACK TINI) ST-04

The SOG-TAC is an invigorating new design that looks like nothing else. It is big but relatively slim and is specifically designed for action. Blade travel is definitely fast and once open it locks up like a floor safe. The machined 6061T6 hard-anodized aluminum is inset with G10 type textured inlays. There is also: a safety button that double locks the blade in the open/closed position, our reversible bayonet style clip and a gorgeous upswept blade. Available with a standard blade, a serrated blade and a tanto-style blade.

Price: $175.00

SOG FLASH II (ALUMINUM HANDLE - BLACK TINI BLADE) STGFSA-98

The Flash family of knives features SOG Assisted Technology™ (S.A.T.), which employs a powerful piston lock that

is easily released with a sliding button. The Flash II (Aluminum Handle- Black TiNi) comes with black TiNi coated 1/2 serrated blade/clip/pivot, and hard-anodized 6061-T6 aluminum handle. All Flash knives come standard with SOG's patent pending, reversible bayonet mounted clip that ensures the lowest, most discreet carry possible. We also had the foresight to incorporate an additional safety lock that gives added security when the blade is closed. Note that when the safety shows red...

Price: $140.00

SOG TIGERSHARK 2.0 TE-01; TIGERSHARK ELITE TE-02

The Tigershark is instantly recognized for its signature handguard and defensive rear point, which are removable for a more streamlined look. But it is also familiar as the largest member of the SEAL series with precise grind lines, scalloped back edge, touch point checkering, and superior ergonomics. The Tigershark is capable of chopping and slicing with an economy of scale and ferocity not available to smaller knives. Still, it's impeccable balance and style create fluidity in the hand that is unexpected and thrilling.

NOTE: Hand guard and rear point are packaged separately and are also removable at any time.

Price: .... $185.00 - $240.00

SOG TRIDENT (BLACK TINI) TF-1; TF-3 TIGERSTRIPE

The SOG Trident uses their well-proven means of delivering a knife blade to the open position with S.A.T. (SOG Assisted Technology™) Now using our patent pending Arc-Actuator™, the Trident locks stronger and releases easier.

SOG/Team Leader TL-01

SOG/Tigershark 2.0 TE-01

SOG/Revolver - SEAL TREV-7

There is also a built-in safety to lock the blade closed. When it shows red, you are ready to go.

What also makes the Trident so unique is the patent pending Groove™ in the handle, which allows the operator to cut paracord, fishing line, etc., without having to open the blade.

The Trident's blade is an evolution as well. Taking key elements from previous blade shapes created a distinct hybrid of form and function. Digi-Grip™ has a variable patterning creates a coarser grip in areas that will require it. The bayonet style clip is easily switched for right/left hand carry or removed for pouch storage.

Price: $110.00

SOG TEAM LEADER (DURATECH™ 20CV) TL-01

The Team Leader exemplifies the exceptional with incredible balance and streamlined aesthetics. What you might not sense when you first pick up this work of art is how exotic the steel is. This is one of the first production knives to be manufactured from DuraTech™ 20CV, a powder metallurgy stainless tool steel. Also available in AUS-8 stainless.

Price: $275.00

SOG REVOLVER - SEAL (BLACK TINI) TREV-7

The SEAL Revolver comes standard with a new look in blade shape that is not only functional, but distinctive. A survival saw serves as a backup in the handle. The blade features a forward thumb rest for increased dexterity and downward pressure. A glass-reinforced Zytel handle hides the stainless steel liners which ensure strength and quality. And as always, SOG edges are razor sharp.

Whether you're camping or crusading, why not pack twice the capability with the SEAL Revolver? It just might transform your idea of what a knife should be. The SOG black TiNi SEAL Revolver was recently chosen to be a part of the Personal Enviromental Protective Survival Equipment (PEPSE) system for Special Operations Forces deployed in cold weather conditions.

Price: $135.00

SOG TWITCH XL (BLACK TINI) TWI-21

The XL is classy...it moves well, looks right, walks the walk, and talks the talk. It is not just a larger version of a Twitch. It is serious business that can more than get the job done. This is a high-tech statement of sophistication with all the bells and whistles that you expect from the designers at SOG, including the SOG Assisted Technology™. The fine construction comes together to make the XL one of the most practical and beautiful knives that you'll ever handle.

Price: $140.00

SPYDERCO BY08 RAVEN

The Raven has an aluminum handle that is both feath-

SOG/Twitch XL TWI-21

Spyderco BY08 Raven

**Spyderco BY175
Cara Cara Rescue**

erweight and feather textured for ultra-light, slip free cutting. The handle's unique feathered pattern radiates bi-directionally outward from the center creating tactile resistance in the palm when cutting in a forward or backward motion. The blade is made with 8Cr13MoV stainless steel with a centerline grind and jimping (crosshatching) where handle and blade connect. Jimping gives the thumb and forefinger traction and cutting manageability over the sharpened edge. Running the length of the handle tucked inside, are full-length steel liners and a Michael Walker-style LinerLock. The comet shaped opening hole is a trademark of the byrd knife line and is synonymous with the stringent quality requirements, high performance materials and manufacturing put into each Byrd knife.

- **Length Overall:** 7 7/8" (200mm)
- **Blade Length:** 3 1/2" (89mm)
- **Blade Steel:** 8CR13MOV
- **Length Closed:** 4 3/8" (111mm)
- **Cutting Edge:** 2 7/8" (73mm)
- **Weight:** 4.3oz (122g)
- **Hole Diameter:** 15/32" (12mm)
- **Blade Thickness:** 1/8" (3mm)
- **Handle Material:** Aluminum

Price: $30.95

SPYDERCO BY175 CARA CARA RESCUE

- **Length Overall:** 8 3/4" (222mm)

- **Blade Length:** 4" (100mm)
- **Blade Steel:** 8CR13MOV
- **Length Closed:** 4 27/32" (123mm)
- **Cutting Edge:** 3 3/8" (86mm)
- **Weight:** 3.7oz (104g)
- **Hole Diameter:** 15/32" (12mm)
- **Blade Thickness:** 1/8" (3mm)
- **Handle Material:** FRN

Price: $31.95

SPYDERCO BY19SBK MEADOWLARK RESCUE

Emergency responders, EMTs, ranchers and river guides by and large favor and purchase round tipped blades because they can't poke or puncture inflatable watercraft, livestock or people. The nature of these professions, place their workers in unpredictable places and situations where cutting without worry about puncturing or poking provides peace of mind. The byrd Line's BY17 Cara Cara Rescue and BY19 Meadowlark Rescue both have Sheepfoot, safety shaped 8Cr13Mov stainless steel blades. They're hollow-ground, plain edge, 50/50 or fully serrated for sliding safely under rope, seatbelts or clothing and offer the highest level cutting performance. Ergonomic comfort is equally important as cutting ability in a rescue knife so the fiberglass reinforced nylon handles are Bi-Directionally Textured™ and have jimping above the Comet Shaped Hole™ and along the finger choil. Both models have a four-way clip that car-

Spyderco C122 Tenacious

**Spyderco BY19SBK
Meadowlark Rescue**

ries: right/lefthand, tip-up/tip-down. A half-moon of steel removed from the locking lever (called a David Boye Dent) lessens the chance of gripping the knife tightly enough during use to inadvertently unlock the blade. Safe and smart.

- **Length Overall:** 7 1/8" (181mm)
- **Blade Length:** 3 1/8" (79mm)
- **Blade Steel:** 8CR13MOV
- **Length Closed:** 4 1/32" (102mm)
- **Cutting Edge:** 2 9/16" (65mm)
- **Weight :** 2.6oz (74g)
- **Hole Diameter:** 15/32" (12mm)
- **Blade Thickness:** 3/32" (2.5mm)
- **Handle Material:** FRN

Price: $27.95

SPYDERCO C122 TENACIOUS

The mid-sized Tenacious has a black G-10 laminate handle, milled with prolonged fatigue-free cutting in mind. Tucked inside are skeletonized steel liners increasing the handle's rigidity and strength without adding non-functioning weight or bulky thickness.

The 8CR13MOV stainless blade is leaf-shaped and ground flat from spine to cutting edge for cutting performance. The blade's shape coupled with an oversized Spyderco Round Hole and textured spine jimping allow you to open the blade and position your thumb on the spine in slip-proof confidence ready for work. A Walker Linerlock (with jimped liner) and a 4-way pocket clip lets you

set your carry and draw preference: Tip-up/tip-down lefthand/right-hand. Screw together construction.

- **Length Overall:** 7 3/4" (197mm)
- **Blade Length:** 3 3/8" (86mm)
- **Blade Steel:** 8CR13MOV
- **Length Closed:** 4 7/16" (113mm)
- **Cutting Edge:** 3 3/8" (86mm)
- **Weight:** 4oz (115g)
- **Hole Diameter:** 1/2" (13mm)
- **Blade Thickness:** 1/8" (3mm)
- **Handle Material:** G-10

Price: $49.95

SPYDERCO FB21 AND FB22 CASPIAN SALT POINTED AND BLUNT

Being underwater changes your perspective by letting you to enter another world. Safely doing that requires the right equipment and divers and paddlers agree knives are essential gear. Serviceable water knives are a dime a dozen but finding one that doesn't rust and stays quick-cutting sharp makes a good water knife a great water knife.

Spyderco's Caspian Salt fixed blade water knives are a solid piece of non-rusting H-1 steel. The industry's new wunderkind for watery applications, H-1 is nitrogen based instead of carbon based. Carbon rusts, but nitrogen doesn't because it doesn't interact with chloride.

Metallurgy lesson aside the knives are built around needs of people who sport in water. The Caspian comes with cut-

Spyderco FB22 Caspian Salt

Spyderco Catbyrd

outs lessening weight with a round cutout hole fitting the index finger (even gloved) like a ring. Once gripped, dropping the knife is next to impossible without fully opening your hand. The index finger hole keeps the knife tucked deep in the palm freeing fingertips and thumb for adjusting gear, picking things up and generating leverage. The handle's solid portion is overlaid in fiberglass reinforced nylon and above the index finger hole is texturing that work together to make it even grippier- a positive feature in cold or moving water.

Two lanyard holes, on the butt end and behind the blade, create additional attachment options for a retrieval-cord or thong. The blade comes CombinationEdged with a line cutter set on the top of the spine.

- **Length Overall:** 7 5/16" (186mm)
- **Blade Length:** 4 1/2" (114mm)
- **Blade Steel:** H-1
- **Cutting Edge:** 3 1/8" (79mm)
- **Weight:** 2.75oz (79g)
- **Hole Diameter:** 15/64" (6mm)
- **Blade Thickness:** 1/8" (3mm)
- **Handle Material:** FRN

Price: $184.95

SPYDERCO CATBYRD

The blade is 8Cr13MoV stainless steel: a recent knife industry creation of high carbon stainless steel similar in performance to AUS-8. It contains molybdenum, vanadium and near 1% carbon for enhancement of the steel's durability and edge retention. Catbyrd's blade is flat-ground, sweeping slightly upward to a Clip-Point tip.

In keeping with the rest of the byrd Line, is the Comet Shaped blade hole for one hand opening and a pocket clip. The clip is positioned for right-handers and carries the knife in pocket with the tip facing upward. The handle is also stainless steel with the backside scale doubling as the liner in an Integral LinerLock. Custom knifemaker Chris Reeve invented this lock design that's brilliant in its simplicity. Using the back steel-side of the handle as the LinerLock's liner not only makes the lock have great strength but limits the number of parts (moving and stationary) needed to build the lock.

On the front of the handle are two pieces of grip tape. Each piece is shaped like the Comet Hole and they spoon each other Yin & Yang-style laying down a gritty sandpapery surface for better grip.

- **Length Overall:** 8" (203mm)
- **Blade Length:** 3 9/16" (90mm)
- **Blade Steel:** 8cr13mov
- **Length Closed:** 4 1/2" (114mm)
- **Cutting Edge:** 3 5/32" (80mm)
- **Weight:** 5.4oz (154g)
- **Hole Diameter:** 1/2" (13mm)
- **Blade Thickness:** 1/8" (3mm)
- **Handle Material:** Stainless Steel

Price: $46.95

INTRODUCTION TO
Tactical Optics
BY EDITORS OF GUN DIGEST

NIGHT VISION

News clips from Desert Storm and the movie "Silence of the Lambs" are what most people think of when night vision is mentioned. Only ten years ago night vision was out of reach of the average individual and the quality of the available optics was not much to write home about.

How does night vision work?

Night vision works by collecting minute particles of light and focusing them into an image intensifier. The image intensifier converts them to electrons. The electrons are then multiplied and projected onto a green phosphorescent screen. When this intensified electron image strikes the phosphor screen, it causes the screen to emit light that is visible to the naked eye.

The whole process is complex and many factors dictate the final outcome, but essentially, night vision takes small electrical charges not detectable to the human senses and multiplying them to a perceptible level.

While the entire process may seem foreign to most of us, we all need to know what separates the $300.00 units for the $3,000.00 units. The differences are really quite easy to understand. Night vision optics have been around for over 50 years and they have gone through many changes. These changes are called "generations" (GEN). With each Generation, the end picture quality, range and light gathering ability has improved. It is these differences combined with the overall size, weight and technical features that dictate the price.

Night Vision - Generation 1

GEN I optics were developed in the 1960s and are still widely used today. They need some visible light to operate and do not function well in extremely dark environments. But for general use with the aid of stars and/or moonlight, combined with extra infrared illumination, they work well for most applications. The biggest advantage to GEN I optics is price. GEN I optics can be had for a quarter of what some of the GEN II and GEN III models cost.

Night Vision - Generation 2

GEN II optics were developed in the 1970's. They have a significantly longer life span than GEN I and do not require visible light to operate, which allows them to work in extremely dark conditions. They also offer a better resolution than GEN I optics and are a good choice for night hunting optics.

Night Vision - Generation 3

GEN III optics are currently the state of the art in night vision. GEN III optics have a greatly increased amount of light gaining ability and resolution (clarity) over all other forms of night vision. For night hunting applications they work extremely well, offering excellent detail and range. The only disadvantage of GEN III optics is the price.

Night Vision – Generation 4

4th generation / Gated Filmless technology represents the biggest technological breakthrough in image intensification of the past 10 years. By removing the ion barrier film and "Gating" the system Gen 4 demonstrates substantial increases in target detection range and resolution, particularly at extremely low light levels. The use of filmless technology and auto-gated power supply in 4th generation image intensifiers result in:

- Up to 100% improvement in photoresponse.
- Superb performance in extremely low light level (better S/N and EBI)
- At least triple high light level resolution (a minimum of 36 lp/mm compared to 12 lp/mm)

With significant improvement in contrast level and in performance under all light conditions, 4th generation represents the top of the line performance in the night vision market. Note: The term 4th generation is used/accepted among Night Vision manufactures to describe gated filmless tubes. However, this designation is widely debated and is currently referred to as Filmless & Gated image intensifiers by the US Military.

Gen 4 technology improves night operational effectiveness for military users of night vision goggles and other night vision devices. The filmless MCP provides a higher signal-to-noise ratio than Gen 3, resulting in better image quality (less scintillation) under low-light conditions. The gated power supply further improves image resolution under high light conditions, and the reduced halo minimizes interference from bright light sources. These improvements also substantially increase the detection range of the systems.

Choosing the Right Optics

Once the differences in Generations are understood, you must decide what you are going to be using the device for. The higher you go, the higher the price. When lives are on the line, that may not be an issue.

BINOCULARS

Power, Field of View and Exit Pupil

Power: The first main comparison used in binoculars is power. Binocular powers are expressed as two numbers such as 8 x 42. The first number, 8 in this example, is the magnification. It expresses the magnification as a factor compared to the naked eye. So an 8 power magnifies the objects in view up to 8 times. An object would appear to be 8 times closer than it would with the naked eye. Therefore, a higher number has a greater magnification.

The second number, 42 in this example, is the diameter of the objective lens in millimeters. So a 42 designation means that the outer lens is 42 mm in diameter. A larger number indicates a larger lens. Large lenses are more bulky, but they also let in more light, making your image clearer - especially in low light conditions.

FOV @ 1000 Yards: Field of View (FOV) is the second most used comparison with binoculars, and it stands for Field of View. What this means is how wide of an area (in ft.) that you can view through the binoculars at 1000 yards. A higher number indicates a wider area, while a smaller number indicates a narrower area. The focal length of the objective lenses and the eyepiece design has the most impact on the actual FOV. The power of the binoculars also has an inverse relationship with FOV. As the magnification increases, a smaller FOV results.

Your choice of FOV depends on your individual use of the binoculars. If you are using them in a wide-open area to scan for mule deer, a narrower field of view is not a big deal. However, if you are scanning a dense forest for hidden black-tailed deer at ranges at or around 100 yards, you will want to select a model that has a wider field of view.

Exit Pupil: Exit pupil is related to the power of the binocular and the size of the objective lens. If you hold a pair of binoculars away from your face, you will see a small circle of bright light in the eyepiece. This is the exit pupil, the size of the beam of light that leaves the binocular. The exit pupil diameter can easily be calculated (in mm) by dividing the diameter of the objective lens by the power. Therefore, a 8x42 binocular has an exit pupil of 5.25mm. On a bright day, the human pupil will vary from 2mm at noon to 4mm later in the day. When your eyes become adapted to dark conditions, the pupil will vary from around 5mm to a maximum of 9mm.

In daylight, having a binocular with a larger exit pupil will have little effect. The only difference you may notice is that you will be able to move a binocular with a larger exit pupil and still maintain the image, which is extremely helpful if you are in unstable conditions, such as in a boat. The main difference occurs in low light conditions. If you plan on using your binoculars near dawn or dusk, which is a time when many hunters depend on their optics, it is recommended that you select an exit pupil greater than 4mm, to fully take advantage of the amount of light your eyes can let in. An exit pupil larger than your pupil's diameter at the time does not result in a brighter image. Your eye can only handle so much.

You can see from the exit pupil calculation that if you choose a higher power binocular, you will also need to increase the size of the objective to maintain the same diameter of light leaving the binocular.

Prisms

As light passes through a pair of binoculars, the image becomes inverted. Erecting prisms are used within the binoculars to correct this problem. The two main types you will find in binoculars are Roof and Porro Prisms.

Roof Prism Binocular

A Roof Prism design reflects the light 5 times, and the resultant light comes out on the same line that it came in on. This straight through design lends itself to slimmer dimensions, a more compact body, and usually, lighter weight, as the objective lens is in direct line with the eyepiece. In general, roof prisms cost more, due to the difficulty of manufacture.

A Porro Prism binocular requires a bit larger body than a roof prism as the light is only reflected 4 times, and it comes out on a different line than it enters the objective. From a side view, the objective lens is usually a small distance above the eyepiece.

Many people debate about which design is better, and it actually depends more on the glass quality, manufacturing tolerances, and individual design as to which delivers the best image. Within Porro prisms, two different types of glass are used, BK-7 and BAK-4.

BK-7 utilizes boro-silicate glass, while BAK-4 uses barium crown glass. The BAK-4 is a finer glass (higher density) and eliminates internal light scattering, therefore producing sharper images than the BK-7 glass. The finer glass in a BAK-4 prism comes at a higher price than ones using BK-7 prisms.

Optical Coatings

The largest limitation of light transmission in binoculars is reflected light. Any time that light strikes a glass surface, up to 5% of the light can be reflected back. In a pair of binoculars, light can pass through at least 10 different glass surfaces. If you do the math, you can see that it is easy to lose 50% of the ambient light. Plus, much of this reflected light remains inside the binocular causing glare and poor contrast.

However, if a thin chemical film (a common one being Magnesium Fluoride) is used to coat the surface of the glass, much of the reflection can be eliminated. The coating reduces light loss and glare, increases light transmission and results in brighter, clearer images. By coating a surface with multiple films, the effect of the coating is increased, at times limiting the amount of reflected light to between 0.25% and 0.5% per glass surface.

The coating must be applied correctly and uniformly, or the effect is lost. You may also no-

tice that certain coatings exhibit different colors. Contrary to popular belief, this does not have a direct effect on the quality. Depending on the chemicals used and number of coatings, colors can vary from violet to blue, to even red, yellow or green.

While any coating will usually increase the performance of a binocular, you need to understand several different definitions to make a full comparison or justify the expense of a certain model.

Coated Optics — Generally means that one or more glass surfaces on at least one lens have received an anti-reflective optical coating.

Fully Coated — Generally means that all glass surfaces have been coated with an anti-reflective optical coating.

Multi-Coated — Generally means that one or more glass surfaces on at least one lens have received multiple anti-reflective optical coatings.

Fully Multi-Coated — Means that all glass surfaces have received multiple anti-reflective optical coatings.

Phase Shift Coating — A phase shift coating is used on the Roof Prism of many newer models to correct for light loss on the horizontal image plane. As light waves come through a Roof Prism, up to 70% of the waves reflected off one roof surface will be ý a wavelength shifted from those coming off the other roof surface.

What does that mean? What can happen is that the phase difference between the horizontal and vertical light in a non-coated Roof Prism can cause a loss of contrast. A phase shift coating in upper-end Roof Prism models corrects this, increasing contrast and image quality, putting them on equal playing fields with high end Porro Prism models.

While phase-coated Prisms will provide more contrast than a non-phase-coated pair, the small phase error on non-phase-coated roof prisms can only be detected if all other manufacturing tolerance errors are minimized. In other words, phase coating a cheap pair of Roof Prism binoculars does little to improve the final image.

Eye Relief

Eye relief is the comfortable distance that a binocular can be held from the eye, while still allowing the viewer to see the entire image. A long eye relief allows for comfortable viewing and is a must for viewing with eyeglasses or sunglasses. Another option to look for is extendable eyepieces or fold down rubber eyecups. These features will allow you to obtain a larger field of view while still keeping your glasses on.

LASER RANGEFINDERS

How do they work?

To simplify, the unit projects an eye-safe laser that is "bounced" off the object being aimed at and received back into the unit. A microprocessor instantly determines the distance to the object based on the length of time the laser beam took to travel to the object and back.

This method is quite accurate, to the tune of plus or minus 1 yard, and very fast. According to the FDA regulations and tests, they are also completely safe. Sorry kids. You're not going to be able to burn up the neighbor's woodpile with one of these units.

As the maximum distance of a unit increases, the laser's actual power remains the same. What you will find with units featuring greater distance reading ability are higher sensitivity receptors receiving the laser beam as it bounces back.

Laser rangefinders differ in features and options. The main difference is distance, of course. Some of the better units incorporate filtering technology that gets accurate readings through rain, haze or dust. Some also have a scan mode, which sends out a continuous laser "stream" (for 10 seconds) to track moving objects, or multiple objects in different places. Another feature is an option to only register objects that are beyond a predetermined distance reducing false readings due to interference by things such as grass, close branches, etc.

So what's new?

Plenty. That first model we got our hands on was a bulky box that only read the distance out to 400 yards or so. Today's rangefinders offer compact size with some models that can fit into the palm of your hand. They also have one feature we think was really lacking from that early model, magnification. Why is that important? If you find an animal or other target with your binoculars, it may be pretty hard to locate it without some sort of magnification. Modern rangefinders offer clear optics for locating the game you want to range.

Most will want the "Big Three" of field optics, meaning quality binoculars, a rangefinder, and a spotting scope. It's rather bulky and awkward to switch quickly from binos to a rangefinder, especially if the target is on the move. Range-finding binoculars bridge the gap and take everything to the next logical level. A look through a website such as Cabela's will show offerings from major optics companies mating a high-end laser rangefinder with a high-end binocular in a package roughly the same size as a compact binocular. The benefit here is you don't have to switch optics when scanning for targets, and you don't have to pack two items.

A relatively new feature deals with the inherit problem with laser range finding technology. That problem is elevation. If you're on a rooftop and you've got a target coming in, you can range it at 100 yards, but is it really 100 yards? We all know that point of aim when shooting up or down hill isn't going to be the same as shooting on flat ground. What these new rangefinders do is compensate for the elevation.

Through the use of a digital inclinometer, you get true readings of horizontal range. This is very important when you've got a rifle in your hands. You'd better know accurately where the bullet is going to go to make the shot. Remember that in shooting, the difference between a great shot and total disaster is inches.

There are limitations that you need to be aware of when making your rangefinder selection. Let's take an 800-yard model for example. Does that mean it will read distance on any object out to 800 yards? No. Why not? Think of it this way. A laser is basically condensed light. As mentioned earlier, rangefinders all project the same basic laser, or light beam. It is the sensitivity of the receptor that determines the effective range the unit will report. So, an 800-yard unit will read the laser reflection from a reflective target at 800 yards.

What does this mean then? Well, you need to practice with your unit. Most companies will give you a pretty close estimate of how far the unit will read with a non-reflective target. An 800-yard unit can effectively read on average targets out to 500 yards, more or less depending on the actual model chosen. Other factors affecting the ranging distance include weather conditions, lighting conditions, target size, angle of inclination, hand steadiness, and let's not forget those all-to-important things that just get in the way, like branches and brush.

Do you need one?

What kind of question is that? Of course you do. All right, "need" and "want" may be two different things, but you'd still be better off with one. Why? How well can you judge distance? Some of you out there might be pretty good at it.

Rangefinders are an invaluable tool for shooting. They allow you to accurately know the distance to your target. This is great for not only judging where you aim, but if you should take a shot at all. Want to sight that rifle in for 100 yards? 200 yards? No sweat. And it is much more accurate than pacing off the distance. Think about bullet drop too. For example, if you're shooting a .300 Win Mag. with a 180-grain bullet, how confident are you in your distances? The bullet is moving pretty fast but the difference in drop from 200 to 300 yards is 3.2 inches to 11.8 inches.

Laser rangefinders have come a long way since they first came out, just like televisions and DVD players. They've advanced the outdoor world so much so that they're right in there as a necessity. The idea behind them forces the question, how'd we ever get along without one? With the models available today at reasonable prices, you don't have to.

OPTICS PRODUCT DIRECTORY

Burris XTR-14

Burris 10X Tactical

Burris 1.6X6 Tactical

Burris Fastfire

BURRIS XTR RIFLESCOPES

Burris has gone to extremes to engineer the ultimate in high-performance optics the XTR Xtreme Tactical Riflescopes. Extra-large, ultra-premium lenses produce unsurpassed resolution, clarity, and brightness. Index-matched HiLume multicoating boosts clarity and, enhanced with new StormCoat™, causes water to bead and shed off for a clearer view when water drops are present.

Outer tube walls are 25% thicker for 42% greater strength. Double-force coil spring suspension locks the inner tube in place for unfailing accuracy.

XTRs also feature side turret-mounted parallax adjustment systems. LRS models have a fully integrated side turret-mounted illumination system. The new 1X-4X XTR equipped with the innovative XTR Ballistic 5.56 Reticle represents the state of the art in tactical optics. The whole package is waterproof, fogproof, shockproof and warranted forever.

The XTR-14 1X-4X riflescope features the XTR Ballistic 5.56 Reticle. A true 1X optic, it is shown matched to XTR Rings and a FastFire reflex sight, which is an offering in this fully-assembled configuration (ideal for M4's and AR15's). It covers the tactical bases from entry work to longrange counter-sniper duties.

This all-new addition to the Fullfield line is built for the mobile shooter who keeps weight to a minimum. High-grade lenses finished with Burris' exclusive index-matched HiLume multicoating for minimal light loss and optimal

clarity. Low-profile TAC-2 adjustment knobs. Available in the proven Ballistic Plex reticle, which is calibrated perfectly to short magnum cartridges.

Color: Olive Drab. Plex, Ballistic PLex, Ballistic Mil-dot

Price: .... $329.99 – 549.99

BURRIS FASTFIRE

Extremely fast, rugged and low profile, the FastFire sight is a sighting solution for pinpoint accuracy on handguns and shotguns. Unlimited field of view and unlimited eye relief. This compact, lightweight red dot has an integrated light sensor that self-adjusts the red dot brightness for optimal performance. Features windage and elevation adjustments, on/off switch and protective sight cover. Operates on CR2032 battery. FastFire Mounts sold separately.

Price: $210

EOTECH HOLOGRAPHIC SIGHTS

The Eotech holographic patterns have been designed to be instantly visible in any light, instinctive to center regardless of shooting angle, and to remain in view while sweeping the engagement zone. Reticles of EOTech HOLOgraphic Weapon Sights are designed as large, see-through patterns to achieve lightning quick reticle to target acquisition without covering or obscuring the point of aim.

The EoTech Holographic Weapon Sight (HWS) employs a true Heads-Up Display that eliminates blind spots, constricted vision, or the tunnel vision associated with tubed

Eotech Holographic Sights

Leupold Mark 4 1.5-5x20mm MR/T M2 Illuminated Reticle

Leupold Tactical Mark 4 CQ/T

leupold Mark 4 8.5-25x50mm ER/T M1 Front Focal Riflescope

sights. All user controls are flush to the Eotech Holographic Weapon Sight's streamline housing with no protruding knobs, battery compartments or mounting rings blocking vision at the target area. True, 2 eyes open shooting is realized with EOTech HWS. Instant threat identification is achieved by maximizing the operator's peripheral vision and ultimately gaining greater control of the engagement zone.

Prices:

EOTech 550:	$449
EOTech 4X Magnifier w/ Flip-to-Side:	$789
L3 EOTech HOLOgraphic 553:	$679
EOTech 550:	$449
EOTech HWS 3X:	$419
EOTech 510/511/512:	$389
EOTech 557:	$569
EOTech 557.4X MPO:	$1099

LEUPOLD TACTICAL MARK 4 CQ/T

The fast target acquisition and illuminated reticle of a red dot sight, the utility of a 1x to 3x riflescope, and the ability to function with or without batteries; this is the Leupold® Mark 4® CQ/T®.

The CQ/T riflescope, parts and accessories fall under the jurisdiction of the U.S. Department of State. Unless required State Department license is obtained, this product is for sale in the U.S.A. only.

Price: $1,099.99

LEUPOLD MARK 4 1.5-5X20MM MR/T M2 ILLUMINATED RETICLE

The illuminated Mil Dot or Tactical Milling Reticle (TMR™) ensures precision shot placement in even the worst light conditions, and is night-vision compatible. These reticles are ideal in tactical situations, yet also provide greater accuracy of range estimation for hunters and target shooters. The Index Matched Lens System® delivers superior resolution from edge to edge of the visual field, along with peak image brightness and optimal contrast in low light. Finger-adjustable 1/2-MOA windage and elevation adjustments with audible, tactile clicks. Engraved Bullet Drop Compensation dial for 5.56mm/.223 Rem, or 7.62mm/.308 win.

Price: $1,874.99

LEUPOLD MARK 4 8.5-25X50MM ER/T M1 FRONT FOCAL RIFLESCOPE

Every feature was put in place for one purpose: to help you get the maximum peformance from your long-range firearms, at the range, hunting, or in a tactical environment. The Leupold® Index Matched Lens System® delivers resolution from edge to edge of the visual field – even at 25x – along with peak image brightness and optimal contrast. Side focus parallax adjustment for fast, easy parallax focusing from 75 yards to infinity, from any shooting position.

Konus M30 4.5X – 16X – 40mm

Konus 7281 M30 Series 6.5X-25X 44mm

Konus 7282 M30 Series 8.5X-32X 52mm

Price: $1,724.99

KONUS M30 4.5X – 16X – 40MM

- Engraved reticle technology
- Built-in anti-canting bubble system
- Locking fast focus ocular
- 45 degree offset illuminator switch
- Flip-Up lens caps
- True 30mm tube (throughout)
- Fully-multi coated hi-def optics
- Locking tactical turret knobs (resettable to zero)
- Mid-sized parallax wheel for easier adjustment and clear visual (down to 10 yards)
- Ultra Blue illumination for dark targets
- Precision 1/8 MOA adjustments
- Includes 4" sunshade
- **Magnification/Objective:** 4.5-16X40 mm
- **Power:** 4.5-16X
- **Objective Diameter:** 40 mm
- **Reticle:** Mil Dot Engraved Ultra Blue illumination
- **Parallax Setting:** 10 yds.inf.
- **Waterproof:** Yes
- **FOV (Field Of View):** 23.1 ft at 100 Yards
- **Eye Relief:** 4 inches
- **M.O.A.:** Precision 1/8 MOA 85 MOA Max
- **Optics:** Fully Multi-Coated
- **Color:** Matte Black
- **Weight:** 26.7 oz.
- **Length:** 14.9 Inches
- **Tube Size:** 30 mm

Price: $529.95

KONUS 7281 M30 SERIES 6.5X-25X 44MM

- Engraved reticle technology
- Built-in anti-canting bubble system
- Locking fast focus ocular
- 45 degree offset illuminator switch
- Flip-Up lens caps
- True 30mm tube (throughout)
- Fully-multi coated hi-def optics
- Locking tactical turret knobs (resettable to zero)
- Includes 4" sunshade
- **Magnification/Objective:** 6.5-25X44 mm
- **Power:** 6.5-25X
- **Objective Diameter:** 44 mm
- **Reticle:** Mil-Dot I.R. Ultra Blue illumination
- **Parallax Setting:** 10 yds.inf.
- **Waterproof:** Yes
- **FOV (Field Of View):** 17.3ft at 100 Yards
- **Eye Relief:** 4 Inches
- **M.O.A.:** Precision 1/8 MOA 50 MOA Max
- **Optics:** Fully-multi coated hi-def optics
- **Color:** Matte Black
- **Weight:** 30 oz.
- **Length:** 17.7 Inches
- **Tube Size:** 30 mm

Price: $629.95

KONUS 7282 M30 SERIES 8.5X-32X 52MM

- Engraved reticle technology
- Built-in anti-canting bubble system
- Locking fast focus ocular
- 45 degree offset illuminator switch

**Schmidt & Bender 1.1–4 x 20
Short Dot with locking turrets**

**Schmidt & Bender 1.1–4 x 20
Short Dot Police Marksman II**

**Schmidt & Bender 1.1–4 x 24
Zenith Short Dot LE**

- Flip-Up lens caps
- True 30mm tube (throughout)
- Fully-multi coated hi-def optics
- Locking tactical turret knobs (resettable to zero)
- Mid-sized parallax wheel for easier adjustment and clear visual (down to 10 yards)
- Ultra Blue illumination for dark targets
- Precision 1/8 MOA adjustments
- Includes 4" sunshade
- **Magnification/Objective:** 8.5-32X52 mm
- **Power:** 8.5-32X
- **Objective Diameter:** 52 mm
- **Reticle:** Mil Dot Engrved Ultra Blue illum
- **Parallax Setting:** 10 yds.inf.
- **Waterproof:** Yes
- **FOV (Field Of View):** 23.1ft at 100 Yards
- **Eye Relief:** 4 inches
- **M.O.A.:** 1/8 MOA adjustments
- **Optics:** Fully Multi Coated
- **Color:** Matte Black
- **Weight:** 26.7 oz.
- **Length:** 14.9 Inches
- **Tube Size:** 30mm

Price: $529.95

SCHMIDT & BENDER 1.1–4 X 20 SHORT DOT POLICE MARKSMAN II

A separate turret with 11 click stops controls the illumination function of a precise red dot at the center of the reticle. Fully variable illumination levels range from barely visible, for use with night vision equipment, to full bright for quick, accurate shots in bright, harsh daylight. With illumination switched off, the Short Dot functions as a standard scope with nonilluminated crosshairs. This gives the

Short Dot "any light, any time" versatility and reliability in any circumstance the shooter may encounter. Four bullet-drop compensators are supplied for 5.56 mm cartridges, including the 62 gr. Green Tip, 75 gr. Hornady TAP, and the SR25 with M118R16 and M118 LR20 loads. Turrets are non-locking.

Price: .... N/A

SCHMIDT & BENDER 1.1–4 X 20 SHORT DOT WITH LOCKING TURRETS

Evolved from the basic Short Dot model, the addition of locking turrets and the CQB reticle results in a highly specialized instrument suitable for high-stress urban and combat situations. You have a choice of rings calibrated for either the M855, 75 gr. TAP or M118LR loads, to cover the popular 5.56 and 7.62 offerings. Locking windage, elevation and illumination turrets insure that the scope's settings will not change even under the most rigorous system.

The reticle is located in the first focal plane, and includes ranging capabilities at higher magnification. At 1.1 power, the skeleton post system virtually disappears for fast, accurate target acquisition. The same highly flexible Flash Dot system as in the standard Short Dot is included.

Price: .... N/A

SCHMIDT & BENDER 1.1–4 X 24 ZENITH SHORT DOT LE

The reticle is located in the second focal plane. At 1.1 power it is more substantial, preferred for quick response when illumination is not required. At 4 power, the illuminated Flash Dot covers only 1.57" at 100 yards (compared to 5.9" for a reticle in the first focal plane). This allows more precise shot placement at longer ranges.

Locking illumination and elevation turrets are standard, calibrated for the M855, 75 gr. TAP or M118LR. Also included is our unique Posicon control, providing a graphic

Schmidt & Bender 3–12 x 50 PM II

Schmidt & Bender 4–16 x 50 PM II

Schmidt & Bender 3–12 x 50 PM II LP

Schmidt & Bender 4–16 x 50 PM II LP

representation of where the reticle lies within its adjustment range. This makes for easier mounting and sighting in. Our Flash Dot illumination system is standard. Offered with reticles FD2 or FD7.

Price: .... N/A

SCHMIDT & BENDER 3–12 X 50 PM II

A versatile scope, allowing precise shot placement to 1000 meters yet still presenting an exceptionally wide field of view at low power. Available with parallax adjustment or with parallax adjustment and illuminated reticles.

Two elevation/windage options are offered; Option One has one-centimeter click values with an elevation range of 220cm at 100m. Option Two has a "double turn" elevation knob with increments of 1/4MOA per click. Elevation range is 56MOA at 100m. Windage is also 1/4MOA per click, with a total adjustment of ±14MOA. Offered with P1 or P3 rangefinding reticles.

Price: .... N/A

SCHMIDT & BENDER 3–12 X 50 PM II LP

Combines parallax compensation, illuminated reticle control and 1/4MOA or centimeter clicks. There are two elevation adjustment options: Option One is calibrated to 0.1 Mil click values. Option Two is calibrated in 1/4MOA click values. Color-coded window indicators graphically illustrate the reticle's position within the overall adjustment travel, preventing the shooter from becoming "lost" within the adjustment range. The entire adjustment range can be covered in just two turns of the elevation knob, while the entire 3-12x magnification range is covered in just one-half turn (180 degrees).

Parallax adjustment is located in its own separate turret, as are the illuminated reticle controls. The reticle brightness is fully adjustable with 11 graduated settings allowing precise selection relative to ambient light. As with all Schmidt

& Bender illuminated reticles, it turns off between settings saving battery power and allowing you to easily return to a pre-selected illumination level. Available with the P3, P4, or P4 Fine reticles.

Price: .... N/A

SCHMIDT & BENDER 4–16 X 50 PM II

A wide magnification range provides versatility from close range shots to distances beyond 1000 meters. A 50mm objective lens provides outstanding performance even under the poorest light conditions. Available in two configurations; parallax adjustment only and parallax and illuminated-reticle adjustment. The 4-16 x 50 is offered with "double turn" elevation

knob with 1/4 MOA clicks and an adjustment range of 56 MOA. The entire 56-minute adjustment range can be covered in just two turns of the elevation knob, while the IAL window illustrates the adjustment position within the overall range. Windage increments are also 1/4 MOA per click, the total adjustment range ±14 MOA. Offered with P1 or P3 reticles.

Price: .... N/A

SCHMIDT & BENDER 4–16 X 50 PM II LP

The Schmidt and Bender 4–16 x 50 in an illuminated reticle LP model. An illuminated reticle and parallax adjustment are standard, each controlled by a separate turret. The LP system features a color-coded elevation knob that gives the shooter instant reference as to where the elevation is set. Just one turn of the knob provides 28 minutes of elevation. A window within the dial then changes to yellow, and one additional turn provides an additional 28 minutes of adjustment. The entire 56-minute adjustment range can be covered in just two turns of the elevation knob. Click values are 1/4 MOA. P3 or P4 Fine reticles available.

Price: .... N/A

Trijicon Accupoint Scopes

2.5x–10x–56mm

BY SCOTT W. WAGNER

We had some rifles come in for this book that needed scopes. All right, we got some rifles in that we KNEW needed scopes. Why? Because we really wanted a good excuse to get a Trijicon AccuPoint scope in to play with.

So what is so special as to peak our interests? Well, anyone who is interested in optics should be interested in these scopes. They have a reputation for extreme clarity, solid construction and then there is that fiber optic thing. We've always liked illuminated reticle scopes and these offer up some of the brightest available and use no batteries.

The Trijicon AccuPoint offers any-light shooting, with fiber-optic and tritium aiming-point illumination, the Trijicon AccuPoint speeds target acquisition and extends available shooting hours. The dual-illumination fiber-optic system automatically adjusts aiming-point brightness to existing light conditions. This provides shooters optimum aiming-point illumination and ideal reticle/target con-

trast. The result: lightning-fast precision aiming in any light without failure-prone batteries.

One thing that blew us away as soon as we opened the box was the eye relief. A good scope will offer a good amount of eye relief so you don't end up with scope brow. The Trijicon scope offered more eye relief than any other scope tested in recent memory. There was well over four inches of eye relief in the 2.5x -10x – 56mm model.

Specifications:

- **Magnification:** 2.5-10
- **Objective Size:** 56
- **Bullet Drop Compensator:** No
- **Length (in):** 13.80
- **Weight (oz):** 22.10
- **Illumination source:** Fiber Optics/Tritium
- **Reticle Pattern:** Triangle
- **Day Reticle Colo:** Amber
- **Night Reticle Color:** Amber
- **Calibration:** N/A
- **Bindon Aiming Concept** Y
- **Eye Relief (in):** 2.8 to 4.1
- **Exit Pupil (mm):** 16.3 to 5.6
- **Field of View (°):** 7.18 to 1.94
- **Field of View @ 100yrds (ft):** 37.6 to 10.1
- **Adjustment @ 100 yds (clicks/in):** 4
- **Tube Size:** 30mm
- **Housing Material:** 6061-T6 aluminum, hard coat anodized per MIL-A-8625, Type III, Class 2 dull & non reflective

Mounted up, this scope was a delight to shoot. Our test model had the single post reticle with the amber triangle. It was bright and clear in any light and stayed bright when the light was very low, making this a great scope for tactical applications.

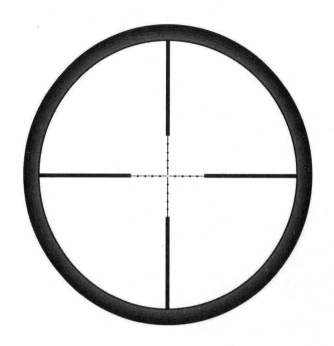

We mounted this scope to a bolt-action rifle as well as two different AR-15 platform guns, one of which was a Bushmaster 450 carbine. The scope mounted up well and aiming was lightning fast. The eye relief made target acquisition immediate and the 56mm objective lens made following moving targets as easy as could be. Forced to find a flaw, the only draw back was weight. This was a hefty scope, but not overly so considering the size.

THE BOTTOM LINE

How well did the scope perform? One of our editors bought the test model. That speaks volumes to us. This is a premium scope and just as good if not better than anything out there. The latest versions are available with a crosshair reticle and are sure to perform just as well.

Schmidt & Bender 5-25 x 56 Police Marksman II LP

Yukon/Yukon-Centurion Systems 24025

25025 Viking 1x24 Goggles.tif @ 54%

SCHMIDT & BENDER 5-25 X 56 POLICE MARKSMAN II LP

This scope offers true 2000-meter capability. Unlike most long-range variables that offer only a 4x magnification multiple, the 5-25 x 56 provides a full 5x and a wider field of view. Parallax adjustment in a separate turret, completely adjustable from 10 meters to infinity. The illuminated reticle has 11 graduated settings offering precise control relative to ambient light. The scope includes Schmidt & Bender's color-coded "Double Turn" elevation knob that gives the shooter instant reference to where the elevation is set. The entire 100-minute adjustment range can be covered in just two turns of the knob. The user will never become "lost" within the adjustment range. The 5–25 x 56 is offered with 56 MOA of 1/4 MOA clicks, or 273cm (93 MOA) of 1cm clicks. Your choice of P3 or P4 reticles.

Price: .... N/A

YUKON/YUKON-CENTURION SYSTEMS 24025

The NVMT 1x24 Head Gear Kit incorporates the element of hands-free night vision with the quality and value of a 1x24 monocular. The NVMT 1x24 monocular uses no magnification so that users can see a clear image with no distortion or change in depth perception. The small, compact monocular is secured to the head gear by a mounting system that sits easily on the front head strap so that the NVMT can be flipped up when not in use or flipped down

when activated; the NVMT head gear is designed to be used with your right eye only and can not be interchanged for the left. The 1x24 also features separately activated Pulse™ system IR illuminator that uses a pulsating infrared beam to enhance night vision viewing capabilities. A simple detaching mechanism allows the monocular to be taken off the mount for hand-held use. Additional accessories for the NVMT 1x24 are the NVMT IR Flashlight, Riflescope Conversion Kit and Digital Camera Adapter.The NVMT Goggle 1x24 is backed by Yukon's Limited Lifetime Warranty.

Price: $400.00

YUKON/YUKON-CENTURION SYSTEMS 25025

The Viking 1x24 NV Goggles are a night vision binocular that allows for incredibly detailed observation ability under the darkness of night that includes a head gear accessory for a flip-up, adjustable and hands-free unit. The Viking 1x24 provides clear viewing in total darkness by utilizing a built-in IR infrared illuminator; when in use the illuminator emits a pulsing frequency that is so energy efficient it creates less battery drainage and prolongs battery life. The ergonomically designed rubberized body is surprisingly lightweight and can be taken on long expeditions both easily and comfortably, and is great for prolonged use with the head gear accessory. The Viking utilizes the revolutionary Eclipse™ Lens Cover System which uses flip-up covers that

Yukon/Yukon-Centurion Systems 26013T

**Yukon/Yukon-Centurion Systems
26014**

can be easily clipped back against the body of the binoculars and rotated out of the user's viewing area while eliminating lens cap hassles. Pin holes in the lens caps allow the Viking to be used in the daytime when the caps are closed. Also featured is a dual diopter adjustment with central focusing knob, fully multi-coated optics and water and fog resistance. The Viking 1x24 NV Goggles are backed by Yukon's Limited Lifetime Warranty.

Price: $750.00

YUKON/YUKON-CENTURION SYSTEMS 26013T

The Varmint Hunter 2.5x50 uses enhanced optics, a durable, titanium body and sleek design to separate itself from any other night vision riflescope. The Varmint Hunter incorporates a long mount into its ergonomic design to allow for more comfort during shooting while also enabling the scope to accommodate the widest range of rifles, including bolt action styles. It is also equipped with a powerful 50mm lens to provide higher resolution and light gathering capabilities, and flip-up lens covers open to reveal quality multi-coated optics and an illuminated reticle. A built-in, powerful Pulse™ infrared illuminator is easily activated to enhance image brightness and increase range in total darkness; a precision windage and elevation adjustment and remote are additional features. The Varmint Hunter is also digital camera adaptable with the digital camera accessory; other accessories include a laser pointer, AK adapter, IR flashlight and doubler lens, which are all sold separately. The Varmint Hunter is backed by Yukon's Limited Lifetime Warranty.

Price: $725.00

YUKON/YUKON-CENTURION SYSTEMS 26014

The NVRS Tactical 2.5x50 uses enhanced optics, a durable, titanium body and sleek design to separate itself from any other night vision riflescope. The NVRS Tactical 2.5x50 has internal focusing ability and incorporates a long mount into its ergonomic design to allow for more comfort during shooting while also enabling the scope to accommodate the widest range of rifles, including bolt action styles. It is also equipped with a powerful 50mm lens to provide higher resolution and light gathering capabilities, and flip-up lens covers open to reveal quality multi-coated optics and an illuminated reticle. A built-in, powerful Pulse™ infrared illuminator is easily activated to enhance image brightness and increase range in total darkness; a precision windage and elevation adjustment and remote are additional features. The NVRS Tactical 2.5x50 is also digital camera adaptable with the digital camera accessory; other accessories include a laser pointer, AK adapter, IR flashlight and doubler lens, which are all sold separately. The NVRS Tactical 2.5x50 is backed by Yukon's Limited Lifetime Warranty.

Price: $800.00

**Yukon/Yukon-Centurion Systems
26021**

**Yukon/Yukon-Centurion Systems
26031**

**Yukon/Yukon-Centurion Systems
26041**

YUKON/YUKON-CENTURION SYSTEMS
26021

The NVRS Tactical 2.5x42 Gen 2+ uses enhanced optics, a durable, titanium body and sleek design to separate itself from any other night vision riflescope. The NVRS Tactical 2.5x42 Gen 2+ incorporates a long mount into its ergonomic design to allow for more comfort during shooting while also enabling the scope to accommodate the widest range of rifles, including bolt action styles. It is also equipped with a powerful 50mm lens to provide higher resolution and light gathering capabilities, and flip-up lens covers open to reveal quality multi-coated optics and an illuminated reticle. A built-in, powerful Pulse™ infrared illuminator is easily activated to enhance image brightness and increase range in total darkness; a precision windage and elevation adjustment and remote are additional features. The NVRS Tactical 2.5x42 Gen 2+ is also digital camera adaptable with the digital camera accessory; other accessories include a laser pointer, AK adapter and IR flashlight, which are all sold separately. The NVRS Tactical 2.5x42 Gen 2+ is backed by Yukon's Limited Lifetime Warranty.

Price: $1,700.00

YUKON/YUKON-CENTURION SYSTEMS
26031

The NVRS Tactical 2.5x42 Gen 3 is the most powerful riflescope in the Titanium line and uses enhanced optics, a durable, titanium body and sleek design to separate itself from any other night vision riflescope. The NVRS Tactical 2.5x42 Gen 3 incorporates a long mount into its ergonomic design to allow for more comfort during shooting while also enabling the scope to accommodate the widest range of rifles, including bolt action styles. It is also equipped with a powerful 50mm lens to provide higher resolution and light gathering capabilities, and flip-up lens covers open to reveal quality multi-coated optics and an illuminated reticle. A built-in, powerful Pulse™ infrared illuminator is easily activated to enhance image brightness and increase range in total darkness; a precision windage and elevation adjustment and remote are additional features. The NVRS Tactical 2.5x42 Gen 3 is also digital camera adaptable with the digital camera accessory; other accessories include a laser pointer, AK adapter and IR flashlight, which are all sold separately. The NVRS Tactical 2.5x42 Gen 3 is backed by Yukon's Limited Lifetime Warranty.

Price: $2,500.00

YUKON/YUKON-CENTURION SYSTEMS
26041

A key component to the originality of the new NVMT is that it sheds the burden of a one-dimensional item and evolves into a multi-functional system allowing the scope to be used virtually anywhere. The NVMT 3x42 Laser Riflescope merges a powerful 3x42 monocular with a detachable eyepiece, rifle mount and laser pointer to create a truly versatile night vision unit. The adjustable laser

Yukon/Yukon-Centurion Systems CS44012

Yukon/Yukon-Centurion Systems CS45002

Yukon/Yukon-Centurion Systems CS45003

pointer's beam acts as a target acquisition guide when the unit is mounted to your riflescope and ensures precision while shooting. As with all monoculars in the NVMT series, the NVMT 3x42 has excellent light amplification performance, amplifying visible light several thousand times, and an exclusive Pulse™ built-in infrared illuminator that expands viewing range and minimizes battery drainage. Fully multi-coated optics decrease glare and improve light transmission to provide an excellent viewing experience while the compact and durable Rubber Armor™ body is small enough to fit in the palm of your hand or in a pocket, yet rugged enough to withstand use. Yukon's NVMT Riflescope is perfect for airsoft, varmint control, paintball or any other night gun sports that require a short range, night vision scope. The NVMT 3x42 Laser Riflescope is backed by Yukon's Limited Lifetime Warranty.

Price: $500.00

YUKON/YUKON-CENTURION SYSTEMS CS44012

The Centurion Systems BORDER PATROL 3.6x68 Gen.2 Long Range Surveillance Night Vision Viewer has a distinguishable, unique panoramic eyepiece, allowing for an increased observation area for extended durations. The Border Patrol Night Vision Viewer is superior for viewing over long distances with exceptional visual comfort, and helps prevent eye fatigue.

Price: $2,400.00

YUKON/YUKON-CENTURION SYSTEMS CS45002

The Centurion Systems DEFENDER 1x24 is the Night Vision Goggle that is the evolved version of the PVS-7 with improved functionality and performance. Available with an extensive choice of image intensifiers, the DEFENDER Night Vision Goggle provides exceptional performance in the most unfavorable conditions. The Centurion Systems DEFENDER 1x24 Night Vision Goggle can also accept a 3x magnifier lens.

Price: $2,750.00

YUKON/YUKON-CENTURION SYSTEMS CS45003

The Centurion Systems DEFENDER 1x24 is the Night Vision Goggles that are the evolved version of the PVS-7 with improved functionality and performance. Available with an extensive choice of image intensifiers, the DEFENDER Night Vision Goggles provide exceptional performance in the most unfavorable conditions. The Centurion Systems DEFENDER 1x24 Night Vision Goggles can also accept a 3x magnifier lens.

Price: $4,500.00

YUKON/YUKON-CENTURION SYSTEMS CS45992

The Centurion Systems GOVERNOR 7x84 Gen.3 Night Vision Binoculars are an extremely effective night vision de-

Yukon/Yukon-Centurion Systems CS45992

Yukon/Yukon-Centurion Systems CS47003

Yukon/Yukon-Centurion Systems CS12001

vice designed for long distance observation. These Night Vision Binoculars incorporate a 165mm F/2.0 objective lens system to provide a high 7x magnification allowing the user to conduct surveillance up to 800 yards.

Price: $5,500.00

YUKON/YUKON-CENTURION SYSTEMS CS47003

The Centurion Systems EXPERT 5-12x83 Day / Night Vision Rifle Scope is deadly accurate at long ranges, and has a special day/night 23 lens zoom optic system.

Price: $6,500.00

YUKON/YUKON-CENTURION SYSTEMS CS12001

The Centurion Systems Sortie™ 7x50 Military Binoculars take a high quality BaK-4 prism, pairs it with incredible, fully multicoated lenses, and transforms them into one of the most extraordinary tactical binoculars ever designed. These military binoculars are reliable to a fault, and provide maximum light transmission and optimal brightness so the user can conduct surveillance and observation in even the most unforgiving terrain.

From early dawn to late dusk, the optimum color fidelity and clarity of image enhance any surveillance mission while a generously long eye relief reduces potential eye strain. Every Centurion Systems Sortie™ 7x50 Military Binoculars incorporate a military grade compass and an approximat-

ing distance reticle to give the user the ability to coordinate live field exercises and fire support while keeping his eyes on the target. This battle tough military binoculars are nitrogen purged, waterproof, fogproof and encased in rubber armor, making it the favorite tactical binocular of sniper teams, infantry units and special forces.

Price: $280.00

YUKON/YUKON-CENTURION SYSTEMS CS45001

The Centurion Systems PVS-7 Night Vision Goggles / Binoculars are engineered to meet MIL-SPEC requirements and standards. The rugged and reliable design ideally accommodates users for extended wear and superior surveillance functions. These Night Vision Goggles have an integrated IR illuminator with an IR "on" indicator, low battery indicator, excess light exposure cut-off sensor and other features. The night nision system is based on the most advanced image intensifiers, with 64-72 lp/mm and a Figure of Merit of no less than 1600. The Centurion Systems PVS-7 Night Vision Goggles / Binoculars also can accept a 3x magnifier lens.

Price: $4,500.00

YUKON/YUKON-CENTURION SYSTEMS CS46002

The Centurion Systems MAGNUM 4x68 Gen.2+ Night Vision Weapon Sight is superior for long range shoot-

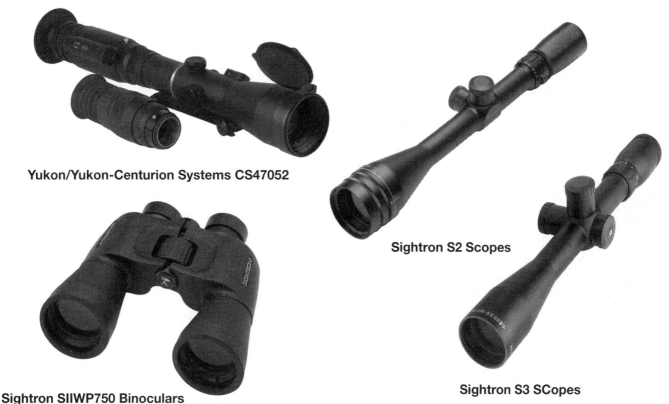

Yukon/Yukon-Centurion Systems CS47052

Sightron S2 Scopes

Sightron SIIWP750 Binoculars

Sightron S3 SCopes

ing, with outstanding accuracy, in the most unfavorable conditions. This Night Vision Weapon Sight is the best in industry power consumption; 120 hours of battery life time.

Price: $3,300.00

YUKON/YUKON-CENTURION SYSTEMS CS47052

The Centurion Systems SHARP SHOOTER Gen.2 Day / Night Riflescope is the most advanced portable sniper system, noted for unparalleled accuracy at long ranges and unique versatility.

Price: $2,100.00

YUKON/YUKON-CENTURION SYSTEMS CS47092

The Centurion Systems MARKSMAN Gen.3 is a revolutionary THREE in ONE: Day Weapon Sight / Night Vision Weapon Sight / Night Vision Monocular.

The innovative design of this Day and Night Vision Weapon Sight meets specific requirements for a Tactical Weapon Day Sight, advanced Night Vision Weapon Sight and Night Vision Monocular.

Price: $7,000.00

SIGHTRON S2 SCOPES

S2 scopes are completely updated with better glass, tighter tolerances and new lens coatings. The S2 was de-

signed to offer maximum light transmission and accuracy. They feature 1/4 MOA adjustments with finger adjustable turrets and are waterproof, fogproof, shockproof and filled with nitrogen. Sightron scopes are covered by a lifetime factory warranty.

Price Range:.................................$349.00 $549.00

SIGHTRON S3 SCOPES

Sightron's S3 scopes are made of quality 6061 T-6 aluminum and are built to take a lifetime of punishment. They also feature ZACT-7 Revcoat™ 7 layer multi-coating process that give an amazing 99% light transmission per lens, so performance under low light is never a problem. The S3 scopes also have Sightron's patented ExacTrack™ windage and elevation system that guarantees that once adjusted, you'll never experience a shift in the point of impact. Both Sightron S3 Scopes are nitrogen charged, waterproof and shockproof and are covered under Sightron's Lifetime Warranty.

Price Range:.................................$600.00 $900.00

SIGHTRON SIIWP750 BINOCULARS

Fully multi-coated lenses, BaK-4 prisms and rubber coated frame allow it to serve in all weather conditions. Water and fogproof. Includes case, neck strap and lifetime warranty.

Price: $129.00

INTRODUCTION TO
Tactical Lights

BY EDITORS OF GUN DIGEST

Flashlights have come a long way. It wasn't that long ago when the top word in a "tactical" light was a light/Billy club that housed several D-cell batteries. The more batteries, the brighter the light, and not to mention the bigger the flashlight. The high output LED bulb and the Lithium Ion battery changed all of that.

For starters, the lights today are bright and compact. You'll often see lumen ratings associated with lights. A lumen is the measured total output of emitted light. Today's tactical lights are extremely bright. This is of high importance for tactical applications, as a brief flash of light from one of these lights will blind a subject instantly in dark situations. Not to mention providing more than adequate lighting for covering your area.

Tactical lights of today are quite often lightweight and fit into the palm of the hand. Most have a pressure switch on the back end to make for easy use when checking a corner, or clearing a room. Many are made of nearly indestructible materials and can serve as a back up weapon should things get to that point. As you'll see, many are constructed with a striking point built into the rim of the flashlight. Gone are the days when you would turn your flash light into a Billy club and repeatedly hit your opponent enough to end the conflict. Now you can strike your attacker with the business end of one of these tactical lights and put them down with one hit. Permanently.

The other things you'll see are weapon-mounting systems. Many hand-held units are available with mounting kits for placement on rifles, shotguns and some handguns, making the perfect entry or defensive weapon. There are also lights designed specifically to go onto today's tactical handguns on the tactical rail many come from the factory with. Several even are available with a light/laser sight com-

bo, such as Streamlight's ultra-slick TLR-2 system. Throw this unit onto your weapon of choice and you have everything you need in a compact package. Remote switching options abound as well making weapon mounted lights very practical for tactical.

As with most things tactical, the market is literally exploding with new products. Flashlights are no exception and it seems every day some company has something new. The applications for these types of lights cross the boundaries too and many companies have models geared toward the hunting and outdoors crowd as well. One thing is certain, these types of lights are definitely not the same thing we had just a few years ago and the future is looking brighter.

Bulbs

Halogen bulbs are made of glass filled with a small amount of halogen gas. The average lifespan of halogen a bulb is 2,500 hours.

Krypton bulbs are made of glass and filled with krypton gas. This technology uses a filament, but produces double the average life of conventional light bulbs with an average life up to 2,000 hours.

Xenon bulbs are made of glass and filled with metal salts and a mixture of noble (non-reactive) gases including xenon, which produce a clear, white light. The average life span of xenon bulbs is 5,000 hours. Xenon is very efficient, when compared to halogen, producing twice the light while consuming half the power.

LEDs are basically a light bulb without a filament to burn out, and since they are very efficient at creating light without heat loss, they don't get hot. The LEDs longevity is further enhanced by its construction. An unbreakable, crystal clear, solid resin encases each LED and makes it nearly indestructible. The drawback to LEDs is their limited output for projecting over a great distance.

All LEDs operate at low temperatures, which make them safe to touch. LEDs have an average lifespan of 100,000 hours of continuous or cumulative use, operate on low voltage DC power, and produce no UV light. Light output of LEDs are measured in lumens; energy input to a lamp is measured in watts. The efficiency of a lamp is expressed as lumens per watt.

NICHIA 5 mm LEDs produce 2-3 lumens of light for each LED. LEDs are also more energy efficient than conventional incandescent light bulbs because most of the energy is turned directly into light; however, single LEDs do not create a significant amount of light.

LUXEON 1-Watt LEDs produce up to 25-30 lumens and provide 10 times the lumens of standard NICHIA LEDs.

LUXEON 3-Watt LEDs have an output of up to 75-80 lumens, or three times the lumens of Luxeon 1 watt LEDs and 25 times the lumens of standard NICHIA LEDs.

LUXEON 5-Watt LEDs have an output of up to 120 lumens, provide four times the lumens of LUXEON 1 watt LEDs and 50 times the lumens of standard NICHIA LEDs, the equivalent of 50, 5mm LEDs.

Lead-Acid Batteries

The cheapest cost of battery power per kilowatt-hour is the traditional lead-acid battery, but remember the earlier discussion of the Mag-Light and the heft of so many D-Cell batteries. The advantage of lightweight batteries must be compared to cost per kilowatt-hour of use and justified by convenience and frequency of use.

Primary (non-rechargeable) batteries are the standard AAA, AA, C, D and 9-volt alkaline units everyone is familiar with. Larger cell batteries provide a lower cost per kilowatt-hour than small cells, but their added size and weight is a disadvantage. The advantages of primary batteries are high energy density, long storage life and immediate operational readiness. No charging or priming time is required before use. Although secondary (rechargeable) batteries have improved, a regular household alkaline battery provides 50% more power than lithium-ion, one of the highest energy-dense secondary batteries.

Lithium Batteries

Lithium batteries lead the world in reliability and safety, providing long-term storage life (up to 10 years) at room temperature and long operational life over a wide range of operating temperatures. The superior chemical and design characteristics of these batteries are well recognized for both performance and power value.

Nickel-Cadmium (NiCad) Batteries

In terms of life cycling, the most enduring power cell is the standard nickel cadmium battery. The down side, is that Nickel-cadmium batteries have a moderate energy density, require periodic full discharges and contain toxic metals.

Nickel-Metal-Hydride Batteries

These batteries perform well in their early stages, but past 300-cycles, they start to deteriorate rapidly.

Lithium-Ion Batteries

In laboratory tests, the lithium-ion battery gets high marks because they offer the highest energy density and contain no toxic metals. Lithium-ion batteries have a lifetime of two to three years and the clock starts ticking as soon as the battery comes off the assembly line. For this reason, do not purchase extra lithium-ion batteries for future use, and always pay attention to the manufacture date.

Pentagonlight Molle Light

Micro Utility/Backup Light Promises Great Potential

BY SCOTT W. WAGNER

One of the biggest product development areas in the law enforcement equipment field has to be in the area of so-called "tactical lighting". For me, in order for a flashlight to be considered "tactical lighting" it must meet or exceed six basic criteria. A true tactical light must be:

1. Compact and easily carried on a duty belt or tactical rig
2. Very bright
3. Very durable, i.e. police/soldier proof
4. Offered in a color that is currently tactically in vogue
5. Marketed primarily to law enforcement, security or the military
6. Offer the very latest in technological improvements

In the olden days, the Kel-Light and Mag Light were considered the tactical lighting of the day. They really met only the criterion of being durable (doubling as an "emergency impact device" when needed), came in black, and were marketed to the law enforcement market. However, they used the same lighting technology with a plain, breakable incandescent bulb and weren't any brighter than the standard three-cell Ace Hardware special. This got better when Krypton gas bulbs were introduced, but these early "tactical lights" really offered no advantage over that Ace Hardware light other than in the area of durability.

The next step toward the true tactical lighting we see today was the introduction of the Mini Mag Light. Here at last was a light that could be carried on the police belt that was always with you no matter what you were doing (anyone ever been in one of those dayshift building searches where you went in without your flashlight because it was light outside – but needed it once you were inside?). My police department

Size comparison, MOLLE Light and Pentagonlight L2 two lithium cell LED Light. Note how sand colored polymer portions of MOLLE Light blend in with the rock. MOLLE Light takes one AA alkaline penlight battery for power.

didn't let us do that; I had to hide my Mini-Mag in a pocket. (The Chief didn't like how it looked on a belt.) That Mini-Mag wasn't a particularly bright light, and you had to use two hands to turn it off or on, but it was relatively durable and made of black aircraft aluminum, like its larger brother. I believe that the Mini-Mag, still in production for the civilian market today, spawned the entire generation of true tactical lighting products that abound in the law enforcement marketplace.

Surefire really brought that movement forward when it introduced their 6p lights with lithium batteries and Xenon gas bulbs, and manufacturers haven't looked back since.

One of those manufacturers is Pentagonlight, a manufacturer of durable tactical lighting both for hand-held and long-gun applications. They have just introduced a brand new light designed for law enforcement tactical and military teams, but which has a wider range of applications as well – the MOLLE Light.

This micro light, with a big light output, utilizes the old 90-degree military (and Boy Scout) angle-head flashlight design, but with 2007 features and increased brightness over its forbears. Designed from the ground up as a backup light (you can't have too many lights when things get hot and heavy) for attachment to MOLLE webbing on tactical armor or load-bearing vests, it weighs only 1.5 ounces and is 3.4 inches in overall length. The actual MOLLE clip that is adjustable around the circumference of the aluminum light body is constructed of spring steel for durability. The LED "bulb" is powered by a single AA Alkaline battery (for easy re-supply around the world) but cranks out up to 40 (yes that's right) Lumens of bright white light for a continuous run time of 5 hours. Some of the early packaging may say 25 lumens, but the LED element has been tuned and updated to the point that peak output normally runs 35 to 40 lumens, according to Pentagonlight™. At that rating, it starts to edge into lighting output ranges occupied by some of the smaller single and double cell lithium models.

There are other features that really distinguish this light and make it a must have is its durable

The MOLLE Light is an essential part of hiking/camping survival gear. With base red filter lens removed, compass is accessible.

construction. Starting with the LED element, it is designed for rough use. The center part of the body is constructed of matte finished aerospace aluminum, with the head and basecap made of polymer. Color choices at this time for the polymer elements are black and desert sand. Neatly concealed as part of the basecap are red or blue lighting filters, which unscrew off the base and screw in place over the lens cap. The Black model has a blue light filter that has some forensic application potential, while the desert sand model has the red filter specifically for night vision. Either filter can be ordered as additional options from Pentagonlight if you wish. Note that when you remove that lens filter from the base, you will find a compass concealed inside! Other features are a built in lanyard ring at the top of the light if you wish that attachment method, and of course the twistable MOLLE Clip, which can also fasten on belts or hiking and fishing vests. I suggested to Pentagonlight that they develop a duty belt holder consisting of a leather or nylon tube, with or without flap that the light can slide inside of with the clip holding it in place outside. This would help to conserve room on those ever more crowded belts. The on/off switch is what I call momentary/push to on. There is no discernable click when moving from the momentary setting to pushing through to continuous. It sits in a pentagon shaped recess on top of the light. In this position the light can be pushed on with the index finger like operating a spray can, or over the top with the thumb. With the thumb method, the MOLLE light can operate as an emergency tactical light applied in the Harries handgun flashlight technique.

Other applications? There are bunches. In addition to being a good survival light for hiking and camping, it would come in handy on a flyfishing vest, or stowed in a tackle box. I am sure hunters would appreciate it as well. It also might work out well attached to the jogging vest I wear when running after dark. With the red filter attached, it would work good attached to the visor in your cruiser for working on late night reports while preserving your night vision, or while flying an aircraft, or for a last minute equipment check in the SWAT Van. The uses are limited only by your imagination.

Author with MOLLE Light clipped high on entry vest

Ever since the introduction of the Mini-Mag Light, as a street officer, I have never been without an on duty backup flashlight carried on my gunbelt (I can do that now). I don't favor rechargeable lights for this purpose, too much to do in the way of maintenance requirements in terms of charging. As a tactical team member, I also favor carrying more than one light source on my person. When I am off duty, I always carry a two-cell tactical light in my pocket. The new MOLLE light has found a home on my MOLLE entry vest and maybe my civilian pocket. When I find the right duty belt holder, it will be there too. The MOLLE light clearly meets all my six requirements of a tactical light. Priced at $32, you can't afford to be without one (or two).

LIGHTS PRODUCT DIRECTORY

Sheffield 1 Watt Tactlite Luxeon Flashlight

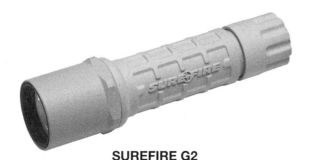

SUREFIRE G2

SUREFIRE G2

SHEFFIELD 1 WATT TACTLITE LUXEON FLASHLIGHT

- 1 Watt Luxeon LED
- 6 tooth strike plate
- 10 times brighter than other LEDS
- 10,000 hour LED life. Runs continuously for 15 hours
- Anodized aluminum non-slip handle
- O-ring sealed and water resistant
- Up to 35 lumens
- 1 AA battery included

Price: .... N/A

SUREFIRE 6P

Compact (pocket sized), high-intensity incandescent flashlight for tactical, self-defense, and general use. Produces a smooth, brilliant, pre-focused tactical-level beam with three times the light of a big two-D-cell flashlight—bright enough to temporarily blind and disorient a person by impairing his night-adapted vision. Light output may be nearly doubled with optional P61 lamp.

Features:

- Rugged aerospace-grade aluminum body, Type II anodized in glossy black
- O-ring sealed, weatherproof
- Tempered Pyrex® window
- **Tailcap switch:** press for momentary-on, twist for constant-on

- Switch lockout prevents accidental activation during transport or storage
- **Max Output:** 65/120 lumens with optional ultra high-output lamp
- **Runtime:** 60/20 minutes with optional ultra high-output lamp
- **Length:** 5.20 inches
- **Weight:** 5.30 ounces
- **Battery:** Two 123A lithiums

Price: $59.00

SUREFIRE G2

Compact (pocket sized), high-intensity incandescent flashlight for tactical, self-defense, and general use. Similar to our 6P but with a tough polymer body. Puts out a smooth, brilliant, pre-focused, tactical-level beam with over three times the light of a big two-D-cell flashlight—bright enough to temporarily blind and disorient a person by impairing his night-adapted vision. Light output may be nearly doubled with optional P61 lamp. Small size, light weight, and high output make it a perfect for camping, backpacking, emergency/disaster-preparedness kits, or everyday carry.

Features:

Rugged, lightweight, corrosion-proof Nitrolon® polymer body, available in black, olive drab, tan, yellow. O-ring sealed, weatherproof. Tailcap switch: press for momentary-on, twist for constant-on. Switch lockout prevents acciden-

SUREFIRE E2L-HA-WH

SUREFIRE G3L-BK

tal activation during transport or storage.

- **Max Output:** 65/120 lumens with optional ultra high-output lamp
- **Runtime:** 60/20 minutes with optional ultra high-output lamp
- **Length:** 5.10 inches
- **Weight:** 4.10 ounces
- **Battery:** Two 123A lithiums

Price: $36.00

SUREFIRE E2L-HA-WH

Compact (pocket sized), dual-output LED flashlight with extended runtime. Its virtually indestructible, two-stage light-emitting diode (LED) light source produces a smooth, pre-focused beam that, at maximum output, is three times brighter than that of a big two-D-cell flashlight. At its low setting it produces a useful three lumens of light and continues producing useful light levels for 100 hours on a set of lithium batteries. Small size (it's lightweight enough to clip to hat brim for hands-free operation), dual output, extended runtime, and 10-year battery shelf life make the E2L perfect for camping, backpacking, travel, emergency/disaster preparedness kits, or as an everyday-carry for general use.

Features:

Dual-output LED light source has no filament to burn out or break, lasts for thousands of hours. Rugged aerospace-grade aluminum body, Mil-Spec Type III hard anodized

in olive drab. O-ring sealed, weatherproof. Total Internal Reflection (TIR) lens. Pocket clip. Tailcap switch: press for momentary-on, press further to click constant-on. Switch lockout prevents accidental activation during transport or storage.

- **Max Output:** High: 60 lumens; Low: 3 lumens
- **Runtime:** High: 11 hours; Low: 100 hours
- **Bezel Diameter:** 1.0 inch
- **Length:** 5.40 inches
- **Weight:** 3.70 ounces

Price: $129.00

SUREFIRE G3L-BK

Compact (palm sized), high-intensity LED flashlight for tactical, outdoor, and general use. Puts out a smooth, brilliant beam with four times the light of a two-D-cell flashlight. Produces tactical-level lighting (enough to temporarily blind and disorient an aggressor) for nearly six hours and useful light levels for an impressive 9.4 hours on a single set of batteries. Features a tough, corrosion-proof Nitrolon® body with molded-in grid and a rugged, aerospace-grade aluminum bezel anodized in black. Light weight, compact size, high output, and extended runtime make the G3 LED a great choice for law enforcement, security, military, and self-defense applications; camping, backpacking, and general outdoor use; and emergency/disaster-preparedness.

Features virtually indestructible, microprocessor-controlled LED has no filament to burn out or break; lasts for

SUREFIRE G3L-BK-KIT01

SUREFIRE L1

thousands of hours. Produces tactical-level light for 5.8 hours on a set of batteries; 9.4 hours of useful light. Precision reflector creates smooth beam without spots or rings. Rugged, lightweight, corrosion-proof Nitrolon® polymer body and anodized aluminum bezel in black. O-ring sealed; weatherproof. Tailcap switch: press for momentary-on, twist for constant-on. Patented switch lockout prevents accidental activation.

- **Max Output:** 80 lumens
- **Runtime:** 9.42 hours (5.8 hrs tactical-level light)
- **Length:** 6.50 inches
- **Weight:** 5.50 ounces
- **Battery:** Three 123A Lithium

Price: $89.00

SUREFIRE G3L-BK-KIT01

Compact (palm sized), high-intensity LED flashlight with an ergonomic holster specially designed for quick deployment of the flashlight—especially when pairing the light with a handgun. Developed for use in law enforcement, where split seconds count, the G3™ LED Holster Kit is also a great choice for anyone who needs a flashlight that produces tactical-level output (enough to temporarily blind an assailant) and an effective, ergonomic way to carry and deploy the light quickly. The G3 LED runs for 9.4 hours on a single set of batteries. The included rugged polymer holster has an integral magazine that holds three spare batteries, giving the G3 LED the capacity to run for over 18 hours in

the field—far longer than a rechargeable flashlight. The reversible, ambidextrous holster is adjustable to accommodate personal preference and to permit maximum ease and speed when drawing the light and pairing it with a handgun, if applicable. The holster accommodates any SureFire flashlight with a 1.25" aluminum bezel. Kit includes flashlight, holster, mounting hardware, manual, and nine SureFire 123A lithium batteries.

Price: $129.00

SUREFIRE L1

Compact (pocket sized), dual-output LED flashlight for backpacking, camping, and general use. Uses a virtually indestructible, power-regulated light emitting diode (LED) light source plus a two-stage tailcap switch for instant selection of desired output level—extremely long-runtime low beam for close-up work or a long-runtime high beam with over three times the light of a big two-D-cell flashlight. Small size, extended runtime, high output, and 10-year battery shelf life make it perfect for emergency/disaster preparedness kits, the outdoors, or everyday carry.

Features LED light source has no filament to burn out or break, lasts for thousands of hours. LED output available in white. Rugged aerospace-grade aluminum body, Mil-Spec Type III hard anodized in olive drab. O-ring sealed, weather proof. Total internal reflection (TIR) lens produces tightly focused beam. Pocket clip. Tailcap switch: press for momentary-on low beam, press further for high beam, twist

Surefire Optimus

for constant-on. Switch lockout prevents accidental activation during transport or storage.

- **Max Output:** High: 65 lumens; Low: 10 lumens
- **Runtime:** High: 1.5 hours; Total: 16 hours
- **Bezel Diameter:** 1.0 inch
- **Length:** 4.52 inches
- **Weight:** 2.9 ounces

Price: $135.00

SUREFIRE OPTIMUS

Eleven settings ensure that the pocket-sized Surefire Optimus is ready for virtually any situation, environment, or circumstance. Set its magnetic selector ring to any of eight preset output levels ranging from two lumens (enough to read a map) to 200 lumens of blinding light that's instantly available by pressing its Max Blast™ tailcap all the way down.

For a tactical advantage that doesn't involve overwhelming an aggressor's eyesight with 200 lumens of electronically regulated LED light, switch the Optimus to its strobe setting and stun him with bright, flickering light designed to disorient and confuse. And should you ever need an emergency beacon, just set the Optimus to its SOS setting and stick it where a passing rescue plane, boat, or vehicle can see it. To help you get the most out of your batteries, the Optimus even features a built-in fuel gauge that lets you know when you should consider switching to a lower output level or changing batteries.

Simply twist its bezel to change the beam's light distribution from spot to flood and any point in between—without any deterioration in beam quality, thanks to SureFire's Vari-Beam™ technology. The Optimus uses precision optics to redistribute the light's energy. The result is a pure beam that's always in focus.

Leave the pocket clip on to carry it in your pocket, or remove it and holster the light. Taking it off also lets you take full advantage of the Optimus' CombatGrip,™ a stepped-down body that provides a secure hold in any weather and makes it easier to pair the Optimus with a handgun.

- **Microprocessor-controlled, virtually indestructible LED**
- **Eight pre-set output levels from 2 to 200 lumens**
- **Vari-Beam™technology changes beam from spot to flood and all points in between—with no degradation in quality**
- **Tactical strobe to disorient an aggressor and flashing SOS beacon for emergency use**
- **Built-in fuel gauge serves as a reminder to power down to a lower output level or change batteries**
- **Attachable/removable pocket clip allows customizable carrying options**
- **CombatGrip™provides one-handed control—especially when pairing flashlight with a firearm (includes two rubber grips:** one for use with pocket clip, one for use without pocket clip)
- **Mil-Spec Type III hard-anodized aerospace-grade aluminum body**
- **Compression-resistant O-ring seals for weatherproofing**
- **Coated, impact-resistant Pyrex® window protects optics and LED and helps maximize light transmission**
- **Tailcap switching:** press for momentary-on at output level determined by selector ring, press all the way for momentary-on max output; twist for constant-on at output level set by selector ring, twist further for constant-on max output
- **Patented lockout tailcap feature prevents accidental activation**
- **Runs on 2 Lithium 123A batteries**

Price: $279.00

Surefire X400

SUREFIRE X300

Surefire E1B Backup

SUREFIRE X300

The SureFire X300™ features a solid-state, electronically regulated LED that generates 110 lumens of tactical-level light — enough to overwhelm an aggressor's night-adapted vision. Its specially developed Total Internal Reflection (TIR) lens creates a bright, tightly focused central beam with plenty of reach and enough surround beam to accommodate peripheral vision. A hard-anodized aerospace-grade aluminum body protects the X300's electronics, and O-ring seals and gaskets make the entire unit waterproof to 22 meters. A tempered Pyrex® window protects its LED and, thanks to a thin layer of anti-reflective coating, helps maximize light transmission. The X300 attaches to both Universal and Picatinny rails in moments, via its proprietary Rail-Lock™ system, and comes with adapter plates for both. An ambidextrous toggle/push switch provides convenient, fail-safe operation. Optional SureFire grip switches, which allow precision control without altering one's grip on the weapon, are also available for many handguns.

Features:

- **Max Output:** 110 lumens (5 times the light of a two-D-cell flashlight); continues producing tactical-level light for 2.4 hours
- **Versatile beam is perfect for longerand close-range applications**
- **Ambidextrous tactical switching enables fail-safe operation under fire**
- **Instantly attaches to most handguns with**

a Universal rail and handguns/long guns with a Picatinny rail
- **1.39" high by 1.43" wide by 3.53" long; weighs 3.7 ounces (with batteries)**
- **Batteries — two SF123 3-volt lithiums with 10-year shelf life**
- **Aerospace-aluminum construction with Mil-Spec, Type III hard-anodized finish**
- **O-ring sealed and gasketed; waterproof to 22 meter**
- **Accepts optional pressure-activated switches for precision control without altering grip on weapon**

Price: $225.00

SUREFIRE X400

The X400 is the same unit as the X300, but is also equipped with a 635nm Red Laser.

Price: $435.00

SUREFIRE E1B BACKUP

Ultra compact (finger length), dual-output LED flashlight with extended runtime and tactical-level output. The E1B was developed as an everyday-carry flashlight for undercover officers and as a backup light for patrol officers — but it's also ideal for outdoor, self-defense, and everyday use by civilians. The Backup features a virtually indestructible, electronically regulated light emitting diode (LED) that,

Streamlight Stinger DS™ LED

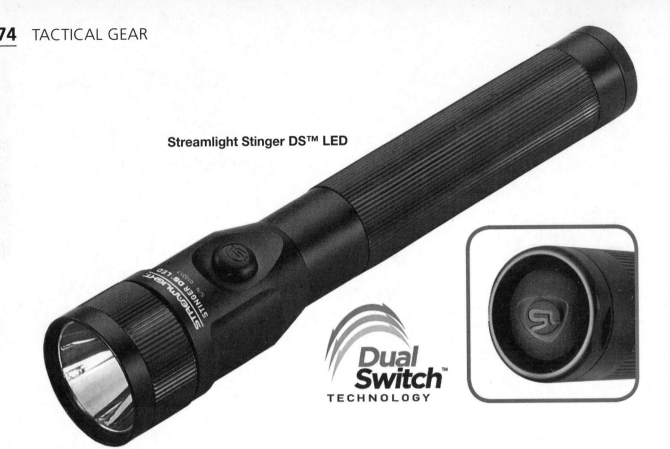

Dual Switch™
TECHNOLOGY

on its "high" setting, produces a smooth, tactical-level beam (enough light to temporarily overwhelm the night-adapted vision of an aggressor) with four times the output, of a two-D-cell flashlight. And it continues generating tactical-light levels for 1.3 hours on a single battery. On its "low" setting, the E1B generates five lumens of light that's perfect for reading a map, checking an ID, or navigating a dark pathway, and generates useful light levels for 37 hours. And the E1B's click-on/off tailcap is programmed to instantly deliver maximum output when its pushbutton is depressed, a critical feature in law enforcement and tactical applications where a lot of light is frequently needed immediately. Rounding out this flashlight's features are its unique "melted" styling — no knurling or sharp edges to catch on clothing — and two-way pocket clip, which lets a user carry the Backup bezel up or down, whichever he or she prefers.

Features:

Virtually indestructible, dual-output light emitting diode has no filament to burn out or break; lasts for thousands of hours. Total Internal Reflection (TIR) lens creates a flawless, bright beam with plenty of reach and enough surround beam to accommodate peripheral vision. Coated Pyrex® window protects the lens and LED and maximizes light transmission. Rugged aerospace-grade aluminum body, Mil-Spec Type III hard anodized in black. Sleek, "melted" body has no knurling or sharp edges to catch on or wear out clothing. O-ring sealed, weatherproof. Two-way pocket clip allows light to be carried bezel up or down. Two-stage tailcap switch: press for momentary-on at high setting, release and press again (within two seconds) for momentary-on at low setting; click for constant-on at high-setting, click off and on again (within two seconds) for constant-on at low setting.

- **Max Output:** 5/80 lumens
- **Runtime:** 37/1.3 hours (low/high settings)
- **Length:** 4.00 inches
- **Weight:** 2.80 ounces
- **Battery:** One 123A lithium

Price: $110.00

STREAMLIGHT STINGER DS™ LED

The Stinger DS™ LED is a rechargeable flashlight with a fully independent dual switch.

- **DUAL SWITCH TECHNOLOGY – Access any of the three variable lighting modes and strobe via the tail cap or the head-mounted switch**
- **Head switch operates independently from the tail cap switch**
- **The combination of a rechargeable battery and a lifetime super high flux LED results in the lowest operating cost of any flashlight made.**
- **Deep-dish parabolic reflector produces a long range targeting beam with optimal**

Streamlight Stylus Pro

peripheral illumination to aid in navigation.
- **Lumens:** 80 typical
- **Runtime:** High – Up to 1.75 hours; Medium – Up to 3.5 hours; Low – up to 6.75 hours; Strobe – Up to 5.5 hours
- Optimized electronics provides regulated intensity
- **Length:** 8.85 " (22.48 cm)
- **Weight:** 12.8 oz (364 grams)
- 6000 series machined aircraft aluminum with non-slip rubberized comfort grip
- Unbreakable Polycarbonate with scratch-resistant coating
- O-Ring sealed construction
- 3 watt super high flux LED, impervious to shock
- 3-cell, 3.6 Volt Nickel cadmium sub-C battery is rechargeable up to 1000 times
- Includes Anti-roll Ring
- Fits existing Stinger chargers
- 10 hours to recharge on 100V, 120V, 230V or 240V AC
- 12V DC 2.5 hour fast charger, 5-bank charger or PiggyBack® charger offered
- Safety wands, ring holder, color filters accessories available

Price: $125.95

STREAMLIGHT STYLUS PRO

Streamlight's new high flux LED light with Proprietary Micro Optical Systems has "Battery-Booster" electronics to provide a super-bright beam.

- Proprietary Micro Optical System (MOS), for optimized output and runtime
- Up to 24 lumens output for up to 7.5 hrs runtime
- Super-bright 1/2 watt, 30,000 hour high flux LED
- An internal polymer body liner and shock proof switch housing allow for operation under the most extreme conditions
- Rubber push button tail cap switch
- O-ring sealed
- Unbreakable polycarbonate lens
- Unbreakable pocket clip
- Belt Holster included
- Corrosion and water resistant construction
- Water resistant per IPX4; in accordance with specification EN 60529:1992
- Shock-proof; drop test verified above the industry standard of six feet
- Type II MIL-SPEC abrasion and corrosion-resistant anodized aircraft aluminum
- Includes (2) "AAA" alkaline batteries and holster
- 1.64 oz. with battery

Streamlight Sidewinder

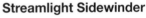

Streamlight The Nano Light

- 5.3" long
- Available in Matte Black
- Limited Lifetime Warranty

Price: $44.95

STREAMLIGHT SIDEWINDER

Sidewinder, the most versatile military light in the world. Twenty flashlights in one! Each LED features 4 levels of output intensities: Low (5%), Medium (20%), Medium-High (50%), High (100%) plus a Strobe function (100%)

- One switch for On-Off, dimming and mode selection functions.
- Pull-to-turn locking rotary color(4)selector knob with tactile indicator for easy operation with gloves
- Double click button to initiate strobe function from "Off" position
- Push and hold button for light output levels from "Off" position
- Sidewinder Light Output and 2 AA Alkaline Battery Run Time
- Also accepts 2 "AA" lithium batteries, which allow extended operation, or extreme temperatures (-40°F 150°F)
- Mounts to MOLLE or ACH for hands-free use
- High-impact, super-tough nylon case; drop-test verified from 30 feet
- Battery polarity indicators for easy

replacement in the dark
- Unbreakable, gasket-sealed polycarbonate lens with scratch-resistant coating
- O-ring sealed for waterproof operation. Meets MIL-STD-810F, Method 512.4
- Tethered tailcap to prevent loss
- Cord attachment hole supports up to 25 lbs
- Articulating 185° rotating head
- Spring steel clip attaches to MOLLE or belt
- Clip can be mounted on either side of the light
- **Dimensions:** 4.63" High; 2.31" Wide
- **Weight:** 4.96 ounces
- Available in Coyote Tan and Green
- US and foreign patents pending
- One year limited warranty

Price: $79.95

STREAMLIGHT THE NANO LIGHT

Truly tiny, the Nanolight® is a weatherproof, personal flashlight featuring a 100,000 hour life LED. Includes a non-rotating snap hook for easy one handed operation when attached to a keychain.

- Easily attaches/detaches to just about anything with convenient pocket clip or key ring
- Up to 8 hrs. run time
- Machined aircraft-grade aluminum with

Streamlight MicroStream

Streamlight Super Tac

- anodized finish
- Powered by 4 alkaline button cells (included)
- 100,000 hr. lifetime high-intensity LED
- LED available in white (10 lumens)
- 1.47" x .51"
- .36 oz.
- Available in black

Price: $19.95

STREAMLIGHT MICROSTREAM

Streamlight's new high-flux LED light with Proprietary Micro Optical Systems has "Battery-Booster" electronics to provide a super-bright beam.

- Proprietary Micro Optical System (MOS), for optimized output and runtime
- Up to 20 lumens output for up to 1.5 hrs runtime
- Super-bright 1/2 watt, 30,000 hour high flux LED
- An internal polymer body liner and shock proof switch housing allow for operation under the most extreme conditions
- Rubber push button tail cap switch
- O-ring sealed
- Unbreakable polycarbonate lens
- Corrosion and water resistant construction
- Water resistant per IPX4; in accordance with specification EN 60529:1992

- Type II MIL-SPEC abrasion and corrosion-resistant anodized aircraft aluminum
- Shock-proof; drop test verified above the industry standard of six feet
- Unbreakable pocket clip
- Key ring and safety lanyard included
- Includes (1) "AAA" alkaline battery
- 1.04 oz with battery
- 3.5" Long
- Available in Matte Black
- Limited Lifetime Warranty

Price: $24.95

STREAMLIGHT SUPER TAC

- Gun Mountable and extremely bright
- Up to 30,000 peak beam candlepower
- C4 LED is 3X brighter than a Super high-flux LED
- 135 Lumens
- **Runtime:** up to 3.5 hours
- Machined Aluminum
- **Length:** 6.62 inches (16.81 cm)
- **Weight:** 7.1 oz (200 g)
- Limited Lifetime Warranty
- Two 3 Volt CR123A Batteries (included)
- Holster Included

Price: $119.95

Streamlight Scorpion LED

Streamlight TLR-1 and TLR-2

STREAMLIGHT TL-2

The brightness of a larger light in a compact size that can be comfortably used with a firearm.

- **Team Soldier Certified Gear**
- **Two 3 volt CR123A lithium batteries with a storage life of 10 years (included)**
- **High-pressure xenon gas-filled bi-pin bulb**
- **Up to 7,900 peak beam candlepower (78 lumens)**
- **Adjustable focus**
- **Spare bulb included**
- **1.3 hrs. continuous run time**
- **Pocket clip, adjustable lanyard**
- **Head:** 1.25;" Body: .9" x Length 4.9"
- **4.2 oz. with batteries**
- **Shock-Proof model available. Designed to withstand even the punishing recoil of a 3" 12 gauge magnum slug.**
  Available in black

Price: $82.95

STREAMLIGHT SCORPION LED

One of the brightest, lightest personal flashlight ever created, the Scorpion® LED is the only tactical light with a rubberized grip and tailcap switch and anti-roll head. Available with a C4 LED.

- **Team Soldier Certified Gear**
- **Anti-roll head**

- **C4 LED is 2X brighter than a Super high-flux LED, delivers 120 lumens**
- **Up to 3.5 hours of runtime to the 10% output level.**
- **5.72"**
- **5.3 oz. with batteries**
- **Two 3 volt CR123A lithium batteries with a storage life of up to 10 years (included)**
- **Machined aluminum covered by a rubber-armored sleeve for a sure grip**
- **O-ring sealed for moisture protection**
- **Available in black**

Price: $59.95

STREAMLIGHT TLR-1 AND TLR-2

Intensly bright, virtually indestructable tactical light, attaches/detaches to almost any gun in seconds. The TLR-2 has the same great features of the TLR-1 with an integrated laser sight for accurate aiming.

- **Powered by two 3-volt CR123 lithium batteries with 10-year storage life**
- **Shockproof super high-flux LED with blinding beam (up to 80 lumens) with bright side-light – will not break or burn out**
- **Up to 2.5 hrs runtime**
- **Rail grip clamp system securely attaches/ detaches quickly and safely with no tools and without putting your hands in front of**

AimShot! Heatseeker

AimShot! Xenon Illuminator
Tactical Flashlight TX 125 & TX 75

muzzle
- Fast, Adjustable, Secure Side mounting to 1913 and Glock style Rails
- Machined aluminum sealed construction with black anodized finsih
- Waterproof to one meter for one hour, dustproof
- Ambidextrous momentary/steady on/off switch
- Highly accurate sight repeatability when remounting
- Fits existing light bearing holsters
- 4.18 oz.
- Lithium Battery Notice under TECH DOCS
- MIL-SPEC 810F Performance Tested

TLR-1 Price: $193.95
TLR-2 Price: $482.95

AIMSHOT! HEATSEEKER

HeatSeeker tracks any heat source up to 300 yards!
Technology for the hunt, security or law enforcement! Heatseeker works by detecting heat sources and motion of heat to help find game and bad guys. Temperatures are read as infrared light waves which appear on the digital bar graph display. A "squelch" alert can also be heard through the ear plug. Detects objects as close as 2' and can reach as far as 900' under optimum conditions.
Features:

- Built-in laser and infrared sighting makes acquiring targets easier
- Infrared laser capability for tracking in total darkness while using night vision
- Adjustable volume, for when silence is critical
- Runs on one 9V battery (included)
- High-impact ABS plastic construction
- 7" long and weighs just 8-1/4 ozs.
- Includes belt pouch, earphone and wrist strap.

Price: $249.99

AIMSHOT! XENON ILLUMINATOR TACTICAL FLASHLIGHT TX 125 & TX 75

The Xenon Illuminator is a bright (165 lumen -TX125, 120 lumen TX75) and shatterproof tactical flashlight with a lightweight aluminum bulb base. A new advanced heat dissipation system has been engineered to increase bulb life and resist flashlight burnout in high temperature environments. Used by military and law enforcement agencies around the world. It provides all the light needed to quickly identify any threats hiding in dimly lit areas. With the universal tactical flashlight glove, you can scan an area with the light while remaining firing-ready.
Features:

- **Dual glass/polycarbonate lens:** shatterproof & high-heat resistance

AimShot! MT61167 Universal Mounting System

- Super-lightweight @ 3 oz
- Made of virtually unbreakable Black Delrin® with non-slip rubber body
- Advanced aluminum heat dissipation system
- 2-position end (constant-on, intermittent)
- Focusable beam Shatter-proof lens and shock-resistant lamp assembly
- Waterproof to 100M
- Belt pouch included

Price: .... $99.99 TX 75; $139.95 TX125

AIMSHOT! MT61167 UNIVERSAL MOUNTING SYSTEM

The AimSHOT mounting system will enable you to mount laser sights on virtually any weapon including pistols, revolvers, rifles, and shotguns. Available in both black and silver, constructed of lightweight aluminum, mounts are equipped with shims to accommodate any pistol or revolver including round and square trigger guards. Rifle mounts include various length screws which adjust to any diameter barrel. For shotguns, the rib vent adaptor will fit any double barrel or rib vent shotgun.

Price: $21.99

BURRIS SHOTCAM

The ShotCam fastens to the picatinny rail of many handguns, shotguns, and carbines. It features three technologies: 120 Lumen Flashlight; Projected Laser Sight; Digital Video Camera, all rolled up into a compact and lightweight package.

One primary application is for law enforcement officers to not only have the benefits of laser and illumination, but to also record on video an entire conflict automatically once a handgun is removed from a holster. Specialized holsters are used with ShotCam which have a special magnet molded into the plastic. A special switch on the ShotCam senses the magnet to put the unit into sleep mode. Once the handgun is removed from the holster the ShotCam is actuated and records up to one hour of video. The video can then be used as evidence to support the officer, department, and government agency. The same could be said for application in a home defense situation.

If a full hour of video is taken, ShotCam stops video recording and goes into a still frame mode capturing a 3.2megapixel photograph of what the gun was pointing at when the shot was fired. The ShotCam can be set to several modes such that any or all of it's features can be activated automatically when unholstering a handgun, or manually. Choose illumination only, laser only, video only, or still frame only, or any combination of these modes. The ShotCam can be quickly removed from a weapon in seconds and used in special situations as an illuminator or camcorder when these features are desired but using a weapon as a pointing devise is inappropriate.

Price: $699

Burris ShotCam

PentAgon Light X2

PENTAGON LIGHT X2

Xenon is the best performing bulb filling gas and provides the maximum lumen per watt over the other gases for incandescent lamps. X2's xenon light source generates an amazing 70 lumens of powerful light collimated by their proprietary reflector designed for focusing the light generated into a smooth intensified light beam.

The light beam is pre-focused at the factory for maximal center intensity in achieving the greatest distance. The lamp assembly is completely isolated from the rest of the light while the batteries are compartmentalized to provide X2 with excellent performance against weapon recoil. The "flaming heat-sink" design of the head ensures adequate heat dissipation for thermal management of the xenon bulb in lengthening its bulb life and optimizing its performance. X2 is crafted out of aerospace grade aluminum tube using precision CNC machine in anti-reflective, anti-corrosive, and anti-abrasive military spec Type III hard anodized exterior finish. All connections are sealed with double O-rings for extra protection against water leakage. X2 is not just a limited use incandenscent light, since its head is interchangeable for alternate light sources from a diverse selection of conversion heads available separately, so your initial investment for a high quality flashlight is maximized. The removable pocket clip can be taken off easily for carrying the light in a holster. X2 is preconfigured with TC4 push on/off PentagonLight™ signature tail-cap switch.

The extended long throw of our tail button switch can easily press slightly for momentary on while allowing click to constant on. The switch is housed in the anti-roll pentagonal shape tail cap making it easy for one-hand operation. Optional tail-caps are available for additional switching functions. Two PentagonLight™ CR-123A lithium batteries with 10-year shelf-life are included. For a similar light but size is the concern, consider X1 Xenon Light. For longer distance and brightness, consider X3 Xenon Light.

Features:
- **Brightness:** 80 Lumens
- **Run-Time:** 60 Minutes
- **Batteries:** Two CR-123A
- **Bezel Size:** 1.25"
- **Length:** 5.5" (140 mm)
- **Weight:** 5.2 oz. (147 g)
- **Xenon Gas-Filled Lamp**
- **Aerospace Grade Aluminum Body**
- **TC4 Push On/Off Tail Switch**
- **Double O-Ring Sealing**
- **Military Spec Type III Hard Anodized Exterior**
- **Removable Pocket Clip**

Price: $89.00

INTRODUCTION TO
Tactical Guns

BY EDITORS OF GUN DIGEST

What are tactical firearms? Straightforward question, isn't it? We just wish there were a straightforward answer!

Nearly any firearm can have a tactical application, depending on the situation. In the 1920s and 1230s, there were few weapons designed expressly for tactical use. Most police departments used stock or slightly-altered versions of popular sportings arms such as the Remington Model 8 rifle, the Winchester Model 1907 carbine, and the Winchester Model 1897 riot gun.

Today, almost every American arms maker offers firearms that can have a tactical application. Nevertheless, a set of standards have evolved for tactical weapons.

Handguns

Tactical handguns are virtually always semi-autos. While more than a few law enforcement personnel undoubtedly carry a Smith & Wesson J-frame somewhere under their gear, we are aware of no organization that issues revolvers as a primary sidearm. It's not a question of reliability but rather of capacity. Five or six shots look pretty pale alongside even a 10-round magazine, to say nothing of the ultra-high-capacity magazines that have become so popular.

The 9mm Parabellum still ranks high in tactical circles, but the .40 S&W has given it a real run for its money. And now the almost century-old .45

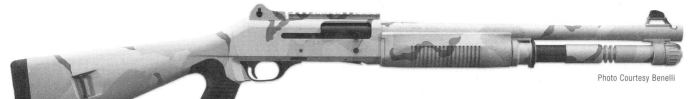

Photo Courtesy Benelli

ACP is gaining in popularity by virtue of its slap-'em-down, flying-bowling-ball nature, and the derivative .45 GAP has quite a few adherents. Some departments favor the .357 SIG, and the FN 5.7 is gaining in popularity due to its excellent penetration. As far as deep-concealment backup autos are concerned, the .380 and .32 ACP remain as popular as ever.

In the following pages, we have limited our listings to models that could make a legitimate claim to being primary or secondary tactical handguns. The list isn't necessariily complete, as new models are being introduced virtually every week.

Rifles

Although there are a number of pump-action rifles that are marketed as tactical weapons, only two types of rifles have been generally accepted as tactical weapons: semi-autos and bolt actions.

As for semi-autos, the AR-style rifle reigns supreme. It has proven itself nearly an ideal platform for close-quarters tactical applications. While most ARs are chambered in .223, the 6.8mm and even the .308 have strong proponents in some quarters.

The carbine chambered in pistol calibers also has a tactical application, albeit a somewhat limited

one. We have included various models chambered in 9mm and .45 ACP because hese weapons are occasionally seen in a secondary role, especially in smaller organizations.

Bolt action rifles, from the .223 to the .50 BMG, have a definite tactical role as sniper weapons.

Shotguns

Most tactical shotguns are pump actions, although a few semi-autos are offered. The pump action apparently has an advantage over other types because of its near-foolproof reliability. As far as chamberings are concerned, the 12 gauge, in either 2.75-, 3-, or 3.5-inch length, has no serious challengers.

Note

In the following section, we have tried to represent tactical weapons at all price points, from entry-level to high end. Some departments, and some individuals, have higher budgets than others, and some of the better tactical weapons are found at the lower end of the price scale.

Photo Courtesy EOTech

The 1911 As a Tactical Pistol

BY ROBERT CAMPBELL

Editor's Note: The 1911 pistol, fast approaching its 100th anniversary, has re-emerged in recent years as a popular choice in tactical pistols. We're delighted to present the following essay from Robert Campbell, a former police officer with plenty of experience with 1911s!

I have asked myself if the handguns I carry are what I need or, rather, if they are merely what is expected of me. I have my answer on those occasions when I test a lesser handgun. I am happy to keep on hand first-class lifesaving gear. I don't dress to impress nor need an ego uplift.

I have turned to the tactical models of modern 1911 handguns for all-around use for good reasons. There are significant differences in the handguns that earn the title "tactical." I have tried to pinpoint the birth of the tactical pistol. It may have had a beginning when Tom Threepersons fitted a special high-profile front sight to his Single Action Army. Or perhaps when Bat Masterson ordered an SAA light on the trigger. But the Tactical Pistol as we know it today began with Jeff Cooper and the Consensus. Cooper and other shooters active at the time reached an agreement on what the 1911 needed: A speed safety, a trigger job, and a good set of sights. If you were going to experiment with exotic bullet styles you needed a feed ramp and chamber polish known as throating. Over the years professionals had their guns nickel- or silver-plated. Some of it was show but some of it was for practical protection of the handgun. Today, we apply a black tactical phosphate or polymer-based finish. The changes in the 1911 did not happen overnight but they have been beneficial. There are quite a few handguns on the mar-

Geometry is everything- the 1911 features a low bore axis and short trigger compression. There is little leverage for the piece to recoil, and the short straight-to-the-rear trigger compression allows good control.

ket that represent the Consensus but stop short of what we refer to as tactical pistols. A top-of-the-line tactical pistol will feature Novak, Heinie or McCormack high visibility sights, a match-grade barrel, and a beavertail grip safety. The design of the pistol is sound, well proven in hard use. The tactical operation of the .45 auto is unquestioned.

When looking at the Tactical Pistol we might ask what the extras accomplish. After all, the guns are not inexpensive. The benefits are defined by the tactical concept. The main benefit is that the pistol is more comfortable to use in prolonged fire. While the pistol will seldom be fired in action, and at those times a few shots will suffice, the skill of the user must be honed by long hours on the range, expending thousands of rounds of ammunition. Ruggedness is but one of the criteria set forth.

One extra is a beavertail grip safety. A well designed grip safety not only funnels the pistol's grip into the hand, it makes certain the safety is properly actuated. The extended slide lock safety or speed safety is an obvious improvement. While some of us find the standard 1911 safety usable, the speed safety as typified by Wilson Combat paddle types are much more functional. It isn't just actuating the safety quickly to take it off safe. When moving or reholstering the gun, it is good to be able to quickly move the gun to on safe. When working on tactical movement or in competition we appreciate the ability to be able to quickly place the gun on safe. A handgun with no safety has no place in tactical operations.

The grip frame of the tactical pistol is often stippled or checkered in the front strap and the rear strap is sometimes checkered as well. The Smith and Alexander magazine guide is the choice of operators who prefer a magazine chute that allows quick, sure loading of the magazine. The Smith and Alexander magazine guide defines the checkered mainspring housing.

This is an Action Works 1911, a first-class pistol for going in harm's way. The sights are Heinie rear and Novak front, the frame is stippled, and the King's beavertail is a worthwhile addition. The trademark Action Work's drop safety is fitted.

Next, we move to the trigger. The person who appreciates good trigger compression and is willing to pay for a top-of-the-line pistol should be able to handle a light, crisp trigger compression. Most modern tactical pistols will have a trigger compression of three and one half to four pounds. The trigger will be very clean, very crisp, and consistent. This is one of the primary advantages of the tactical pistol. It is made for operators who appreciate the handgun and who can handle the handgun's trigger action well.

The sights of the tactical pistol are also very important. Handgun sights have evolved a great deal in recent years. The embryonic sights found on the Government Issue 1911 are seldom found any more except on low-budget pistols. Even the least expensive handguns from the major makers have some type of high-visibility sight. Novak sights were among the first and remain a good choice. High-visibility sights are also designed to be snag-free and relatively low profile in order to allow a smooth draw from concealed carry. So, we find two attributes that would be mutually exclusive without good engineering: high-visibility and low-profile. The best sights accomplish each requirement well. The sights offer an excellent sight picture and allow the user to get good sight alignment and make a good shot.

The exact size of the sight channel is also important. If the tunnel is too long or deep in the rear sight, shadows will intrude and the sight picture is compromised. The front sight is usually a square post. Quite often, the Novak front sight is used even when a Heinie rear sight is chosen. This works well. Some tactical pistols have fiber optic front sights, a great advance for aging eyes.

Sight options vary. As an example, the High Standard G-Man, a top-quality Tactical Pistol, comes standard with self-luminous iron sights. The Kimber Custom II version chosen by LAPD SWAT is fitted with Meprolight self-luminous sights. Tritium sights are not fitted to every tactical tactical handgun but should be. Trijicon refits are popular, so are the Wilson Combat Nite Eyes.

Then we come to the handgun's grip. Smooth grips and ivory grips are often found on prized 1911

pistols but not the tactical pistol. The grips may be of plastic, Micarta, or wood, but they will have sufficient purchase for an operator to hold the handgun in firing, whether his hands are sweaty, cold, or tired. There are many good choices. Some of the grip panels are raspy for average hands. Many of us work on the keyboard more than with tools, and our hands are not conditioned for such rough use. A half checkered, half smooth grip such as the Ahrends may be considered ideal for most of us. The Ahrends tactical grips feature a cut-out section to allow the thumb to quickly access the magazine release, a good touch.

Ahrends' special half-checkered handgun grip is for those who debate between smooth and checkered grips. Some feel that a smooth grip allows the shooter to quickly reposition his hands. I myself have no problem in repositioning my hand when using checkered grips. I simply release my

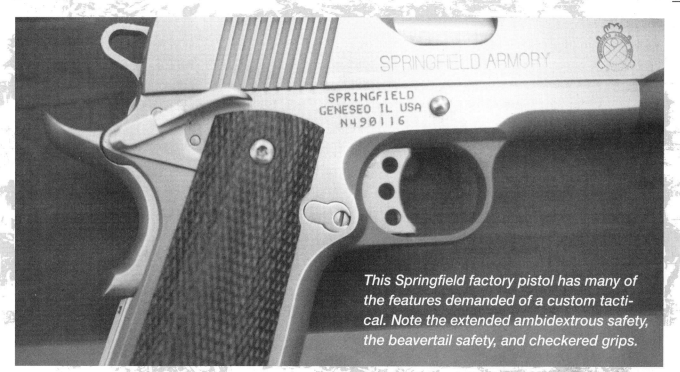

This Springfield factory pistol has many of the features demanded of a custom tactical. Note the extended ambidextrous safety, the beavertail safety, and checkered grips.

grip when need be if I have to reposition my grip as when speed loading or in other handling movements. There are enough choices to allow a wide range of personal preference, but a tactical pistol should have checkered or abrasive grips to ensure good control.

The barrel is sometimes called the heart of the 1911. While this is true, the fitting of the barrel is as important as the quality of the barrel. The other additions to the tactical handgun help practical accuracy. A smooth trigger compression and good sights make the gun easier to shoot well. Tightening the slide and frame or fitting a custom barrel increases the intrinsic accuracy of the handgun. Off the bench, from a solid rest, the differences in sights and trigger action are not as important. We can manage a heavy trigger or squint into small sights. But offhand, firing under time constraints, firing on the move, and from awkward positions, the smoother trigger and good sights are a great aid.

A match-grade barrel increases the intrinsic ability of the handgun to group its shots close together. Custom 1911 barrels are delivered oversize if the barrel is fitted to the piece in a custom shop. Drop-in barrels have more generous dimensions and while they may require some fitting, they will often fit into GI specification pistols. I have used

A true tactical should have a stippled front strap such as the 1911 in the background, but we can get by with Pachmayrs.

barrels from Bar-Sto, Nowlin, and Kart with good results, in both .38 Super and .45 ACP and also several 1911 9mm and Glock barrels from Bar-Sto. A well-fitted barrel results in less wear than a standard barrel. A tightly fitted barrel returns more precisely to the same position after firing. This adds up to greater accuracy, less wear, and of course more expense in fitting. The more tightly fitted gun is just as reliable if not more so than many other 1911s. This was proven in FBI testing. Pistols with tightly fitted match-grade barrels capable of grouping five rounds of ammunition into 1.25 inches at 25 yards fired 20,000 rounds of ammunition during these tests. There were no malfunctions among several of the top pistols and the Springfield pistol with Nowlin barrel passed the test with flying colors, to be adopted as the FBI HRT Hostage Rescue Team) pistol.

At this point, it may be a fair question to ask where you can purchase a tactical pistol ready to go. There are several choices, all of them good. If you have the time and funds to invest in the best, then the Action Works, of Chino Valley, Arizona, will build a .45 automatic pistol to your specifications. There is time, experience and finesse involved in building "serious handguns for serious times" and the Action Works enjoys an enviable reputation. My personal Action Works .45 is a fine example of understatement. The pistol has a very nice, crisp trigger action that has survived thousands of rounds of ammunition and high visibility sights. The beavertail is well fitted and certain features such as a carefully stippled grip strap and custom slide lock safety add up to a handgun that performs exceptionally well. Any problem spots, sharp edges or burrs were addressed by Don Williams and the rest is pure improvement. This type of pistol is available as a package of certain standard features, but you can go wilder with more improvements custom work – and work it really is – if you wish.

In a high-end production pistol, if there is such a thing, the Rock River Arms pistols have earned an enviable reputation. You may build your own tactical pistol from a RRA frame and slide and

A more involved pistol from the Action Works, with front-frame checkering, the mark of a fine pistolsmith. Note the squared trigger guard. This is a shorter 1911, so this is probably a short Tactical intended for concealed carry.

I have taken this route, with a RRA frame and slide and Bar-Sto barrel presently en route to the Action Works. The frame arrived with a custom grade checkered front strap and a number of top grade internals, including a Smith and Alexander beavertails safety, standard on the RRA line.

The Wilson Combat CQB (Close Quarters Battle) pistol is a highly respected handgun, capable and ready to go without additional work or parts from the factory. It is not cheap but it is excellent. The Wilson Combat pistol helps define a tactical pistol: excellent sights and trigger compression, a positive enhanced safety, a beavertail safety, and some means of enhancing the user's purchase on the handgun.

BUILD YOUR OWN

The 1911 allows the user to build a Tactical Pistol a piece at a time. Still, you should begin with a quality handgun. Some time ago, I wished to assay the performance of the FBI pistol, but found the $1000+ tap of the Bureau Model a bit steep. After all, there have seldom been terror attacks in my neighborhood and my difficulties in police work were handled with pretty ordinary 1911s. The compelling need was less than the curiosity. But I was able to find a basic list of the parts that went into the pistol, and turned out a very decent handgun.

I began with a Springfield Loaded Model. This pistol featured Novak rear sights but curiously, a standard staked on post front. The pistol also featured forward slide serrations, which operators feel are a requirement for gloved hand use. The extended safety was nice but the extended slide lock could be done without. The pistol came with a standard beavertail, which worked just fine with the Smith and Alexander magazine guide. After fitting the FBI-specification magazine guide I fitted certain Wilson Combat internal parts including an extractor, ejector, and sear. I also added Herett's checkered grips, again FBI-specification. This resulted in a considerably improved handgun. The S&A mag guide is the cat's pajamas when engaging in speed runs, and let me make the point again: We may not find ourselves in a situation requiring copious amounts of .45 caliber ammunition to solve a problem but in training and in administrative handling the mag chute makes things go much smoother. As a bonus, the grip feels much better in the hand. Overall, the Smith and Alexander magazine guide is on my short list of must-have items.

As issued the Springfield would group five shots of Winchester USA ball into about 3 inches at 25 yards. The premium Partition Gold Winchester load, a recently introduced load with much potential, did better: 2.5 inches. This is adequate for a service handgun and better than many, but far from the 1.25-inch group specified by the FBI. I turned to Nowlin for an FBI-specification match-grade barrel. Fitting such a barrel is cut and dried for me, file, polish, and check, and the best results are obtained by allowing Nowlin to fit the barrel to your pistol, or the Action Works will oblige as well. In the end, the pistol operated as specified with the FBI-style barrel, at least with certain loads. These are the results from my FBI version Springfield, fired at 25 yards from a benchrest (five shots fired, average of three groups):

Conley Precision 230-grain ball	1.8 inches
C and R ammo 230-grain JHP	1.5 inches
Winchester 230-grain USA	2.0 inches
Winchester 230-grain SXT	1.25 inches
Winchester 230-grain SXT +P	1.3 inches

I was able to meet the requirements set for by the FBI with one load, and since that load happens to be the choice of LAPD SWAT, I am satisfied. The Springfield still lacks the space-age Teflon finish applied to the Bureau guns, but my friends at Bear Coat can apply such a finish when I am ready. While many tactical handguns are supplied in stainless steel, and this makes good sense, quite a few have the corrosion-resistant Teflon-based finish offered by Bear Coat. This finish is self-lubricating and requires little maintenance. It is a winner on all counts.

The tactical pistol is not for everyone, any more than Lance Armstrong's racing bike would appeal to the casual rider. But for those going in harm's way or simply desiring the best handgun available, this is the ticket.

OTHER CHOICES

Recently, Kimber published an ad stating that the 1911 is the choice of special teams. Those using other handguns wish they had the 1911. This is completely true. However, yeoman work has been done by another handgun. The Browning High Power was the choice of the FBI HRT long ago, and the Novak-modified High Powers were excellent handguns. Within the limitations of the 9mm Luger cartridge, they served the FBI, and bone stock military pistols served the SAS in Europe. A decade or more ago, the Action Works performed a trigger action on my personal High Power and fitted Novak self luminous iron sights. This was all that was needed to produce a first-class 9mm pistol. I qualified with this handgun on several occasions, and more than once fired a four inch 50 yard group using Pro Load 124 grain JHP ammunition. This is outstanding performance. The pistol went well over 20,000 trouble-free rounds in my service, including a busy training schedule and in testing 9mm ammunition for two police agencies. Remember, this is without major internal modification. After a time, I noticed the "edge" was gone in accuracy but the pistol still turned in consistent 2-inch groups with several loadings.

From the Action Works, a Tactical Pistol built on a Series 80 Colt. The front slide serrations, high visibility sights, frame stippling, checkered grips, and beavertail safety define a Tactical.

A Tale of Three 45's (Make that Five...)

BY DERREK SIGLER

When we set out to pull together information for this book, the one thing we wanted to do was get in some of the cool stuff and test it. After all, what would be the point of writing a book if we didn't get to play with some cool toys? So when Smith & Wesson offered up one of their new M&P .45s, we were eager to say yes. Add to that H&K's willingness to supply one of their new .45s and we were chomping at the bit to get to the range. And just then, Taurus dropped off a new stainless model of their new 1911. For gun guys, this was "it."

OUT OF THE BOX

The first thing we noticed was how each gun felt in our hands the moment we picked it up for the first time. The Taurus felt like a 1911 should, very slim and with classic, dare we say graceful lines. The H&K felt much like a Sig Sauer to us. Comfortable, but not quite perfect. The Smith M&P fit our hands right off the bat.

Heckler & Koch HK45

Now the 1911 has a plethora of grips available to customize the fit. Both the H&K and the M&P had exchangeable back straps that came with each gun that could work to fit the shooter's hand. The standard grip on the M&P was our favorite, while we did swap out the H&K's grip. All three fit very well and we had no real complaints there. If we were to pick one as the best for our hands, it would be the Smith.

IN THIS CORNER:

The Heckler & Koch HK45

The HK45 was developed to meet the needs of the most distinguished, elite U.S. military operators. The HK45 is available in any one of the 10, HK specific variants, including the double-action and single-action Law Enforcement Modification known as the LEM. Left, right and ambidextrous control levers provide safety and/or de-cocking functions and can be fitted to the pistol by simply changing parts.

An internal mechanical recoil reduction system reduces the recoil forces imparted to the weapon and shooter by as much as 30%, improving shooter control during rapid firing.

Some of the numerous features of the HK45:

- Ergonomical grip profiles
- Replaceable grip panel
- Integrated Picatinny rail molded into the polymer frame dust cover
- Enlarged ambidextrous magazine levers
- Improved ergonomic control levers

(safety and/or decocking)

- Low-profile, drift adjustable, 3-dot sight
- Contoured and radiused slide with forward grasping grooves
- Ambidextrous slide release
- Overall length 7.52"
- Overall height 5.83"
- Overall width 1.42"
- Barrel length 4.53"
- Sight radius 6.61"
- Weight w/ magazine 1.73 lb
- Magazine 0.20 lb

The Taurus 1911

The Taurus 1911

The Taurus 1911 offers hammer-forged – not cast – ordnance-grade steel frames, slides and barrels. They machine each and every part to tolerance levels that surpass even today's industry standards. They then hand-fit and tune each gun, using quality parts that are built 100% on site. Then they mark the slide, barrel and frame with matching serial numbers.

- Model: 1911
- Caliber: .45 ACP
- Capacity: 8+1
- Barrel Length: 5"
- Action: SA
- Finish: Blue Steel or Stainless
- Grips: Checkered Black
- Weight: 38 oz
- Construction: Steel
- Frame: Large
- Front Sight: Heinie
- Rear Sight: Straight-8
- Trigger Type: Ventilated
- Length: 8-1/2"
- Width: 1-1/2"
- Height: 5.45"
- Rate of Twist: 1:16"
- Grooves: 6

The Smith & Wesson M&P

The M&Ps feature a reinforced polymer chassis, superb ergonomics, ambidextrous controls, and proven safety features. In the design of the M&P, S&W considered the needs of military and law enforcement from every conceivable angle.

- The M&P 45 is available with or without a thumb safety, and in several variants to meet the needs of Law Enforcement, Military and the shooter.
- Model: M&P
- Caliber: .45ACP
- Capacity: 10-14 Rounds
- Action: Striker Fire Action
- Barrel Length: 4"
- Front Sight: Steel Ramp Dovetail
- Rear Sight: Steel Lo-Mount Carry
- Overall Length: 7 1/2"

The Smith & Wesson M&P

- Weight: 27.7 oz. (Empty Mag: 3.0 oz., Full Mag: Approx. 10 oz.)
- Grip: (3) Interchangeable Palmswell Grip Sizes
- Frame: Polymer
- Material: Stainless Steel Slide & Barrel
- Finish: Black Melonite®, 68 HRc

EXTRAS AND DO-DADS

Each gun came with two magazines, although the 1911 being a single-stack handgun, the ammo capacity is reduced. To be honest, we didn't really notice all that much. We found the 1911 magazines to be the easier to load and the Smith's to be the more difficult if we had to make a choice.

LIGHT SHOW

The H&K and the M&P both have a built-in tactical rail for mounting a light or laser sight. The 1911 didn't, although Taurus does offer it with a tactical rail. We would like to play with one of those one of these days. For testing sake, we used Streamlight's awesome TSR-2 light/laser combo. We have used several of these combo light/sights before and think this one is the slickest unit out there. Not too big, not too small and incredibly easy to use. They have more switching options than any other light we've seen either.

SHUT UP AND PULL THE TRIGGER

With clips loaded with Hornady TAP ammo, Ray Ban eye protection and Howard Leight's awesome Impact Sport ear protection, it was time to pull the trigger. We fired a three-shot group from each gun at a 15-yard target. We seemed to shoot about the same with the 1911 and the M&P. The H&K was very close though. The next volley was a three-shot rapid-fire test. Now the M&P and the H&K were almost identical, while the 1911 was just a hair off. The H&K's recoil reduction system was nice and was noticeable. It easily won the recoil war.

The Smith seemed to have the best trigger for us. No creep and a crisp break. The H&K has an excellent trigger as well, but we felt the pull was a little longer, and the H&K has a hammer that can be cocked for better trigger action in single-action style shooting. The Taurus 1911 has one of the best triggers we've used in a production 1911 and it made us check and recheck the suggested retail price to see if we were reading it right.

The day wore on; the ammo piles dwindled, and we were glad that recoil doesn't have a negative effect on us for the most part. The bottom line is this. If you're hoping we can say which of the three was the best, we can't. They were each very good, solid guns. Do we have a favorite? Yes, we are partial to the Smith M&P. But we would happily carry either of the other two with no doubt whatsoever. Every round of ammo fired and hit the target pretty much where it was aimed. Each gun was flawless in action and just plain fun to shoot.

THE LATE ENTRANTS

After we did the initial test and the initial story was written, two more guns showed up on the doorstep that you should be aware of. Glock sent in a Model 21 and FNH sent over one of their FNP 45s.

The Glock 21 is, well, a Glock. Glocks are the original and standard of the polymer pistol crowd. They have a strong following and are known the world over for reliability and functionality. This handgun was no different.

Contrary to conventional wisdom, the trigger is the only operating element. All three pistol safeties are deactivated when the trigger is pulled and automatically activated when it is released.

As for the finish, Glock provides their hi-tech surface refinement for barrel and slide. Apart from optimum corrosion protection and anti-reflective finish, a degree of hardness of 64 HRC – close to that of a diamond – is achieved.

The polymer frame is corrosion resistant, tougher than steel and still 86% lighter. More than 20 years ago, Glock pistols were the first industrially manufactured handguns with high-tech polymer frames.

- Caliber: .45 Auto
- System: Safe Action
- Weight: 745 G / 26.28 Oz.
- Loaded (mag) 1085 G / 38.28 Oz.

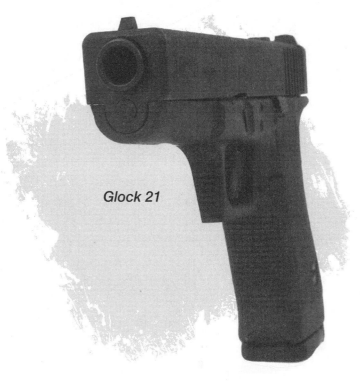

Glock 21

- Length: 193 Mm / 7.59 In.
- Height: 139 Mm / 5.47 In.
- Mag. Capacity (STD.): 13
- Width: 32.5 Mm / 1.27 In.
- Barrel Height: 32 Mm / 1.26 In.
- Trigger Pull: 2.5 Kg / 5.5 Lbs.
- Trigger Travel: 12.5 Mm / 0.5 In.
- Line Of Sight: 172 Mm / 6.77 In.
- Barrel Length: 117 Mm / 4.60 In.
- Barrel Rifling: Right Hand, Octagonal
- Length Of Twist: 400 Mm / 15.75 In.

FNP-45

FNH

The FNP-45 features traditional double-action/single-action (DA/SA) operation, a high-capacity polymer frame with interchangeable backstrap inserts, accessory rail and ambidextrous frame-mounted decocking levers and magazine release. The FNH-45's barrel is hammer-forged and the stainless steel slide has a hard, matte black Melonite® finish for added durability, or is available with a stainless steel slide, which is what we tested. The FNP-45 also offers a loaded chamber indicator on the external extractor. A variety of standard and night sights are available. All FNH pistols come standard with three magazines and a lockable hard case.

- Caliber: 45 ACP
- Magazine Capacity: 14
- Barrel Length: 4 1/2"
- Overall Length: 7 7/8"
- Weight: 32.4 oz.
- Operating Principle: DA/SA
- Stock Finish: Polymer Frame
- Grip: Interchangeable arched and flat backstrap insert

We ran both of these pistols through their paces and came away with mixed feelings. It had to be us, and our hands, but the Glock didn't fit well. The grip felt block and too wide to get a secure purchase; as a result, the pistol twisted in our hands. And a gun that doesn't fit well won't shoot well. This is in no means a slight against Glock, so Glock fans can stop writing that flaming email right now. It just didn't work well for us.

The opposite could be said for the FNH. It fit us very well and therefore shot very well. The trigger was superb and the gun never missed a beat, or a target for that matter. We ran several loads through it from several manufacturers and never once experienced anything out of the ordinary.

All five of these 45 caliber autos were top notch and it shows that when it comes to a .45, there are many great choices on the market. Get the one that fits you best and go to work.

The AR-24

Armalite's New Pistol is Ready to Fight

BY DAVE MORELLI

We all know Armalite as a producer of quality AR-15 style rifles. The firm has now become producers of a quality handgun, the AR-24. Resembling the CZ-75 in appearance and function, and I must admit I have never shot a CZ-75, the AR-24s that I had opportunity to evaluate were quite impressive defensive tools. I shot the full-size and compact and really had a good time running some lead downrange.

The fullsized with its forged steel frame and slide weighs in at 34.9 ounces with the compact coming in a about 1.5 ounces less. The guns come in 9mm and the full-size carrries 15 rounds. Both guns are great for concealability with the compact having a bit shorter barrel and grip. The compact comes with an extended magazine to accommodate a

comfortable grip. I fit my hand well and I didn't feel cramped shooting it. Both guns feel good in the hand and the laser cut ebony-colored wood grips felt tight in either right or left hand.

I shot both ball ammo and Winchester 115-grain Silver Tip ammo through the pistols and reliability was excellent with no jams or malfunctions. The gun was accurate and easy to handle with very little felt recoil. Slow aimed fire was accurate and quick defensive fire was easily controlled. Double taps printed side-by-side and hip rocks and Mo-

The compact version of the AR-24 uses an extended grip on the base of the magazine to fill your hand nicely. This gun is a dream to shoot.

zambique felt really good and smooth.

We don't hear as much about the 9mm as we used to since the 40 S&W hit the law enforcement community, but it hasn't become any less effective. Loaded with the right stuff, like the Silver Tip, and put in the right place, a 9mm round can change the bad guy's mind. I've always thought bigger was better but as far as defensive handgun rounds go, they are all marginal at best. I have trained many folks in defensive shooting and I figure the biggest round you can consistently put on center mass is a better philosophy. My personal experience with the Winchester Silver Tip in 9mm is, it works.

The triggers on these Armalite pistols were adequate. The double-action of the pistol was like most, heavy for the first round but then the gun fires single-action from then on. The Compact's trigger was a bit over 5 pounds and the full size was right at 5. This is a good trigger for defensive purposes and my 1911 triggers are in the 4-pound range. The triggers were crisp and had little creep which will do more for the feel of a trigger than reducing weight. The hammers rotated back slightly making them slightly positive and would be a safe carry tool.

The safety, located right where my shooting hand thumb would rest, made us 1911 shooters feel at home. It operates similar to the 1911, down for fire and up for safe. I didn't have to retrain my thumb like I did when we went to the Beretta. The AR-24 doesn't have a decock device like other double actions, but the safety can be engaged while the hammer is cocked. Other safeties include a half cock

At the range, the AR-24 did everything that was ask of it. This group is typical of what the gun can do in defensive situations.

notch, firing pin block and loaded chamber indicator.

The low-profile sights on the full size were just what I like for a carry gun. The 3-dot system lines up quickly, and the rounded edges and low profile make for easier concealed carry. The compact I tested had adjustable 3-dot sights but I would get a compact with the combat sights as it is more likely to be a concealed carry piece. Tritium night sights would be my only addition in this department.

I really enjoyed shooting the first line of Armalite's pistols and believe they did a great job in producing a quality defensive tool. I would feel confident carrying it on duty or for protection of myself or my family. I shot a hundred rounds through each of them with out a hitch and they were plenty reliable and accurate. I kind of put reliable a bit in front of accurate for a defensive gun because they got to go bang before accuracy counts for anything.

As for this brief evaluation, the AR-24 is a fine pistol; solid in every respect. For those who want a 9mm double-action auto, this gun will do everything you could ask of it. The lack of a decocking mechanism, might give some people pause, but with the safety locking up the whole works, even if the hammer is cocked, you are in a pretty good place as far as that goes. Accuracy is all you could ask for out of a box-stock gun and the functional quality is pure Armalite. It looks like they have a winner.

HANDGUNS PRODUCT DIRECTORY

BAER 1911 STINGER PISTOL

BERETTA MODEL PX4 STORM

AUTO-ORDNANCE 1911A1 AUTOMATIC PISTOL

AUTO-ORDNANCE 1911A1 AUTOMATIC PISTOL

Caliber: 45 ACP, 7-shot magazine. Barrel: 5". Weight: 39 oz. Length: 8.5" overall. Grips: Brown checkered plastic with medallion. Sights: Blade front, rear drift-adjustable for windage. Features: Same specs as 1911A1 military guns-parts interchangeable. Frame and slide blued; each radius has non-glare finish. Made in U.S.A. by Kahr Arms.

> **Price:** 1911SE Standard, blued $609.00
>
> **Price:** 1911WGSE Deluxe, black textured wraparound grips $615.00
>
> **Price:** 1911PKZSEW Parkerized, intr. 2007 .... $662.00

BAER 1911 ULTIMATE RECON PISTOL

Caliber: 45 ACP, 7- or 10-shot magazine. Barrel: 5". Weight: 37 oz. Length: 8.5" overall. Grips: Checkered cocobolo. Sights: Baer improved ramp-style dovetailed front, Novak low-mount rear. Features: NM Caspian frame, slide and barrel with stainless bushing. Baer speed trigger with 4-lb. pull. Includes integral Picatinny rail and Sure-Fire X-200 light. Made in U.S.A. by Les Baer Custom, Inc. Introduced 2006.

> **Price:** Bead blast blued $2,988.00
>
> **Price:** Bead blast chrome $3,230.00

BAER 1911 S.R.P. PISTOL

Caliber: 45 ACP. Barrel: 5". Weight: 37 oz. Length: 8.5"

overall. Grips: Checkered walnut. Sights: Trijicon night sights. Features: Similar to the F.B.I. contract gun except uses Baer forged steel frame. Has Baer match barrel with supported chamber, Complete tactical action. Has Baer Ultra Coat finish. Introduced 1996. Made in U.S.A. by Les Baer Custom, Inc.

> **Price:** Government or Comanche length $2,339.00

BAER 1911 STINGER PISTOL

Caliber: 45 ACP, 7-round magazine. Barrel: 5". Weight: 34 oz. Length: 8.5" overall. Grips: Checkered cocobolo. Sights: Baer dovetailed front, low-mount Bo-Mar rear with hidden leaf. Features: Baer NM frame. Baer Commanche slide, Officer's style grip frame, beveled mag well. Made in U.S.A. by Les Baer Custom, Inc.

> **Price:** Blued $1,666.00
>
> **Price:** Stainless $1,675.00

BERETTA MODEL 92FS PISTOL

Caliber: 9mm Para., 10-shot magazine. Barrel: 4.9". Weight: 34 oz. Length: 8.5" overall. Grips: Checkered black plastic. Sights: Blade front, rear adjustable for windage. Tritium night sights available. Features: Double action. Extractor acts as chamber loaded indicator, squared trigger guard, grooved front and backstraps, inertia firing pin. Matte or blued finish. Introduced 1977. Made in U.S.A.

> **Price:** With plastic grips $650.00

BERETTA MODEL M9

BERSA THUNDER 45
ULTRA COMPACT PISTOL

BERETTA MODEL M9A1

BERETTA MODEL
92FS PISTOL

BERETTA MODEL PX4 STORM

Caliber: 9mm, 40 S&W. Capacity: 17 (9mm); 14 (40 S&W). Barrel: 4". Weight: 27.5 oz. Grips: Black checkered w/3 interchangeable backstraps. Sights: 3-dot ystems coated in Superluminova; removable front and rear sights. Features: DA/SA, manual safety/hammer decocking lever (ambi) and automatic firing pin block safety. Picatinny rail. Comes with two magazines (17/10 in 9mm and 14/10 in 40 S&W). Removable hammer unit. American made by Beretta. Introduced 2005.

Price: $598.00

Price: Subcompact, intr. 2007 .... $575.00

BERETTA MODEL M9

Caliber: 9mm. Capacity: 15. Barrel: 4.9". Weight: 32.2-35.3 oz. Grips: Plastic. Sights: Dot and post, low profile, windage adjustable rear. Features: DA/SA, forged aluminum alloy frame, delayed locking-bolt system, manual safety doubles as decocking lever, combat-style trigger guard, loaded chamber indicator. Comes with two magazines (15/10). American made by Beretta. Introduced 2005.

Price: $750.00

BERETTA MODEL M9A1

Caliber: 9mm. Capacity: 15. Barrel: 4.9". Weight: 32.2-35.3 oz. Grips: Plastic. Sights: Dot and post, low profile, windage adjustable rear. Features: Same as M9, but also

includes integral Mil-Std-1913 Picatinny rail, has checkered frontstrap and backstrap. Comes with two magazines (15/10). American made by Beretta. Introduced 2005.

Price: $750.00

BERSA THUNDER 45
ULTRA COMPACT PISTOL

Caliber: 45 ACP. Barrel: 3.6". Weight: 27 oz. Length: 6.7" overall. Grips: Anatomicaly designed polymer. Sights: White outline rear. Features: Double action; firing pin safeties, integral locking system. Available in matte, satin nickel, gold, or duo-tone. Introduced 2003. Imported from Argentina by Eagle Imports, Inc.

Price: Thunder 45, matte blue $441.95

Price: Thunder 45, duo-tone $499.95

Price: Thunder 45, Satin nickel $466.95

BROWNING HI-POWER 9MM
AUTOMATIC PISTOL

Caliber: 9mm Para., 13-round magazine; 40 S&W, 10-round magazine. Barrel: 4-5/8". Weight: 32 to 39 oz. Overall length: 7-3/4". Metal Finishes: Blued (Standard); black-epoxy/silver-chrome (Practical); black-epoxy (Mark III). Grips: Molded (Mark III); wraparound Pachmayr (Practical); or walnut grips (Standard). Sights: Fixed (Practical, Mark III, Standard); low-mount adjustable rear (Standard). Cable lock supplied. Features: External hammer with half-cock

**BROWNING
PRO-9 PISTOL**

**CHARLES DALY M-5
GOVERNMENT**

**BROWNING
HI-POWER 9MM
AUTOMATIC PISTOL**

**CHARLES DALY ENHANCED
1911 PISTOL**

and thumb safeties. Fixed rear sight model available. Commander-style (Practical) or spur-type hammer, single action. Includes gun lock. Imported from Belgium by Browning.

Price: Mark III	....	$813.00
Price: Standard, fixed sights	....	$836.00
Price: Standard, adjustable sights	....	$896.00

BROWNING PRO-9, PRO-40 PISTOLS

Caliber: 9mm Luger, 16-round magazine; 40 S&W, 14-round magazine. Barrel: 4". Weight: 30-33 oz. Overall length: 7.25". Features: Polymer frame, stainless-steel frames and barrels, double-action, ambidextrous decocker and safety. Fixed, 3-dot-style sights, 6" sight radius. Molded composite grips with interchangeable backstrap inserts. Cable lock supplied.

Price: $628.00

CHARLES DALY ENHANCED 1911 PISTOLS

Caliber: 45 ACP. Barrel: 5". Weight: 38 oz. Length: 8-3/4" overall. Grips: Checkered double diamond hardwood. Sights: Dovetailed front and dovetailed snag-free low profile rear sights, 3-dot system. Features: Extended high-rise beavertail grip safety, combat trigger, combat hammer, beveled magazine well, flared and lowered ejection port. Field Grade models are satin-finished blued steel. EMS series includes an ambidextrous safety, 4" barrel, 8-shot magazine. ECS series has a contoured left hand safety, 3.5"

barrel, 6-shot magazine Two magazines, lockable carrying case. Introduced 1998. Empire series are stainless versions. Imported from the Philippines by K.B.I., Inc.

Price: EFS, blued, 39.5 oz., 5" barrel	....	$529.00
Price: EMS, blued, 37 oz., 4" barrel	....	$529.00
Price: ECS, blued, 34.5 oz., 3.5" barrel	....	$529.00
Price: EFS Empire, stainless, 38.5 oz., 5" barrel	....	$629.00
Price: EMS Empire, matte stainless, 36.5 oz., 4" barrel	....	$619.00
Price: ECS Empire, matte stainless, 33.5 oz., 3.5" barrel	....	$619.00

CHARLES DALY HP 9MM SINGLE-ACTION PISTOL

Caliber: 9mm, 10 round magazine. Barrel: 4.6". Weight: 34.5 oz. Length: 7-3/8" overall. Grips: Uncle Mike's padded rubber grip panels. Sights: XS Express Sight system set into front and rear dovetails. Features: John Browning design. Matte-blued steel frame and slide, thumb safety. Made in the U.S. by K.B.I., Inc.

Price: Hi-Power w/XS Sights $549.00

CHARLES DALY M-5 POLYMER-FRAMED HI-CAP 1911 PISTOL

Caliber: 9mm, 12-round magazine; 40 S&W 17-round magazine; 45 ACP, 13-round magazine. Barrel: 5". Weight: 33.5 oz. Length: 8.5" overall. Grips: Checkered polymer.

CHARLES DALY M-5 COMMANDER

CHARLES DALY M-5 ULTRA X

COLT XSE GOVERNMENT

COLT MODEL 1991 MODEL O

Sights: Blade front, adjustable low-profile rear. Features: Stainless steel beaver-tail grip safety, rounded trigger-guard, tapered bull barrel, full-length guide rod, matte blue finish on frame and slide. 40 S&W models in M-5 Govt. 1911, M-5 Commander, and M-5 IPSC introduced 2006; M-5 Ultra X Compact in 9mm and 45 ACP introduced 2006; M-5 IPSC .45 ACP introduced 2006. Made in Israel by BUL, imported by K.B.I., Inc.

Price: M-5 Govt. 1911, 40 S&W/45 ACP,
   matte blue $719.00
Price: M-5 Commander, 40 S&W/45 ACP,
   matte blue $719.00
Price: M-5 Ultra X Compact, 9mm, 3.1" barrel,
   7" OAL, 28 oz. $719.00
Price: M-5 Ultra X Compact, 45 ACP, 3.1" barrel,
   7" OAL, 28 oz. $719.00
Price: M-5 IPSC, 40 S&W/45 ACP, 5" barrel,
   8.5" OAL, 33.5 oz. $1,499.00

COLT MODEL 1991 MODEL O AUTO PISTOL

Caliber: 45 ACP, 7-shot magazine. Barrel: 5". Weight: 38 oz. Length: 8.5" overall. Grips: Checkered black composition. Sights: Ramped blade front, fixed square notch rear, high profile. Features: Matte finish. Continuation of serial number range used on original G.I. 1911A1 guns. Comes with one magazine and molded carrying case. Introduced 1991.

Price: Blue $786.00
Price: Stainless $839.00

COLT XSE SERIES MODEL O AUTO PISTOLS

Caliber: 45 ACP, 8-shot magazine. Barrel: 4.25", 5". Grips: Checkered, double diamond rosewood. Sights: Drift-adjustable 3-dot combat. Features: Brushed stainless finish; adjustable, two-cut aluminum trigger; extended ambidextrous thumb safety; upswept beavertail with palm swell; elongated slot hammer. Introduced 1999. From Colt's Mfg. Co., Inc.

Price: XSE Government (5" bbl.) $944.00
Price: XSE Government (4.25" bbl.) $944.00

COLT XSE LIGHTWEIGHT COMMANDER AUTO PISTOL

Caliber: 45 ACP, 8-shot. Barrel: 4-1/4". Weight: 26 oz. Length: 7-3/4" overall. Grips: Double diamond checkered rosewood. Sights: Fixed, glare-proofed blade front, square notch rear; 3-dot system. Features: Brushed stainless slide, nickeled aluminum frame; McCormick elongated slot enhanced hammer, McCormick two-cut adjustable aluminum hammer. Made in U.S.A. by Colt's Mfg. Co., Inc.

Price: Stainless $944.00

COLT DEFENDER

Caliber: 45 ACP, 7-shot magazine. Barrel: 3". Weight:

**COLT SPECIAL COMBAT
GOVERNMENT**

COLT SERIES 70

COLT DEFENDER

**DESERT EAGLE
MARK XIX**

22-1/2 oz. Length: 6-3/4" overall. Grips: Pebble-finish rubber wraparound with finger grooves. Sights: White dot front, snag-free Colt competition rear. Features: Stainless finish; aluminum frame; combat-style hammer; Hi Ride grip safety, extended manual safety, disconnect safety. Introduced 1998. Made in U.S.A. by Colt's Mfg. Co., Inc.

Price: $885.00

COLT SERIES 70

Caliber: 45 ACP. Barrel: 5". Weight: NA. Length: NA. Grips: Rosewood with double diamond checkering pattern. Sights: Fixed. Features: Custom replica of the Original Series 70 pistol with a Series 70 firing system, original rollmarks. Introduced 2002. Made in U.S.A. by Colt's Mfg. Co., Inc.

Price: Blued $919.00
Price: Stainless $950.00

COLT SPECIAL COMBAT GOVERNMENT

Caliber: 45 ACP, 38 Super. Barrel: 5". Weight: 39 oz. Length: 8-1/2". Grips: Rosewood w/double diamond checkering pattern. Sights: Clark dovetail, front; Bo-Mar adjustable, rear. Features: A competition-ready pistol with enhancements such as skeletonized trigger, upswept grip safety, custom tuned action, polished feed ramp. Blue or satin nickel finish. Introduced 2003. Made in U.S.A. by Colt's Mfg. Co.

Price: $1,543.00

DESERT EAGLE MARK XIX PISTOL

Caliber: 357 Mag., 9-shot; 44 Mag., 8-shot; 50 AE, 7-shot. Barrel: 6", 10", interchangeable. Weight: 357 Mag.-62 oz.; 44 Mag.-69 oz.; 50 AE-72 oz. Length: 10-1/4" overall (6" bbl.). Grips: Polymer; rubber available. Sights: Blade on ramp front, combat-style rear. Adjustable available. Features: Interchangeable barrels; rotating three-lug bolt; ambidextrous safety; adjustable trigger. Military epoxy finish. Satin, bright nickel, chrome, brushed, matte or black finishes available. 10" barrel extra. Imported from Israel by Magnum Research, Inc.

Price: 357, 6" bbl., standard pistol $1,369.00
Price: 44 Mag., 6", standard pistol $1,369.00
Price: 50 Magnum, 6" bbl., standard pistol $1,369.00

DESERT BABY EAGLE PISTOLS

Caliber: 9mm Para., 40 S&W, 45 ACP, 10-round magazine. Barrel: 3.5", 3.7", 4.72". Weight: 26.8-39.8 oz. Length: 7.25" to 8.25" overall. Grips: Polymer. Sights: Drift-adjustable rear, blade front. Features: Steel frame and slide; slide safety; decocker. Reintroduced in 1999. Imported from Israel by Magnum Research, Inc.

Price: Standard (9mm or 40 cal.; 4.72" barrel,
8.25" overall) $549.00
Price: Semi-Compact (9mm, 40 or 45 cal.; 3.7" barrel,

DESERT BABY EAGLE

**EAA WITNESS FULL SIZE
AUTO PISTOL**

**EAA WITNESS COMPACT
AUTO PISTOL**

7.75" overall) $549.00

Price: Compact (9mm or 40 cal.; 3.5" barrel,
7.25" overall) $549.00

Price: Polymer (9mm or 40 cal; polymer frame; 3.25" barrel,
7.25" overall) $549.00

EAA WITNESS FULL SIZE AUTO PISTOL

Caliber: 9mm Para., 38 Super, 18-shot magazine; 40 S&W, 10mm, 15-shot magazine; 45 ACP, 10-shot magazine. Barrel: 4.50". Weight: 35.33 oz. Length: 8.10" overall. Grips: Checkered rubber. Sights: Undercut blade front, open rear adjustable for windage. Features: Double-action/single-action trigger system; round trigger guard; frame-mounted safety. Introduced 1991. Polymer frame introduced 2005. Imported from Italy by European American Armory.

Price: 9mm, 38 Super, 10mm, 40 S&W, 45 ACP,
full-size steel frame, Wonder finish $459.00

Price: 45/22 22 LR, full-size steel frame, blued $429.00

Price: 9mm, 40 S&W, 45 ACP, full-size
polymer frame $429.00

EAA WITNESS COMPACT AUTO PISTOL

Caliber: 9mm Para., 40 S&W, 10mm, 12-shot magazine; 45 ACP, 8-shot magazine. Barrel: 3.6". Weight: 30 oz. Length: 7.3" overall. Otherwise similar to Full Size Witness. Polymer frame introduced 2005. Imported from Italy by

European American Armory.

Price: 9mm, 10mm, 40 S&W, 45 ACP, steel frame,
Wonder finish $459.00

Price: 9mm, 40 S&W, 45 ACP, polymer frame $429.00

EAA WITNESS-P CARRY AUTO PISTOL

Caliber: 10mm, 15-shot magazine; 45 ACP, 10-shot magazine. Barrel: 3.6". Weight: 27 oz. Length: 7.5" overall. Otherwise similar to Full Size Witness. Polymer frame introduced 2005. Imported from Italy by European American Armory.

Price: 10mm, 45 ACP, polymer frame, from $469.00

EAA WITNESS GOLD TEAM AUTO

Caliber: 9mm Para., 9x21, 38 Super, 40 S&W, 45 ACP. Barrel: 5.1". Weight: 44 oz. Length: 10.5" overall. Grips: Checkered walnut, competition-style. Sights: Square post front, fully adjustable rear. Features: Triple-chamber cone compensator; competition SA trigger; extended safety and magazine release; competition hammer; beveled magazine well; beavertail grip. Hand-fitted major components. Hard chrome finish. Match-grade barrel. From E.A.A. Custom Shop. Introduced 1992. From European American Armory.

Price: $1,699.00

ED BROWN CLASSIC CUSTOM

Caliber: 45 ACP, 7 shot. Barrel: 5". Weight: 40 oz. Stocks:

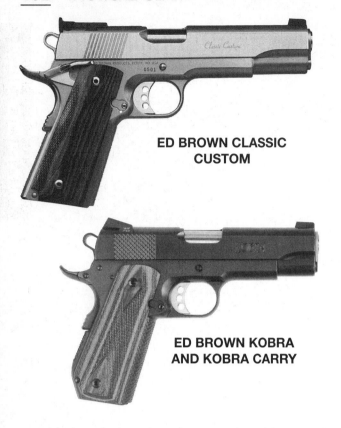

ED BROWN CLASSIC CUSTOM

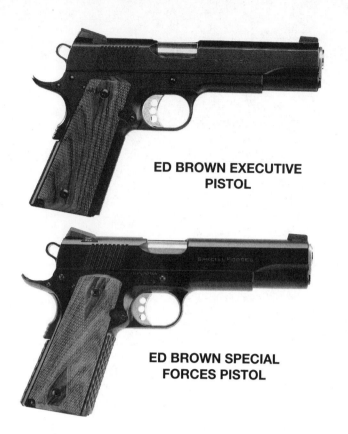

ED BROWN EXECUTIVE PISTOL

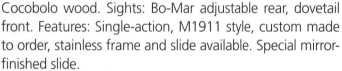

ED BROWN KOBRA AND KOBRA CARRY

ED BROWN SPECIAL FORCES PISTOL

Cocobolo wood. Sights: Bo-Mar adjustable rear, dovetail front. Features: Single-action, M1911 style, custom made to order, stainless frame and slide available. Special mirror-finished slide.

> **Price:** Model CC-BB, blued $2,895.00
> **Price:** Model CC-SB, blued and stainless $2,995.00
> **Price:** Model CC-SS, stainless $3,095.00

ED BROWN KOBRA AND KOBRA CARRY

Caliber: 45 ACP, 7-shot magazine. Barrel: 5" (Kobra); 4.25" (Kobra Carry). Weight: 39 oz. (Kobra); 34 oz. (Kobra Carry). Grips: Hogue exotic wood. Sights: Ramp, front; fixed Novak low-mount night sights, rear. Features: Has snakeskin pattern serrations on forestrap and mainspring housing, dehorned edges, beavertail grip safety.

> **Price:** Kobra K-BB, blued $1,995.00
> **Price:** Kobra K-SB, stainless and blued $2,095.00
> **Price:** Kobra K-SS, stainless $2,195.00
> **Price:** Kobra Carry KC-BB, blued $2,095.00

ED BROWN EXECUTIVE PISTOLS

Similar to other Ed Brown products, but with 25-lpi checkered frame and mainspring housing.

> **Price:** Elite blued, blued/stainless, or
> stainless, from $2,195.00
> **Price:** Carry blued, blued/stainless, or
> stainless, from $2,295.00

> **Price:** Target blued, blued/stainless, or stainless,
> intr. 2006, ... $2,470.00

ED BROWN SPECIAL FORCES PISTOL

Similar to other Ed Brown products, but with Chain-Link treatment on forestrap and mainspring housing. Slide coated with Gen III finish. "Square cut" serrations on rear of slide only. Dehorned. Introduced 2006.

> **Price:** SF-BB blued $1,995.00

GLOCK 17/17C AUTO PISTOL

Caliber: 9mm Para., 17/19/33-shot magazines. Barrel: 4.49". Weight: 22.04 oz. (without magazine). Length: 7.32" overall. Grips: Black polymer. Sights: Dot on front blade, white outline rear adjustable for windage. Features: Polymer frame, steel slide; double-action trigger with "Safe Action" system; mechanical firing pin safety, drop safety; simple takedown without tools; locked breech, recoil operated action. ILS designation refers to Internal Locking System. Adopted by Austrian armed forces 1983. NATO approved 1984. Imported from Austria by Glock, Inc.

> **Price:** Fixed sight $599.00
> **Price:** Fixed sight w/ILS $624.00
> **Price:** Adjustable sight $617.00
> **Price:** Adjustable sight w/ILS $642.00
> **Price:** Night sight $646.00

GLOCK 17 AUTO PISTOL

GLOCK 17C AUTO PISTOL

GLOCK 26 AUTO PISTOL

GLOCK 22/22C AUTO PISTOL

Price: Night sight w/ILS	$671.00
Price: 17C Compensated (fixed sight)	$621.00
Price: 17C Compensated (fixed sight) w/ILS	$646.00

GLOCK 19/19C AUTO PISTOL

Caliber: 9mm Para., 15/17/19/33-shot magazines. Barrel: 4.02". Weight: 20.99 oz. (without magazine). Length: 6.85" overall. Compact version of Glock 17. Pricing the same as Model 17. Imported from Austria by Glock, Inc.

Price: Fixed sight	$599.00
Price: 19C Compensated (fixed sight)	$621.00

GLOCK 26 AUTO PISTOL

Caliber: 9mm Para. 10/12/15/17/19/33-shot magazines. Barrel: 3.46". Weight: 19.75 oz. Length: 6.29" overall. Subcompact version of Glock 17. Pricing the same as Model 17. Imported from Austria by Glock, Inc.

Price: Fixed sight	$599.00

GLOCK 34 AUTO PISTOL

Caliber: 9mm Para. 17/19/33-shot magazines. Barrel: 5.32". Weight: 22.9 oz. Length: 8.15" overall. Competition version of Glock 17 with extended barrel, slide, and sight radius dimensions. Imported from Austria by Glock, Inc.

Price: Adjustable sight	$679.00
Price: Adjustable sight w/ILS	$704.00

GLOCK 22/22C AUTO PISTOL

Caliber: 40 S&W, 15/17-shot magazines. Barrel: 4.49". Weight: 22.92 oz. (without magazine). Length: 7.32" overall. Features: Otherwise similar to Model 17, including pricing. Imported from Austria by Glock, Inc. Introduced 1990.

Price: Fixed sight	$599.00
Price: Fixed sight w/ILS	$624.00
Price: Adjustable sight	$617.00
Price: Adjustable sight w/ILS	$642.00
Price: Night sight	$646.00
Price: Night sight w/ILS	$671.00
Price: 22C Compensated (fixed sight)	$621.00
Price: 22C Compensated (fixed sight) w/ILS	$646.00

GLOCK 23/23C AUTO PISTOL

Caliber: 40 S&W, 13/15/17-shot magazines. Barrel: 4.02". Weight: 21.16 oz. (without magazine). Length: 6.85" overall. Features: Otherwise similar to Model 22, including pricing. Compact version of Glock 22. Imported from Austria by Glock, Inc. Introduced 1990.

Price: Fixed sight	$599.00
Price: 23C Compensated (fixed sight)	$621.00

GLOCK 27 AUTO PISTOL

Caliber: 40 S&W, 9/11/13/15/17-shot magazines.

**GLOCK 35
AUTO PISTOL**

**GLOCK 20/20C 10MM
AUTO PISTOL**

**GLOCK 21
AUTO PISTOL**

**GLOCK 30
AUTO PISTOL**

Barrel: 3.46". Weight: 19.75 oz. (without magazine). Length: 6.29" overall. Features: Otherwise similar to Model 22, including pricing. Subcompact version of Glock 22. Imported from Austria by Glock, Inc. Introduced 1996.

    Price: Fixed sight $599.00

GLOCK 35 AUTO PISTOL

Caliber: 40 S&W, 15/17-shot magazines. Barrel: 5.32". Weight: 24.52 oz. (without magazine). Length: 8.15" overall. Features: Otherwise similar to Model 22. Competition version of Glock 22 with extended barrel, slide, and sight radius dimensions. Imported from Austria by Glock, Inc. Introduced 1996.

    Price: Fixed sight $679.00
    Price: Adjustable sight w/ILS $704.00

GLOCK 20/20C 10MM AUTO PISTOL

Caliber: 10mm, 15-shot magazines. Barrel: 4.6". Weight: 27.68 oz. (without magazine). Length: 7.59" overall. Features: Otherwise similar to Model 17. Imported from Austria by Glock, Inc. Introduced 1990.

    Price: Fixed sight $637.00
    Price: Fixed sight w/ILS $662.00
    Price: Adjustable sight $655.00
    Price: Adjustable sight w/ILS $680.00
    Price: Night sight $684.00

    Price: Night sight w/ILS $709.00
    Price: 20C Compensated (fixed sight) $676.00
    Price: 20C Compensated (fixed sight) w/ILS $701.00

GLOCK 29 AUTO PISTOL

Caliber: 10mm, 10/15-shot magazines. Barrel: 3.78". Weight: 24.69 oz. (without magazine). Length: 6.77" overall. Features: Otherwise similar to Model 20, including pricing. Subcompact version of Glock 20. Imported from Austria by Glock, Inc. Introduced 1997.

    Price: Fixed sight $637.00

GLOCK 21/21C AUTO PISTOL

Caliber: 45 ACP, 13-shot magazines. Barrel: 4.6". Weight: 26.28 oz. (without magazine). Length: 7.59" overall. Features: Otherwise similar to Model 17. Imported from Austria by Glock, Inc. Introduced 1991.

    Price: Fixed sight $637.00
    Price: Fixed sight w/ILS $662.00
    Price: Adjustable sight $655.00
    Price: Adjustable sight w/ILS $680.00
    Price: Night sight $684.00
    Price: Night sight w/ILS $709.00
    Price: 21C Compensated (fixed sight) $676.00
    Price: 21C Compensated (fixed sight) w/ILS $701.00

GLOCK 29
AUTO PISTOL

GLOCK 31
AUTO PISTOL

GLOCK 37
AUTO PISTOL

GLOCK 38
AUTO PISTOL

GLOCK 30 AUTO PISTOL

Caliber: 45 ACP, 9/10/13-shot magazines. Barrel: 3.78". Weight: 23.99 oz. (without magazine). Length: 6.77" overall. Features: Otherwise similar to Model 21, including pricing. Subcompact version of Glock 21. Imported from Austria by Glock, Inc. Introduced 1997.

Price: Fixed sight $637.00

GLOCK 36 AUTO PISTOL

Caliber: 45 ACP, 6-shot magazines. Barrel: 3.78". Weight: 20.11 oz. (without magazine). Length: 6.77" overall. Features: Single-stack magazine, slimmer grip than Glock 21/30. Subcompact. Imported from Austria by Glock, Inc. Introduced 1997.

Price: Fixed sight $637.00

GLOCK 37 AUTO PISTOL

Caliber: 45 GAP, 10-shot magazines. Barrel: 4.49". Weight: 25.95 oz. (without magazine). Length: 7.32" overall. Features: Otherwise similar to Model 17. Imported from Austria by Glock, Inc. Introduced 2005.

Price: Fixed sight $614.00
Price: Fixed sight w/ILS $639.00
Price: Adjustable sight $632.00
Price: Adjustable sight w/ILS $657.00
Price: Night sight $661.00

Price: Night sight w/ILS $686.00

GLOCK 38 AUTO PISTOL

Caliber: 45 GAP, 8/10-shot magazines. Barrel: 4.02". Weight: 24.16 oz. (without magazine). Length: 6.85" overall. Features: Otherwise similar to Model 37. Compact. Imported from Austria by Glock, Inc.

Price: Fixed sight $614.00

GLOCK 39 AUTO PISTOL

Caliber: 45 GAP, 6/8/10-shot magazines. Barrel: 3.46". Weight: 19.33 oz. (without magazine). Length: 6.3" overall. Features: Otherwise similar to Model 37. Subcompact. Imported from Austria by Glock, Inc.

Price: Fixed sight $614.00

GLOCK 31/31C AUTO PISTOL

Caliber: 357 Auto, 15/17-shot magazines. Barrel: 4.49". Weight: 23.28 oz. (without magazine). Length: 7.32" overall. Features: Otherwise similar to Model 17. Imported from Austria by Glock, Inc.

Price: Fixed sight $599.00
Price: Fixed sight w/ILS $624.00
Price: Adjustable sight $617.00
Price: Adjustable sight w/ILS $642.00
Price: Night sight $646.00
Price: Night sight w/ILS $671.00

HECKLER & KOCH USP ELITE AUTO PISTOL

HECKLER & KOCH USP COMPACT AUTO PISTOL

HECKLER & KOCH MARK 23 SPECIAL OPERATIONS PISTOL

HECKLER & KOCH USP45 TACTICAL PISTOL

Price: 31C Compensated (fixed sight) **$621.00**

Price: 31C Compensated (fixed sight) w/ILS **$646.00**

GLOCK 32/32C AUTO PISTOL

Caliber: 357 Auto, 13/15/17-shot magazines. Barrel: 4.02". Weight: 21.52 oz. (without magazine). Length: 6.85" overall. Features: Otherwise similar to Model 31. Compact. Imported from Austria by Glock, Inc.

Price: Fixed sight **$599.00**

Price: 32C Compensated (fixed sight) **$621.00**

GLOCK 33 AUTO PISTOL

Caliber: 357 Auto, 9/11/13/15/17-shot magazines. Barrel: 3.46". Weight: 19.75 oz. (without magazine). Length: 6.29" overall. Features: Otherwise similar to Model 31. Subcompact. Imported from Austria by Glock, Inc.

Price: Fixed sight **$599.00**

HECKLER & KOCH USP AUTO PISTOL

Caliber: 9mm Para., 15-shot magazine; 40 S&W, 13-shot magazine; 45 ACP, 12-shot magazine. Barrel: 4.25-4.41". Weight: 1.65 lbs. Length: 7.64-7.87" overall. Grips: Non-slip stippled black polymer. Sights: Blade front, rear adjustable for windage. Features: New HK design with polymer frame, modified Browning action with recoil reduction system, single control lever. Special "hostile environment" finish on all metal parts. Available in SA/DA, DAO, left- and

right-hand versions. Introduced 1993. 45 ACP Introduced 1995. Imported from Germany by Heckler & Koch, Inc.

Price: USP 45 .... **$839.00**

Price: USP 40 and USP 9mm **$769.00**

HECKLER & KOCH USP COMPACT AUTO PISTOL

Caliber: 9mm Para., 13-shot magazine; 40 S&W and .357 SIG, 12-shot magazine; 45 ACP, 8-shot magazine. Similar to the USP except the 9mm Para., 357 SIG, and 40 S&W have 3.58" barrels, measure 6.81" overall, and weigh 1.47 lbs. (9mm). Introduced 1996. 45 ACP measures 7.09" overall. Introduced 1998. Imported from Germany by Heckler & Koch, Inc.

Price: USP Compact 45 .... **$874.00**

Price: USP Compact 9mm Para., 357 SIG,
and 40 S&W **$799.00**

HECKLER & KOCH USP45 TACTICAL PISTOL

Caliber: 40 S&W, 13-shot magazine; 45 ACP, 12-shot magazine. Barrel: 4.90-5.09". Weight: 1.9 lbs. Length: 8.64" overall. Grips: Non-slip stippled polymer. Sights: Blade front, fully adjustable target rear. Features: Has extended threaded barrel with rubber O-ring; adjustable trigger; extended magazine floorplate; adjustable trigger stop; polymer frame. Introduced 1998. Imported from Germany by Heckler & Koch, Inc.

**HI-POINT C-9 MODEL 9MM
COMPACT PISTOL**

**HI-POINT FIREARMS
40SW/POLY
AND 45 AUTO PISTOL**

HECKLER & KOCH P2000 SK AUTO PISTOL

Price: USP Tactical 45 .... $1,115.00
Price: USP Tactical 40 .... $1,019.00

HECKLER & KOCH USP COMPACT TACTICAL PISTOL

Caliber: 45 ACP, 8-shot magazine. Similar to the USP Tactical except measures 7.72" overall, weighs 1.72 lbs. Introduced 2006. Imported from Germany by Heckler & Koch, Inc.

Price: USP Compact Tactical $1,115.00

HECKLER & KOCH MARK 23 SPECIAL OPERATIONS PISTOL

Caliber: 45 ACP, 12-shot magazine. Barrel: 5.87". Weight: 2.42 lbs. Length: 9.65" overall. Grips: Integral with frame; black polymer. Sights: Blade front, rear drift adjustable for windage; 3-dot. Features: Civilian version of the SOCOM pistol. Polymer frame; double action; exposed hammer; short recoil, modified Browning action. Introduced 1996. Imported from Germany by Heckler & Koch, Inc.

Price: $2,412.00

HECKLER & KOCH P2000 AUTO PISTOL

Caliber: 9mm Para., 13-shot magazine; 40 S&W and

.357 SIG, 12-shot magazine. Barrel: 3.62". Weight: 1.5 lbs. Length: 7" overall. Grips: Interchangeable panels. Sights: Fixed Patridge style, drift adjustable for windage, standard 3-dot. Incorporates features of HK USP Compact pistol, including Law Enforcement Modification (LEM) trigger, double-action hammer system, ambidextrous magazine release, dual slide-release levers, accessory mounting rails, recurved, hook trigger guard, fiber-reinforced polymer frame, modular grip with exchangeable back straps, nitro-carburized finish, lock-out safety device. Introduced 2003. Imported from Germany by Heckler & Koch, Inc.

Price: $887.00
Price: P2000 LEM DAO, 357 SIG, intr. 2006 .... $887.00
Price: P2000 SA/DA, 357 SIG, intr. 2006 .... $887.00

HECKLER & KOCH P2000 SK AUTO PISTOL

Caliber: 9mm Para., 10-shot magazine; 40 S&W and .357 SIG, 9-shot magazine. Barrel: 3.27". Weight: 1.3 lbs. Length: 6.42" overall. Sights: Fixed Patridge style, drift adjustable. Features: Standard accessory rails, ambidextrous slide release, polymer frame, polygonal bore profile. Smaller version of P2000. Introduced 2005. Imported from Germany by Heckler & Koch, Inc.

Price: $929.00

KAHR TP45 PISTOL

KAHR PM SERIES PISTOLS

KAHR MK SERIES MICRO PISTOLS

HI-POINT FIREARMS MODEL 9MM COMPACT PISTOL

Caliber: 9mm Para., 8-shot magazine. Barrel: 3.5". Weight: 25 oz. Length: 6.75" overall. Grips: Textured plastic. Sights: Combat-style adjustable 3-dot system; low profile. Features: Single-action design; frame-mounted magazine release; polymer frame. Scratch-resistant matte finish. Introduced 1993. Comps are similar except they have a 4" barrel with muzzle brake/compensator. Compensator is slotted for laser or flashlight mounting. Introduced 1998. Made in U.S.A. by MKS Supply, Inc.

Price: C-9 9mm		$140.00
Price: C-9 Comp		$169.00
Price: C-9 Comp-L w/laser sight		$219.00

HI-POINT FIREARMS 40SW/POLY AND 45 AUTO PISTOLS

Caliber: 40 S&W, 8-shot magazine; 45 ACP (9-shot). Barrel: 4.5". Weight: 32 oz. Length: 7.72" overall. Sights: Adjustable 3-dot. Features: Polymer frames, last round lock-open, grip mounted magazine release, magazine disconnect safety, integrated accessory rail, trigger lock. Introduced 2002. Made in U.S.A. by MKS Supply, Inc.

Price: 40SW Poly		$179.00
Price: 40SW Poly w/laser		$239.00
Price: 45 ACP		$179.00
Price: 45 ACP w/laser		$239.00

KAHR K SERIES AUTO PISTOLS

Caliber: K9: 9mm Para., 7-shot; K40: 40 S&W, 6-shot magazine. Barrel: 3.5". Weight: 25 oz. Length: 6" overall. Grips: Wraparound textured soft polymer. Sights: Blade front, rear drift adjustable for windage; bar-dot combat style. Features: Trigger-cocking double-action mechanism with passive firing pin block. Made of 4140 ordnance steel with matte black finish. Contact maker for complete price list. Introduced 1994. Made in U.S.A. by Kahr Arms.

Price: K9093C K9, matte stainless steel		$741.00
Price: K9093NC K9, matte stainless steel w/tritium night sights		$853.00
Price: K9094C K9 matte blackened stainless stee .		$772.00
Price: K9098 K9 Elite 2003, stainless steel		$806.00
Price: K4043 K40, matte stainless steel		$741.00
Price: K4043N K40, matte stainless steel w/tritium night sights		$853.00
Price: K4044 K40, matte blackened stainless steel		$772.00
Price: K4048 K40 Elite 2003, stainless steel		$806.00

KAHR MK SERIES MICRO PISTOLS

Similar to the K9/K40 except is 5.35" overall, 4" high, with a 3.08" barrel. Weighs 23.1 oz. Has snag-free bar-dot sights, polished feed ramp, dual recoil spring system, DA-only trigger. Comes with 5-round flush baseplate and

KAHR P SERIES PISTOLS

KAHR PM SERIES PISTOLS

KAHR CW SERIES PISTOL

6-shot grip extension magazine. Introduced 1998. Made in U.S.A. by Kahr Arms.

Price: M9093 MK9, matte stainless steel $741.00

Price: M9093N MK9, matte stainless steel, tritium
night sights $853.00

Price: M9093-BOX MK9, matte stainless steel frame,
matte black slide $475.00

Price: M9098 MK9 Elite 2003, stainless steel $806.00

Price: M4043 MK40, matte stainless steel $741.00

Price: M4043N MK40, matte stainless steel, tritium
night sights $853.00

Price: M4048 MK40 Elite 2003, stainless steel $806.00

KAHR P SERIES PISTOLS

Caliber: 9x19, 40 S&W. Similar to K9/K40 steel frame pistol except has polymer frame, matte stainless steel slide. Barrel length 3.5"; overall length 5.8"; weighs 17 oz. Includes two 7-shot magazines, hard polymer case, trigger lock. Introduced 2000. Made in U.S.A. by Kahr Arms.

Price: KP9093 P9 .... $697.00

Price: KP9093N P9, tritium night sight $808.00

Price: KPS9093 P9 Covert, shortened grip,
15 oz., 6+1 .... $697.00

Price: KP4043 P40 .... $697.00

Price: KPS4043N P40 Covert, shortened grip, tritium
night sights $697.00

KAHR PM SERIES PISTOLS

Caliber: 9x19, 40 S&W. Similar to P-Series pistols except has smaller polymer frame (Polymer Micro). Barrel length 3.08"; overall length 5.35"; weighs 17 oz. Includes two 7-shot magazines, hard polymer case, trigger lock. Introduced 2000. Made in U.S.A. by Kahr Arms.

Price: PM9093 PM9 .... $728.00

Price: PM9093N PM9, tritium night sight $839.00

Price: PM4043 PM40 .... $728.00

Price: PM45 (2007) $814.00

KAHR CW SERIES PISTOL

Caliber: 9mm Para., 7-shot magazine; 40 S&W, 6-shot magazine. Barrel: 3.5-3.6". Weight: 17.7-18.7 oz. Length: 5.9-6.36" overall. Grips: Textured polymer. Similar to P-Series, but CW Series have conventional rifling, metal-injection-molded slide stop lever, no front dovetail cut, one magazine. CW40 introduced 2006. Made in U.S.A. by Kahr Arms.

Price: CW9093 CW9 .... $533.00

Price: CW4043 CW40 .... $533.00

KEL-TEC P-11 AUTO PISTOL

Caliber: 9mm Para., 10-shot magazine. Barrel: 3.1". Weight: 14 oz. Length: 5.6" overall. Grips: Checkered black polymer. Sights: Blade front, rear adjustable for windage. Features: Ordnance steel slide, aluminum frame. Double-

KIMBER COMPACT STAINLESS II AUTO PISTOL

KEL-TEC PF-9 PISTOL

KEL-TEC P-11 AUTO PISTOL

action-only trigger mechanism. Introduced 1995. Made in U.S.A. by Kel-Tec CNC Industries, Inc.

Price: Blue/Hard Chrome/
Parkerized .... $320.00/$375.00/$362.00

KEL-TEC PF-9 PISTOL

Caliber: 9mm Luger; 7 rounds. Weight: 12.7 oz. Sights: Rear sight adjustable for windage and elevation. Barrel Length: 3.1". Length: 5.85". Features: Barrel, locking system, slide stop, assembly pin, front sight, recoil springs and guide rod adapted from P-11. Trigger system with integral hammer block and the extraction system adapted from P-3AT. MIL-STD-1913 Picatinny rail. Made in U.S.A. by Kel-Tec CNC Industries, Inc.

Price: Blue/Parkerized/Hard
Chrome .... $314.00/$355.00/$368.00

KIMBER COMPACT STAINLESS II AUTO PISTOL

Stainless steel frame, 4-inch bbl., grip is .400" shorter than standard, no front serrations. Weighs 34 oz. 45 ACP only. Introduced in 1998. Made in U.S.A. by Kimber Mfg., Inc.

Price: $907.00

KIMBER TEN II HIGH CAPACITY POLYMER PISTOL

Similar to Custom II, Pro Carry II and Ultra Carry II depending on barrel length. Thirteen-round magazine ca-

pacity (double stack and flush fitting). Polymer grip frame molded over stainless steel or aluminum (BP Ten pistols only) frame insert. Checkered front strap and belly of trigger guard. All models have fixed sights except Gold Match Ten II, which has adjustable sight. Frame grip dimensions approximately that of the standard 1911. Weight: 24 to 34 oz. Improved version of the Kimber Polymer series. Made in U.S.A. by Kimber Mfg., Inc.

Price: Pro Carry Ten II $794.00
Price: Stainless Ten II $786.00

KIMBER GOLD COMBAT II AUTO PISTOL

Similar to Gold Match II except designed for concealed carry. Extended and beveled magazine well, Meprolight Tritium night sights; premium aluminum trigger; 30 lpi front strap checkering; extended magazine well. Introduced 1999. Made in U.S.A. by Kimber Mfg., Inc.

Price: Gold Combat II $1,733.00
Price: Gold Combat Stainless II $1,674.00

KIMBER CDP II SERIES AUTO PISTOL

Similar to Custom II, but designed for concealed carry. Aluminum frame. Standard features include stainless steel slide, fixed Meprolight tritium 3-dot (green) dovetail-mounted night sights, match grade barrel and chamber, 30 LPI front strap checkering, two-tone finish, ambidextrous thumb safety, hand-checkered double diamond rosewood grips. In-

KIMBER GOLD COMBAT II AUTO PISTOL

KIMBER CDP II SERIES AUTO PISTOL

KIMBER TEN II HIGH CAPACITY POLYMER PISTOL

KIMBER ECLIPSE II SERIES AUTO PISTOL

troduced in 2000. Made in U.S.A. by Kimber Mfg., Inc.

Price: Ultra CDP II 40 S&W $1,215.00

Price: Ultra CDP II (3" barrel, short grip) $1,177.00

Price: Compact CDP II (4" barrel, short grip) $1,177.00

Price: Pro CDP II (4" barrel, full length grip) $1,177.00

Price: Custom CDP II (5" barrel, full length grip) .. $1,177.00

KIMBER ECLIPSE II SERIES AUTO PISTOL

Similar to Custom II and other stainless Kimber pistols. Stainless slide and frame, black oxide, two-tone finish. Gray/black laminated grips. 30 lpi front strap checkering. All models have night sights; Target versions have Meprolight adjustable Bar/Dot version. Made in U.S.A. by Kimber Mfg., Inc.

Price: Eclipse Ultra II (3" barrel, short grip) $1,085.00

Price: Eclipse Pro II (4" barrel, full length grip) $1,085.00

Price: Eclipse Pro Target II (4" barrel, full length grip, adjustable sight) $1,189.00

Price: Eclipse Custom II (5" barrel, full length grip) $1,105.00

Price: Eclipse Target II (5" barrel, full length grip, adjustable sight) $1,189.00

Price: Eclipse Custom II (10mm) $1,220.00

OLYMPIC ARMS ENFORCER 1911 PISTOL

Caliber: 45 ACP, 6-shot magazine. Barrel: 4" bull stain-

less steel. Weight: 35 oz. Length: 7.75" overall. Grips: Smooth walnut with etched black widow spider icon. Sights: Ramped blade front, LPA adjustable rear. Features: Compact Enforcer frame. Busingless bull barrel with triplex counter-wound self-contained recoil system. Matched frame and slide, fitted and head-spaced barrel, complete ramp and throat jobs, lowered and widened ejection port, beveled mag well, hand-stoned-to-match hammer and sear, lightweight longshoe over-travel adjusted trigger, shaped and tensioned extractor, extended thumb safety, wide beavertail grip safety and full length guide rod. Made in U.S.A. by Olympic Arms.

Price: $750.00

OLYMPIC ARMS COHORT PISTOL

Caliber: 45 ACP, 7-shot magazine. Barrel: 4" bull stainless steel. Weight: 36 oz. Length: 7.75" overall. Grips: Fully checkered walnut. Sights: Ramped blade front, LPA adjustable rear. Features: Full size 1911 frame. Bushingless bull barrel with triplex counter-wound self-contained recoil system. Matched frame and slide, fitted and head-spaced barrel, complete ramp and throat jobs, lowered and widened ejection port, beveled mag well, hand-stoned-to-match hammer and sear, lightweight long-shoe over-travel adjusted trigger, shaped and tensioned extractor, extended thumb safety, wide beavertail grip safety and full length guide rod. Made in U.S.A. by Olympic Arms.

Price: $779.00

OLYMPIC ARMS ENFORCER 1911 PISTOL

OLYMPIC ARMS BIG DEUCE PISTOL

OLYMPIC ARMS COHORT PISTOL

PARA-ORDNANCE LDA HI-CAPACITY AUTO PISTOL

OLYMPIC ARMS BIG DEUCE PISTOL

Caliber: 45 ACP, 7-shot magazine. Barrel: 6"stainless steel. Weight: 44 oz. Length: 9.75" overall. Grips: Double diamond checkered exotic cocobolo wood. Sights: Ramped blade front, LPA adjustable rear. Features: Carbon steel parkerized slide with satin bead blast finish full size frame. Matched frame and slide, fitted and head-spaced barrel, complete ramp and throat jobs, lowered and widened ejection port, beveld mag well, hand-stoned-to-match hammer and sear, lightweight long-shoe over-travel adjusted trigger, shaped and tensioned extractor, extended thumb safety, wide beavertail grip safety and full length guide rod. Made in U.S.A. by Olympic Arms.

Price: $834.00

PARA-ORDNANCE PXT 1911 SINGLE-ACTION SINGLE-STACK AUTO PISTOLS

Caliber: 38 Super, 45 ACP. Barrel: 3.5", 4.25", 5". Weight: 28-40 oz. Length: 7.1-8.5" overall. Grips: Checkered cocobolo, textured composition, Mother of Pearl synthetic. Sights: Blade front, low-profile Novak Extreme Duty adjustable rear. High visibility 3-dot system. Features: Available with alloy, steel or stainless steel frames. Skeletonized trigger, spurred hammer. Manual thumb, grip and firing pin lock safeties. Full-length guide rod. PXT designates new Para Power Extractor through-

out the line. Introduced 2004. Made in Canada by Para-Ordnance.

Price: SSP-SE1 (2006), midnight blue,
7+1, 5" barrel $1,094.00

Price: OPS, stainless, Griptor grooves front
strap (2006) $1,043.00

Price: LTC, blued or stainless, 7+1,
4.25" barrel .... $884.00 to 1,043.00

Price: SSP, blued or stainless, 7+1,
4.25" barrel .... $884.00 to 1,043.00

PARA-ORDNANCE PXT 1911 SINGLE-ACTION HIGH-CAPACITY AUTO PISTOLS

Caliber: 9mm, 45 ACP, 10//14/18-shot magazines. Barrel: 3", 5". Weight: 34-40 oz. Length: 7.1-8.5" overall. Grips: Textured composition. Sights: Blade front, low-profile Novak Extreme Duty adjustable rear or fixed sights. High visibility 3-dot system. Features: Available with alloy, steel or stainless steel frames. Skeletonized match trigger, spurred hammer, flared ejection port. Manual thumb, grip and firing pin lock safeties. Full-length guide rod. Introduced 2004. Made in Canada by Para-Ordnance.

Price: P14-45MB (2006), midnight blue,
14+1, 5" barrel $899.00

Price: P14-45 stainless, 14+1, 5" barrel $998.00

Price: P18-9 stainless,18+1 9mm, 5" barrel $1,049.00

**PARA-ORDNANCE LDA
SINGLE-STACK CARRY
AUTO PISTOL**

**PARA-ORDNANCE
NITE HAWG**

**PARA-ORDNANCE LDA
HIGH-CAP
CARRY AUTO PISTOL**

**PARA-ORDNANCE LITE
HAWG**

PARA-ORDNANCE LDA SINGLE-STACK CARRY AUTO PISTOLS

Similar to PXT-series except has double-action trigger mechanism, flush hammers, brushed stainless finish, checkered composition grips. Available in 45 ACP. Introduced 1999. Made in Canada by Para-Ordnance.

Price: Carry, 6+1, 3" barrel, stainless $1,049.00

Price: Carry, 6+1, 3" barrel, covert black $1,133.00

Price: CCO, 7+1, 3.5" barrel $1,049.00

Price: CCW, 7+1, 4.5" barrel $1,049.00

PARA-ORDNANCE LDA HIGH-CAP CARRY AUTO PISTOLS

Similar to LDA-series with double-action trigger mechanism. Also, bobbed beavertail, high-cap mags. Available in 9mm Para., 45 ACP. Introduced 1999. Made in Canada by Para-Ordnance.

Price: Carry 12, 12+1, 3.5" barrel, stainless $1,133.00

Price: Tac-Four, 13+1, 4.5" barrel, stainless $1,028.00

Price: C TX189B, 18+1, 5" barrel, covert black, Novak sights $1,163.00

PARA-ORDNANCE LDA SINGLE-STACK AUTO PISTOLS

Similar to LDA-series with double-action trigger mechanism. Cocobolo and polymer grips. Available in 45 ACP. Introduced 1999. Made in Canada by Para-Ordnance.

Price: Black Watch Companion, 7+1, 3.5" barrel $1,133.00

Price: Tac-S, 7+1, 4.5" barrel, Spec Ops matte finish $944.00

Price: Tac-S, 7+1, 4.5" barrel, stainless $1,028.00

Price: Limited, 7+1, 5" barrel, stainless $1,193.00

PARA-ORDNANCE LDA HI-CAPACITY AUTO PISTOLS

Similar to LDA-series with double-action trigger mechanism. Polymer grips. Available in 9mm, 40 S&W, 45 ACP. Introduced 1999. Made in Canada by Para-Ordnance.

Price: Colonel, 14+1, 4.25" barrel $944.00

Price: Hi-Cap 45, 14+1, 5" barrel, stainless $1,028.00

Price: Hi-Cap 9, 18+1, 5" barrel, covert black finish $944.00

Price: Hi-Cap LTD 45 45 ACP, 14+1, 5" barrel, stainless $1,193.00

Price: Hi-Cap LTD 40 40 S&W, 15+1, 5" barrel, stainless $1,193.00

Price: Hi-Cap LTD 9 9mm, 18+1, 5" barrel, stainless $1,193.00

PARA-ORDNANCE LDA LIGHT RAIL PISTOLS

Similar to PXT and LDA-series above, with built-in light

**PARA-ORDNANCE
NITE-TAC 40**

**PARA-ORDNANCE
WARTHOG**

**PARA-ORDNANCE
WARTHOG 1911**

**PARA-ORDNANCE
WARTHOG 9MM**

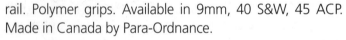

rail. Polymer grips. Available in 9mm, 40 S&W, 45 ACP. Made in Canada by Para-Ordnance.

Price: Nite-Tac 45, 14+1 45 ACP, 5" barrel,
covert black $1,034.00

Price: Nite-Tac 40, 16+1 40 S&W, 5" barrel,
stainless (2006) $1,103.00

Price: Nite-Tac 9, 16+1 9mm, 5" barrel,
stainless (2006) $1,103.00

PARA-ORDNANCE WARTHOG

Caliber: 9mm, 45 ACP, 6, 10, or 12-shot magazines. Barrel: 3". Weight: 24 to 31.5 oz. Length: 6.5". Grips: Varies by model. Features: Single action. Made in Canada by Para-Ordnance.

Price: Slim Hawg (2006) single stack .45 ACP,
stainless, 6+1 .... $1,043.00

Price: Nite Hawg .45 ACP, black finish, 10+1 .... $1,013.00

Price: Warthog .45 ACP, Regal finish, 10+1 .... $884.00

Price: Stainless Warthog .45 ACP (2006),
brushed finish, 10+1 .... $989.00

Price: Hawg 9 9mm Regal finish, alloy
frame, 12+1 .... $884.00

Price: Lite Hawg 9 9mm (2006) black finish, alloy
frame, 12+1 .... $1,049.00

ROCK RIVER ARMS BASIC CARRY AUTO PISTOL

Caliber: 45 ACP. Barrel: NA. Weight: NA. Length: NA. Grips: Rosewood, checkered. Sights: dovetail front sight, Heinie rear sight. Features: NM frame with 20-, 25- or 30-LPI checkered front strap, 5-inch slide with double serrations, lowered and flared ejection port, throated NM Kart barrel with NM bushing, match Commander hammer and match sear, aluminum speed trigger, dehorned, Parkerized finish, one magazine, accuracy guarantee. 3.5 lb. Trigger pull. Introduced 2006. Made in U.S.A. From Rock River Arms.

Price: PS2700 .... $1,540.00

RUGER P89 AUTOLOADING PISTOL

Caliber: 9mm Para., 15-shot magazine. Barrel: 4.50". Weight: 32 oz. Length: 7.75" overall. Grips: Grooved black synthetic composition. Sights: Square post front, square notch rear adjustable for windage, both with white dot inserts. Features: Double action, ambidextrous slide-mounted safety-levers. Slide 4140 chrome-moly steel or 400-series stainless steel, frame lightweight aluminum alloy. Ambi-

**RUGER P89 AUTO-
LOADING PISTOL**

**RUGER KP94 AUTO-
LOADING PISTOL**

**RUGER P90 MANUAL
SAFETY MODEL AU-
TOLOADING PISTOL**

**RUGER P95 AUTO-
LOADING PISTOL**

dextrous magazine release. Blue, stainless steel. Introduced 1986; stainless 1990.

> **Price:** P89, blue, extra mag and mag loader, plastic
> case locks $475.00

> **Price:** KP89, stainless, extra mag and mag loader,
> plastic case locks $525.00

RUGER P89D DECOCKER AUTOLOADING PISTOL

Similar to standard P89 except has ambidextrous de-cocking levers in place of regular slide-mounted safe-ty. Decocking levers move firing pin inside slide where hammer cannot reach. Blue, stainless steel. Introduced 1990.

> **Price:** P89D, blue, extra mag and mag loader, plastic
> case locks $475.00

> **Price:** KP89D, stainless, extra mag and mag loader,
> plastic case locks $525.00

RUGER P90 MANUAL SAFETY MODEL AUTOLOADING PISTOL

Caliber: 45 ACP, 8-shot magazine. Barrel: 4.50". Weight: 33.5 oz. Length: 7.75" overall. Grips: Grooved black syn-

thetic composition. Sights: Square post front, square notch rear adjustable for windage, both with white dot. Features: Double action; ambidextrous slide-mounted safety-levers. Stainless steel only. Introduced 1991.

> **Price:** KP90 with extra mag, loader, case
> and gunlock $565.00

> **Price:** P90 (blue) $525.00

RUGER KP94 AUTOLOADING PISTOL

Sized midway between full-size P-Series and compact KP94. 4.25" barrel, 7.5" overall length, weighs about 34 oz. KP94 manual safety model. Slide gripping grooves roll over top of slide. KP94 has ambidextrous safety-levers; Matte finish stainless slide, barrel, alloy frame. Also blue. Includes hard case and lock. Introduced 1994. Made in U.S.A. by Sturm, Ruger & Co.

> **Price:** P944, blue (manual safety) $495.00

> **Price:** KP944 (40-caliber) (manual safety-stainless) $575.00

RUGER P95 AUTOLOADING PISTOL

Caliber: 9mm Para., 15-shot magazine. Barrel: 3.9". Weight: 27 oz. Length: 7.25" overall. Grips: Grooved; integral with frame. Sights: Blade front, rear drift adjust-

**SABRE DEFENCE
SPHINX 3000 9MM**

**SIGARMS P220 CARRY
AUTO PISTOL**

**SABRE DEFENCE
SPHINX 3000 P45 ACP**

**SIGARMS P220
AUTO PISTOL**

able for windage; 3-dot system. Features: Molded polymer grip frame, stainless steel or chrome-moly slide. Suitable for +P+ ammunition. Safety model, decocker. Introduced 1996. Made in U.S.A. by Sturm, Ruger & Co. Comes with lockable plastic case, spare magazine, loader and lock, Picatinny rails.

> **Price:** P95DPR15 decocker only **$445.00**
> **Price:** P95PR15 stainless steel decocker only **$480.00**
> **Price:** KP95PR15 safety model, stainless steel **$480.00**
> **Price:** P95PR15 safety model, blued finish **$445.00**

SABRE DEFENCE SPHINX 3000 PISTOLS

Caliber: 9mm, 45 ACP., 10-shot magazine. Barrel: 4.43". Weight: 39.15 oz. Length: 8.27" overall. Grips: Textured polymer. Sights: Fixed Trijicon Night Sights. Features: CNC engineered from stainless steel billet; grip frame in stainless steel, titanium or high-strength aluminum. Integrated accessory rail, high-cut beavertail, decocking lever. Made in Switzerland. Imported by Sabre Defence Industries.

> **Price:** 45 ACP (2007) **$2,990.00**
> **Price:** 9mm Standard, titanium w/decocker **$2,700.00**
> **Price:** 9mm Tactical, 3.74" barrel **$2,425.00**

SIGARMS REVOLUTION PISTOLS

Caliber: 45 ACP, 8-shot magazine. Barrel: 5". Weight: 40.3 oz. Length: 8.65" overall. Grips: Checkered wood grips. Sights: Novak night sights. Blade front, drift adjustable rear for windage. Features: Single-action 1911. Hand-fitted dehorned stainless-steel frame and slide; match-grade barrel, hammer/sear set and trigger; 25-lpi front strap checkering, 20-lpi mainspring housing checkering. Beavertail grip safety with speed bump, extended thumb safety, firing pin safety and hammer intercept notch. Introduced 2005. XO series has contrast sights, Ergo Grip XT textured polymer grips. Target line features adjustable target night sights, match barrel, custom wood grips, non-railed frame in stainless or Nitron finishes. TTT series is two-tone 1911 with Nitron slide and black controls on stainless frame. Includes burled maple grips, adjustable combat night sights. STX line available from SIGARMS Custom Shop; two-tone 1911, non-railed, Nitron slide, stainless frame, burled maple grips. Polished cocking serrations, flat-top slide, magwell. Carry line has Novak night sights, lanyard attachment point, gray diamondwood or rosewood grips, 8+1 capacity. Compact series has 6+1 capacity, 7.7" OAL, 4.25" barrel, slim-profile wood grips, weighs 30.3 oz. RCS line (Revolu-

**SIGARMS P220 EQUINOX
AUTO PISTOL**

**SIGARMS P220 ELITE
AUTO PISTOL**

**SIGARMS REVOLUTION
PISTOL**

**SIG-SAUER P229 DA
AUTO PISTOL**

tion Compact SAS) is Customs Shop version with anti-snag dehorning. Stainless or Nitron finish, Novak night sights, slim-profile gray diamondwood or rosewood grips. 6+1 capacity. Imported from Germany by SIGARMS, Inc.

Price: Revolution Nitron finish, w/ or w/o
Picatinny rail $1,069.00

Price: Revolution Stainless, w/ or w/o
Picatinny rail $1,050.00

Price: Revolution XO Black $890.00

Price: Revolution XO Stainless, intr. 2006 .... $860.00

Price: Revolution Target Nitron, intr. 2006 .... $1,100.00

Price: Revolution TTT, intr. 2006 .... $1,070.00

Price: Revolution STX, intr. 2006 .... $1,300.00

Price: Revolution Carry Nitron, 4.25" barrel,
intr. 2006 .... $1,070.00

Price: Revolution Compact, Nitron finish $1,080.00

Price: Revolution RCS, Nitron finish $1,150.00

SIGARMS P220 AUTO PISTOLS

Caliber: 45 ACP, (7- or 8-shot magazine). Barrel: 4.4". Weight: 27.8 oz. Length: 7.8" overall. Grips: Checkered black plastic. Sights: Blade front, drift adjustable rear for windage. Optional Siglite night sights. Features: Double action. Stainless-steel slide, Nitron finish, alloy frame, M1913 Picatinny rail; safety system of decocking lever, automatic firing pin safety block, safety intercept notch, and trigger bar disconnector. Squared combat-type trigger guard. Slide stays open after last shot. Introduced 1976. P220 SAS Anti-Snag has dehorned stainless steel slide, front Siglite Night Sight, rounded trigger guard, dust cover, Custom Shop wood grips. Equinox line is Custom Shop product with Nitron stainless-steel slide with a black hard-anodized alloy frame, brush-polished flats and nickel accents. Truglo tritium fiber-optic front sight, rear Siglite night sight, gray laminated wood grips with checkering and stippling. Imported from Germany by SIGARMS, Inc.

Price: P220R $840.00

Price: P220R Two-Tone, matte-stainless slide,
black alloy frame $840.00

Price: P220 Stainless $935.00

Price: P220 Crimson Trace, w/lasergrips $1,150.00

Price: P220 SAS Anti-Snag $1,000.00

Price: P220 Two-Tone SAO, single action, intr.
2006, from $929.00

SMITH & WESSON M&P COMPACT AUTO PISTOL

SMITH & WESSON MODEL 910 DA AUTO PISTOL

SMITH & WESSON MODEL 3913 TRADITIONAL DOUBLE ACTION

Price: P220R DAK (intr. 2006) **$840.00**

Price: P220R Equinox (intr. 2006) **$1,070.00**

SIGARMS P220 CARRY AUTO PISTOLS

Caliber: 45 ACP, 8-shot magazine. Barrel: 3.9". Weight: NA. Length: 7.1" overall. Grips: Checkered black plastic. Sights: Blade front, drift adjustable rear for windage. Optional Siglite night sights. Features: Similar to full-size P220, except is "Commander" size. Single stack, DA/SA operation, Nitron finish, Picatinny rail, and either post and dot contrast or 3-dot Siglite night sights. Introduced 2005. Imported from Germany by SIGARMS, Inc.

Price: P220 Carry, from **$840.00**

Price: P220 Carry Two-Tone, from **$915.00**

Price: P220 Carry Equinox, wood grips,
two tone, from **$1,070.00**

SIG-SAUER P229 DA AUTO PISTOL

Similar to the P228 except chambered for 9mm Para. (10- or 15-round magazines), 40 S&W, 357 SIG (10- or 12-round magazines). Has 3.86" barrel, 7.1" overall length and 3.35" height. Weight is 32.4 oz. Introduced 1991. Frame made in Germany, stainless steel slide assembly made in U.S.; pistol assembled in U.S. From SIGARMS, Inc.

Price: P229R, from $840.00

Price: P229R Crimson Trace, w/lasergrips, from . **$1,150.00**

SIG-SAUER SP2022 PISTOLS

Caliber: 9mm Para., 357 SIG, 40 S&W, 10-, 12-, or 15-shot magazines. Barrel: 3.9". Weight: 30.2 oz. Length: 7.4" overall. Grips: Composite and rubberized one-piece. Sights: Blade front, rear adjustable for windage. Optional Siglite night sights. Features: Polymer frame, stainless steel slide; integral frame accessory rail; replaceable steel frame rails; left- or right-handed magazine release, two interchangeable grips. From SIGARMS, Inc.

Price: SP2009, Nitron finish, from **$640.00**

SIG-SAUER P226 PISTOLS

Similar to the P220 pistol except has 4.4" barrel, measures 7.7" overall, weighs 34 oz. Chambered in 9mm, 357 SIG, or 40 S&W. X-Five series has factory tuned single-action trigger, 5" slide and barrel, ergonomic wood Nill grips with beavertail, ambidextrous thumb safety and stainless slide and frame with magwell, low-profile adjustable target sights, front cocking serrations and a 25-meter factory test

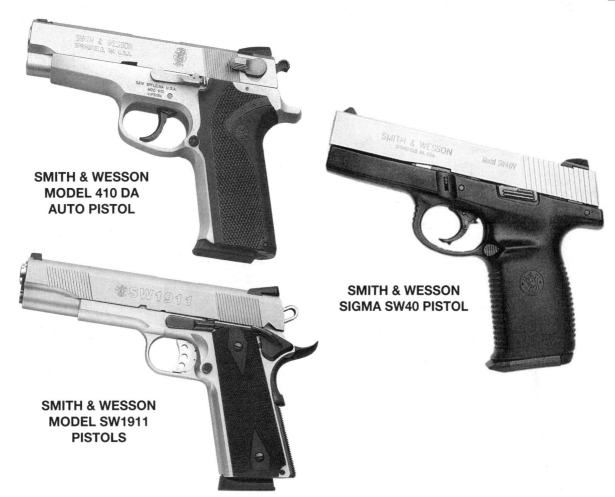

SMITH & WESSON MODEL 410 DA AUTO PISTOL

SMITH & WESSON SIGMA SW40 PISTOL

SMITH & WESSON MODEL SW1911 PISTOLS

target. Imported from Germany by SIGARMS, Inc.

Price: P226R, Nitron finish, night sights	....	$915.00
Price: P226R Two Tone, Nitron/stainless finish	......	$969.00
Price: P226 Stainless, from	....	$935.00
Price: P226 X-Five	....	$2,500.00
Price: P226 X-Five Tactical, Ilaflon finish, high cap, from	....	$1,500.00

SIG-SAUER P239 PISTOL

Caliber: 9mm Para., 8-shot, 357 SIG 40 S&W, 7-shot magazine. Barrel: 3.6". Weight: 25.2 oz. Length: 6.6" overall. Grips: Checkered black composite. Sights: Blade front, rear adjustable for windage. Optional Siglite night sights. Features: SA/DA or DAO; blackened stainless steel slide, aluminum alloy frame. Introduced 1996. Made in U.S.A. by SIGARMS, Inc.

Price: P239	....	$739.00
Price: P239 Two-Tone, w/night sights	....	$895.00
Price: P239 DAK, double action	....	$739.00

SMITH & WESSON M&P AUTO PISTOLS

Caliber: 9mm, 40 S&W, 357 SIG. Barrel: 4.25". Weight:

24.25 oz. Length: 7.5" overall. Grips: One-piece Xenoy, wraparound with straight backstrap. Sights: Ramp dovetail mount front; tritium sights optional; Novak Lo-mount Carry rear. Features: Zytel polymer frame, embedded stainless steel chassis; stainless steel slide and barrel, stainless steel structural components, black Melonite finish, reversible magazine catch, 3 interchangeable palmswell grip sizes, universal rail, sear deactivation lever, internal lock system, magazine disconnect. Ships with 2 magazines. Internal lock models available. Overall height: 5.5"; width: 1.2"; sight radius: 6.4". Introduced November 2005. 45 ACP version introduced 2007, 10+1 or 14+1 capacity. Barrel: 4.5". Length: 8.05". Weight: 29.6 ounces. Features: Picatinny-style equipment rail; black or bi-tone, dark-earth-brown frame. Bi-tone M&P45 includes ambidextrous, frame-mounted thumb safety, take down tool with lanyard attachment. Compact 9mm/357 SIG/40 S&W versions introduced 2007. Compacts have 3.5" barrel, OAL 6.7". 10+1 or 12+1 capacity. Weight: 21.7 ounces. Features: Picatinny-style equipment rail. Made in U.S.A. by Smith & Wesson.

Price:	....	$624.00
Price: M&P 45 Bi-tone (2007)	....	$678.00
Price: M&P Compacts (2007)	....	$624.00

SPRINGFIELD ARMORY XD 45 W/EXTENDED MAGAZINE

SMITH & WESSON MODEL 908 AUTO PISTOL

SPRINGFIELD ARMORY XD 45

SMITH & WESSON MODEL 457 TDA AUTO PISTOL

Caliber: 45 ACP, 7-shot magazine. Barrel: 3-3/4". Weight: 29 oz. Length: 7-1/4" overall. Grips: One-piece Xenoy, wraparound with straight backstrap. Sights: Post front, fixed rear, 3-dot system. Features: Aluminum alloy frame, matte blue carbon steel slide; bobbed hammer; smooth trigger. Introduced 1996. Made in U.S.A. by Smith & Wesson.

> **Price:** Model 457, black matte finish $711.00
> **Price:** Model 457S, matte finish stainless $711.00

SMITH & WESSON MODEL 908 AUTO PISTOL

Caliber: 9mm Para., 8-shot magazine. Barrel: 3-1/2". Weight: 24 oz. Length: 6-13/16". Grips: One-piece Xenoy, wraparound with straight backstrap. Sights: Post front, fixed rear, 3-dot system. Features: Aluminum alloy frame, matte blue carbon steel slide; bobbed hammer; smooth trigger. Introduced 1996. Made in U.S.A. by Smith & Wesson.

> **Price:** Model 908, black matte finish $648.00
> **Price:** Model 908S, stainless matte finish $648.00
> **Price:** Model 908S Carry Combo, with holster $672.00

SMITH & WESSON MODEL 4013 TSW AUTO

Caliber: 40 S&W, 9-shot magazine. Barrel: 3-1/2". Weight: 26.8 oz. Length: 6 3/4" overall. Grips: Xenoy one-piece wraparound. Sights: Novak 3-dot system. Features: Traditional double-action system; stainless slide, alloy frame; fixed barrel bushing; ambidextrous decocker; reversible magazine catch, equipment rail. Introduced 1997. Made in U.S.A. by Smith & Wesson.

> **Price:** Model 4013 TSW $1,027.00

SMITH & WESSON MODEL 410 DA AUTO PISTOL

Caliber: 40 S&W, 10-shot magazine. Barrel: 4". Weight: 28.5 oz. Length: 7.5". Grips: One-piece Xenoy, wraparound with straight backstrap. Sights: Post front, fixed rear; 3-dot system. Features: Aluminum alloy frame; blued carbon steel slide; traditional double action with left-side slide-mounted decocking lever. Introduced 1996. Made in U.S.A. by Smith & Wesson.

> **Price:** From $687.00

SMITH & WESSON MODEL 910 DA AUTO PISTOL

Caliber: 9mm Para., 10-shot magazine. Barrel: 4". Weight: 28 oz. Length: 7-3/8" overall. Grips: One-piece Xenoy, wraparound with straight backstrap. Sights: Post front with white dot, fixed 2-dot rear. Features: Alloy frame, blue carbon steel slide. Slide-mounted decocking lever. Introduced 1995.

> **Price:** From $616.00

GEAR GALLERY

FIREARMS, KNIVES, EQUIPMENT & MORE

Sabre Defense Precision Marksman in .5.56 NATO or 6.5 Grendel.

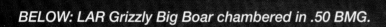

BELOW: LAR Grizzly Big Boar chambered in .50 BMG.

Barrett Model 95 in .50 BMG.

Heckler & Koch USC semi-auto carbine in .45 ACP.

H&K P-2000 in 9mm.

Opposite Left and Above: KA-BAR tactical drop-point with Springfield Armory XD 9mm with Crimson Trace LaserGrips and Sure-Fire X300 Weapon Light.

Right: Kimber SIS (Special Investigation Section) in .45 ACP.

DPMS A-15 in 5.56 with
SureFire Weapon Light and
full tactical entry rig.

Buck Metro knife (top); Columbia River Knife & Tool Wild Weasel Plain Edge (bottom), shown open and closed.

Ontario XM-1 folding tactical knives, plain edge and serrated.

Boker Chad Los Banos tactical folder (top); Ontario SP2 Air Force Survival Knife (center): Zero Tolerance Ranger Green (bottom).

NVRS 2.5x50 night vision rifle scope (left); EOTech HWS Holographic Weapon Sight (right).

6P LED

SureFire 6P LED tactical flashlight (center); bottom right inset: Steiner Nighthunter night vision binocular (left); Impact Sport sound-amplifying electronic earmuffs (center); Cabela's VLR Laser Rangefinder (right).

Opposite Page: Clockwise from upper left: Paulson DK-5 Tactical Face Shield; Truspec Tactical Response Uniform; Paulson Manufacturing 510-TN Tactical Goggle with Nose Shield; Blackhawk! 32HC Head Cover; RBR Tactical Padded Neck Protector IIA.

Right Page: Blackhawk! Viking 1X24 night vision binoculars; ZW5 5" Side Zip Boot; Revision Desert Locust protective ballistic eyewear (note shotgun pellet impact).

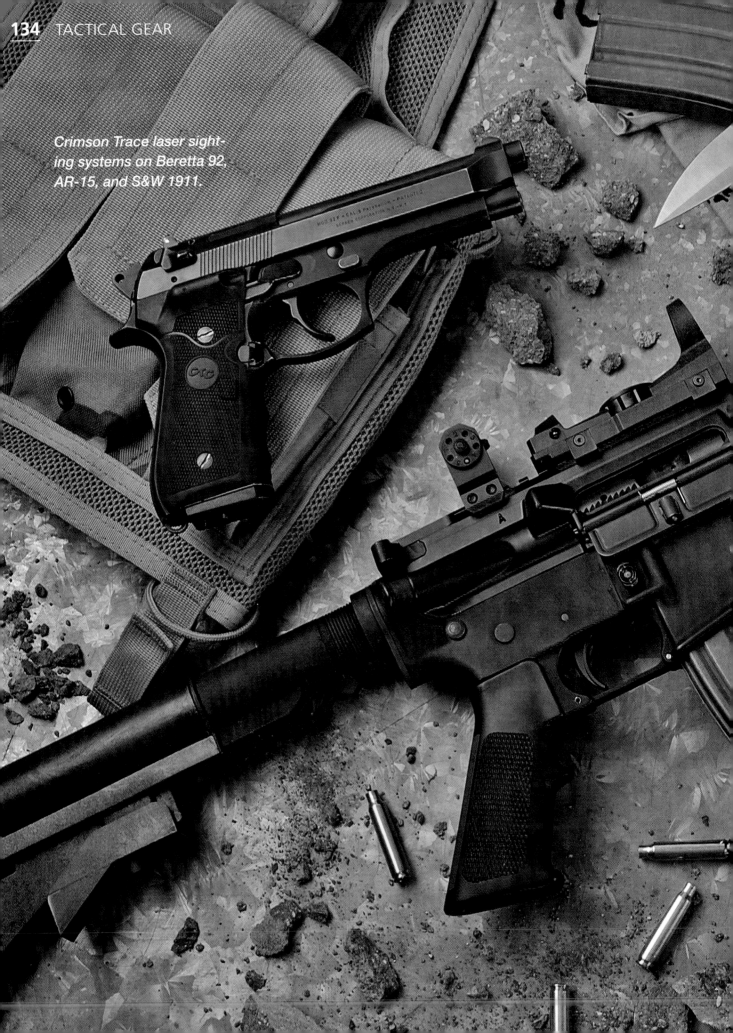

Crimson Trace laser sighting systems on Beretta 92, AR-15, and S&W 1911.

From Top: EOTech HWS holographic sight on Mossberg Model 930 Rolling Thunder with collapsible stock; Recon Scout remote video reconnaissance robot camera; Heckler & Koch HK 4.6 x 30mm MP7A1; Benelli M4 12-gauge tactical shotgun.

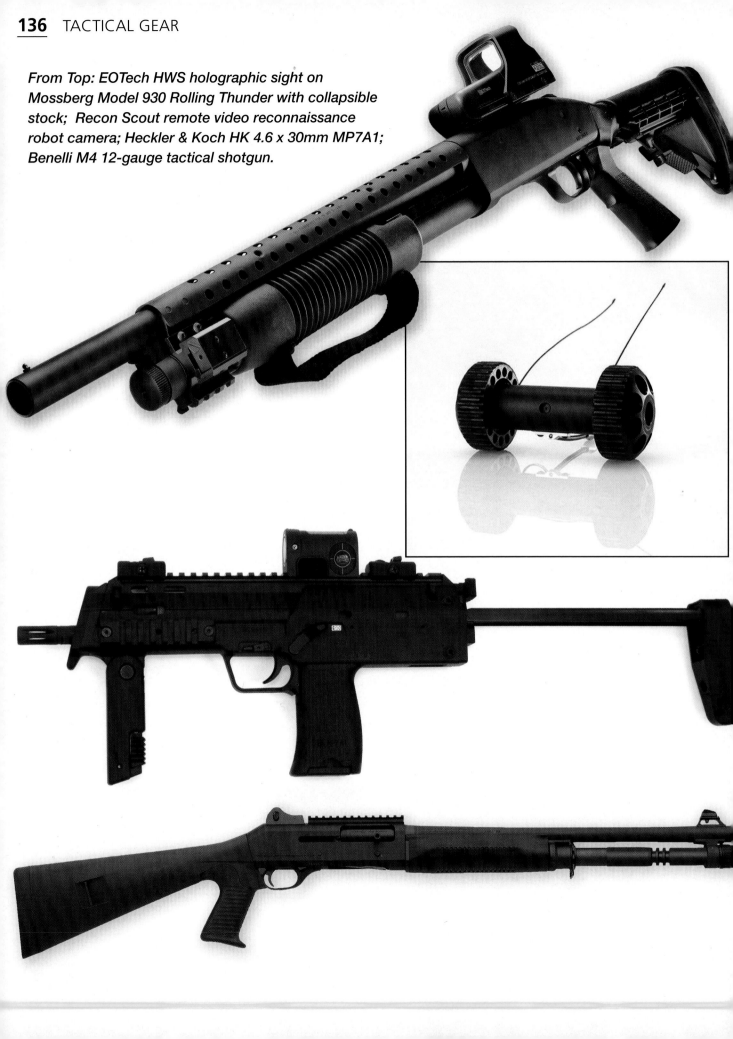

**SPRINGFIELD ARMORY
XD 40**

**SPRINGFIELD ARMORY
XD 45 GAP**

SMITH & WESSON MODEL 3913 TRADITIONAL DOUBLE ACTIONS

Caliber: 9mm Para., 8-shot magazine. Barrel: 3-1/2". Weight: 24.8 oz. Length: 6-3/4" overall. Grips: One-piece Delrin wraparound, textured surface. Sights: Post front with white dot, Novak LoMount Carry with two dots. Features: TSW has aluminum alloy frame, stainless slide. Bobbed hammer with no half-cock notch; smooth .304" trigger with rounded edges. Straight backstrap. Equipment rail. Extra magazine included. Introduced 1989. The 3913-LS Ladysmith has frame that is upswept at the front, rounded trigger guard. Comes in frosted stainless steel with matching gray grips. Grips are ergonomically correct for a woman's hand. Novak LoMount Carry rear sight adjustable for windage. Extra magazine included. Introduced 1990.

Price: 3913TSW $924.00
Price: 3913-LS $909.00

SMITH & WESSON MODEL SW1911 PISTOLS

Caliber: 45 ACP, 8 rounds. Barrel: 5". Weight: 39 oz. Length: 8.7". Grips: Wood or rubber. Sights: Novak Lo-Mount Carry, white dot front. Features: Large stainless frame and slide with matte finish, single-side external safety. No. 108284 has adjustable target rear sight, ambidextrous safety levers, 20-lpi checkered front strap, comes with two 8-round magazines. DK model (Doug Koenig) also has oversized magazine well, Doug Koenig speed hammer, flat competition speed trigger with overtravel stop, rosewood

grips with Smith & Wesson silver medallions, oversized magazine well, special serial number run. No. 108295 has olive drab Crimson Trace lasergrips. No. 108299 has carbon-steel frame and slide with polished flats on slide, standard GI recoil guide, laminated double-diamond walnut grips with silver Smith & Wesson medallions, adjustable target sights. Tactical Rail No. 108293 has a Picatinny rail, black Melonite finish, Novak Lo-Mount Carry Sights, scandium alloy frame. Tactical Rail Stainless introduced 2006. SW1911PD gun is Commander size, scandium-alloy frame, 4.25" barrel, 8" OAL, 28.0 oz., non-reflective black matte finish. Gunsite edition has scandium alloy frame, beveled edges, solid match aluminum trigger, Herrett's logoed tactical oval walnut stocks, special serial number run, brass bead Novak front sight. SC model has 4.25" barrel, scandium alloy frame, stainless-steel slide, non-reflective matte finish.

Price: From $1,011.00

SMITH & WESSON ENHANCED SIGMA SERIES DAO PISTOLS

Caliber: 9mm Para., 40 S&W; 10-, 16-shot magazine. Barrel: 4". Weight: 24.7 oz. Length: 7-1/4" overall. Grips: Integral. Sights: White dot front, fixed rear; 3-dot system. Tritium night sights available. Features: Ergonomic polymer frame; low barrel centerline; internal striker firing system; corrosion-resistant slide; Teflon-filled, electroless-nickel coated magazine, equipment rail. Introduced 1994. Made

SPRINGFIELD ARMORY CUSTOM LOADED FULL-SIZE 1911A1 TACTICAL COMBAT

SPRINGFIELD ARMORY CUSTOM LOADED FULL-SIZE 1911A1 WITH ADJUSTABLE SIGHTS

SPRINGFIELD ARMORY CUSTOM LOADED FULL-SIZE 1911A1 AUTO PISTOL

in U.S.A. by Smith & Wesson.

Price: From $419.00

SMITH & WESSON MODEL CS9 CHIEF'S SPECIAL AUTO

Caliber: 9mm Para., 7-shot magazine. Barrel: 3". Weight: 20.8 oz. Length: 6-1/4" overall. Grips: Hogue wraparound rubber. Sights: White dot front, fixed 2-dot rear. Features: Traditional double-action trigger mechanism. Alloy frame, stainless slide. Ambidextrous safety. Introduced 1999. Made in U.S.A. by Smith & Wesson.

Price: Stainless $782.00

SMITH & WESSON MODEL CS45 CHIEF'S SPECIAL AUTO

Caliber:45 ACP, 6-shot magazine. Weight: 23.9 oz. Features: Introduced 1999. Made in U.S.A. by Smith & Wesson.

Price: Stainless $830.00

SPRINGFIELD ARMORY XD POLYMER AUTO PISTOLS

Caliber: 9mm Para., 357 SIG, 40 S&W, 45 ACP, 45 GAP. Barrel: 3", 4", 5". Weight: 20.5-31 oz. Length: 6.26-8" overall. Grips: Textured polymer. Sights: Varies by model; Fixed sights are dovetail front and rear steel 3-dot units. Features: Three sizes in X-Treme Duty (XD) line: Sub-Compact (3" barrel), Service (4" barrel), Tactical (5" barrel). Three ported models available. Ergonomic polymer frame, hammer-forged barrel, no-tool disassembly, ambidextrous magazine release, visual/tactile loaded chamber indicator, visual/tactile striker status indicator, grip safety, XD gear system included. Introduced 2004. XD 45 introduced 2006. Compact line introduced 2007. Compacts ship with one extended magazine (13) and one compact magazine (10). From Springfield Armory.

Price: Sub-Compact Black 9mm, fixed sights $536.00

Price: Sub-Compact Black 9mm/40 S&W, Heinie night sights $633.00

Price: Sub-Compact Bi-Tone 9mm/40 S&W, fixed sights $566.00

Price: Sub-Compact OD Green 9mm/40 S&W, fixed sights $536.00

Price: Service Black 9mm/40 S&W/357 SIG, fixed sights $536.00

Price: Service Black 45 ACP, fixed sights $559.00

Price: Service Black 45 GAP, fixed sights $536.00

Price: Service Black 9mm/40 S&W, Heinie night sights $626.00

Price: Service Bi-Tone 9mm/40 S&W/357 SIG/45 GAP, fixed sights $566.00

Price: Service Bi-Tone 45 ACP, fixed sights $595.00

Price: Service OD Green 9mm/40 S&W/357 SIG/45 GAP, fixed sights $536.00

Price: V-10 Ported Black 9mm/40 S&W/357 SIG $566.00

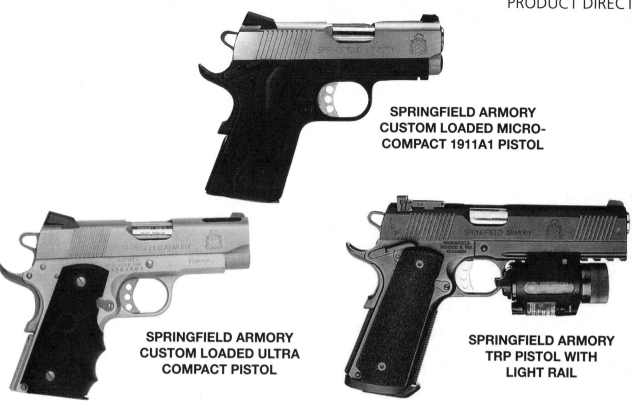

SPRINGFIELD ARMORY CUSTOM LOADED MICRO-COMPACT 1911A1 PISTOL

SPRINGFIELD ARMORY CUSTOM LOADED ULTRA COMPACT PISTOL

SPRINGFIELD ARMORY TRP PISTOL WITH LIGHT RAIL

Price: Tactical Black 45 ACP, fixed sights $595.00

Price: Tactical Black 9mm/40 S&W/357 SIG, fixed sights $566.00

Price: Tactical Bi-Tone 45 ACP/45 GAP, fixed sights .... $626.00/$595.00

Price: Tactical OD Green 9mm/40 S&W/357 SIG/45 GAP, fixed sights $566.00

Price: Tactical OD Green 45 ACP, fixed sights $595.00

Price: Compact, 4" barrel (2007) $589.00

Price: Compact, 5" barrel (2007) $619.00

Price: Compact, 5" barrel, Trijicon night sights (2007) $709.00

SPRINGFIELD ARMORY CUSTOM LOADED FULL-SIZE 1911A1 AUTO PISTOL

Caliber: 9mm Para., 9-shot; 45 ACP, 7-shot. Barrel: 5". Weight: 30-42 oz. Length: 8.5" overall. Grips: Cocobolo, polymer. Sights: Fixed 3-dot system or adjustable. Features: Beveled magazine well; lowered and flared ejection port. All forged parts, including frame, barrel, slide. All new production. Introduced 1990. From Springfield Armory.

Price: Tactical Combat Black Stainless Steel, fixed sights $904.00

Price: Stainless Steel, fixed sights $902.00

Price: Service Model 5" Lightweight, bi-tone finish . $934.00

Price: Stainless Steel, adjustable target sights $966.00

Price: Black Stainless, adjustable Bo-Mar rear, 3-dot tritium $1,124.00

Price: Stainless Steel 9mm, fixed combat sights $976.00

SPRINGFIELD ARMORY GI 45 1911A1 AUTO PISTOLS

Caliber: 45 ACP; 6-, 7-, 13-shot magazines. Barrel: 3", 4", 5". Weight: 28-36 oz. Length: 5.5-8.5" overall. Grips: Checkered double-diamond walnut, "U.S" logo. Sights: Fixed GI style. Features: Similar to WWII GI-issue 45s at hammer, beavertail, mainspring housing. From Springfield Armory. Enhanced Micro Pistol (EMP) introduced 2007.

Price: GI .45 4" Lightweight Champion, 7+1, 28 oz. $564.00

Price: GI .45 5" High Capacity, 13+1, 36 oz. $617.00

Price: GI .45 5" OD Green, 7+1, 36 oz. $564.00

Price: GI .45 3" Micro Compact, 6+1, 32 oz. $608.00

Price: EMP 9mm 3", (2007) $940.00

SPRINGFIELD ARMORY MIL-SPEC 1911A1 AUTO PISTOLS

Caliber: 38 Super, 9-shot magazines; 45 ACP, 7-shot magazines. Barrel: 5". Weight: 35.6-39 oz. Length: 8.5-8.625" overall. Features: Similar to GI 45s. From Springfield Armory.

Price: Mil-Spec Parkerized, 7+1, 35.6 oz. $660.00

Price: Mil-Spec Stainless Steel, 7+1, 36 oz. $724.00

STI TROJAN-6 INCH

STI EXECUTIVE PISTOL

STI TROJAN-5 INCH

Price: Mil-Spec 38 Super, Nickel finish,
9+1, 39 oz. $1,254.00

SPRINGFIELD ARMORY CUSTOM LOADED CHAMPION 1911A1 PISTOL

Similar to standard 1911A1, slide and barrel are 4". 7.5" OAL. Available in 45 ACP only. Novak Night Sights. Delta hammer and cocobolo grips. Parkerized or stainless. Introduced 1989.

Price: Stainless, 34 oz. $952.00
Price: Lightweight, 28 oz. $913.00

SPRINGFIELD ARMORY CUSTOM LOADED ULTRA COMPACT PISTOL

Similar to 1911A1 Compact, shorter slide, 3.5" barrel, 6+1, 7" OAL. Beavertail grip safety, beveled magazine well, fixed sights. Videki speed trigger, flared ejection port, stainless steel frame, blued slide, match grade barrel, rubber grips. Introduced 1996. From Springfield Armory.

Price: Stainless Steel $952.00

SPRINGFIELD ARMORY CUSTOM LOADED MICRO-COMPACT 1911A1 PISTOL

Caliber: 45 ACP, 6+1 capacity. Barrel: 3" 1:16 LH. Weight: 24-32 oz. Length: 4.7". Grips: Slimline cocobolo. Sights: Novak LoMount tritium. Dovetail front. Features: Aluminum hard-coat anodized alloy frame, forged steel slide, forged barrel, ambi-thumb safety, Extreme Carry Bevel dehorning. Lockable plastic case, 2 magazines.

Price: Bi-Tone Operator w/light rail $1,284.00
Price: Lightweight Bi-Tone $1,220.00

SPRINGFIELD ARMORY TRP PISTOLS

Similar to 1911A1 except 45 ACP only, checkered front strap and main-spring housing, Novak Night Sight combat rear sight and matching dove-tailed front sight, tuned, polished extractor, oversize barrel link; lightweight speed trigger and combat action job, match barrel and bushing, extended ambidextrous thumb safety and fitted beavertail grip safety. Checkered cocobolo wood grips, comes with two Wilson 7-shot magazines. Frame is engraved "Tactical," both sides of frame with "TRP." Introduced 1998. TRP-Pro Model meets FBI specifications for SWAT Hostage Rescue Team. From Springfield Armory.

Price: Standard with Armory Kote finish $1,606.00
Price: Standard, stainless steel $1,606.00
Price: Standard with Operator Light Rail
Armory Kote $1,689.00
Price: TRP-Pro, Armory Kote finish $2,395.00

SPRINGFIELD ARMORY LOADED OPERATOR 1911A1 PISTOL

Similar to Full-Size 1911A1, except light-mounting rail is forged into frame. From Springfield Armory.

STOEGER COUGAR

TAURUS MODEL 24/7

TAURUS MODEL 1911

Price: Loaded Full-Size MC Operator, 42 oz.,
8.5" OAL $1,254.00
Price: TRP Light Rail Armory Kote, 42 oz. $1,689.00
Price: Micro Compact LW, w/XML Mini Light,
32 oz., 6.7 OAL $1,284.00

STI EXECUTIVE PISTOL

Caliber: 40 S&W. Barrel: 5" bull. Weight: 39 oz. Length: 8-5/8". Grips: Gray polymer. Sights: Dawson fiber optic, front; STI adjustable rear. Features: Stainless mag. well, front and rear serrations on slide. Made in U.S.A. by STI.

Price: $2,389.00

STI TROJAN

Caliber: 9mm, 38 Super, 40S&W, 45 ACP. Barrel: 5", 6". Weight: 36 oz. Length: 8.5". Grips: Rosewood. Sights: STI front with STI adjustable rear. Features: Stippled front strap, flat top slide, one-piece steel guide rod.

Price: (Trojan 5") $1,024.00
Price: (Trojan 6", not available in 38 Super) $1,344.00

STOEGER COUGAR

Caliber: 9mm, 40 S&W. Capacity: 15 (9mm); 11 (40 S&W). Barrel: 3.6". Length: 7.0". Weight: 32.5 oz. Grips: Black checkered w/3 interchangeable backstraps. Sights: 3-dot . Features: Aluminum frame, DA/SA, ambisafety. Comes with two magazines. Same design as Beretta-made

version. Rotating barrel, hard-chromed bores, removable front sight, combat trigger, Made in Turkey, imported by Benelli USA. Introduced 2007.

Price: $370.00

TAURUS MODEL 800 SERIES

Caliber: 9mm, 40 S&W, 45 ACP. Barrel: 4". Weight: 32 oz. Length: 8.25". Grips: Checkered. Sights: Novak. Features: DA/SA. Blue and Stainless Steel finish. Introduced in 2007. Imported from Brazil by Taurus International.

Price: 809B, 9mm, Blue, 17+1 .... NA
Price: 809SS, 9mm, Stainless Steel, 17+1 .... NA
Price: 840B, .40 cal., Blue, 15+1 .... NA
Price: 840SS, .40 cal., Stainless Steel, 15+1 .... NA
Price: 845B, .45 ACP, Blue, 12+1 .... NA
Price: 845SS, .45ACP, Stainless Steel, 12+1 .... NA

TAURUS MODEL 1911

Caliber: 45 ACP, 8+1 capacity. Barrel: 5". Weight: 33 oz. Length: 8.5". Grips: Checkered Black. Sights: Heinie Straight 8. Features: SA. Blue, Stainless Steel, Duotone Blue, and Blue/Gray finish. Standard/Picatinny Rail, Standard Frame, Alloy Frame, and Alloy/Picatinny Rail. Introduced in 2007. Imported from Brazil by Taurus International.

Price: 1911B-1, Blue   NA
Price: 1911SS, Stainless Steel .... NA

**TAURUS MODEL 92
AUTO PISTOL**

**TAURUS MODEL 99
AUTO PISTOL**

**TAURUS MODEL 111
MILLENNIUM PRO
AUTO PISTOL**

Price: 1911SS-1, Stainless Steel .... NA
Price: 1911 DT, Duotone Blue .... NA
Price: 1911 AL, Blue/Gray .... NA
Price: 1911 ALR, Blue/Gray .... NA

TAURUS MODEL 917

Caliber: 9mm, 19+1 capacity. Barrel: 4.3". Weight: 32.2 oz. Length: 8.5". Grips: Checkered Rubber. Sights: Fixed. Features: SA/DA. Blue and Stainless Steel finish. Medium Frame. Introduced in 2007. Imported from Brazil by Taurus International.

   Price: 917B-20, Blue .... NA

TAURUS MODEL 24/7

Caliber: 9mm, 40 S&W, 45 ACP. Barrel: 4". Weight: 27.2 oz. Length: 7-1/8". Grips: "Ribber" rubber-finned overlay on polymer. Sights: Adjustable. Features: SA/DA; accessory rail, four safeties, blue or stainless finish. One-piece guide rod, flush-fit magazine, flared bushingless barrel, Picatinny accessory rail, manual safety, user changeable sights, loaded chamber indicator, tuned ejector and lowered port, one piece guide rod and flat wound captive spring. Introduced 2003. Long Slide models have 5" barrels, measure 8-1/8" overall, weigh 27.2 oz. Imported from Brazil by Taurus International.

   Price: 40BP, 40 S&W, blued, 10+1 or 15+1 ...... **$503.00**

Price: 40SSP, 40 S&W, stainless slide, 10+1
            or 15+1 .... **$520.00**
Price: 45BP, 45 ACP, blued, 10+1 or 12+1 .... **$503.00**
Price: Long Slide OSS-D45, 45 ACP, blued, 10+1 or
            12+1, intr. 2007 .... NA

TAURUS MODEL 92
AUTO PISTOL

Caliber: 9mm Para., 10- or 17-shot mags. Barrel: 5". Weight: 34 oz. Length: 8.5" overall. Grips: Checkered rubber, rosewood, mother-of-pearl. Sights: Fixed notch rear. 3-dot sight system. Also offered with micrometer-click adjustable night sights. Features: Double action, ambidextrous 3-way hammer drop safety, allows cocked & locked carry. Blue, stainless steel, blue with gold highlights, stainless steel with gold highlights, forged aluminum frame, integral key-lock. .22 LR conversion kit available. Imported from Brazil by Taurus International.

   Price: Blued or Stainless .... **$602.00 to $664.00**

TAURUS MODEL 99
AUTO PISTOL

Similar to 92, fully adjustable rear sight.

   Price: Blue .... **$617.00 to $633.00**
   Price: 22 Conversion kit for PT 92 and PT99
              (includes barrel and slide) **$266.00**

TAURUS 145 MILLENNIUM AUTO PISTOL

TAURUS MODEL 911 AUTO PISTOL

TAURUS 745 MILLENNIUM AUTO PISTOL

TAURUS MODEL 100/101 AUTO PISTOL

Caliber: 40 S&W, 10- or 11-shot mags. Barrel: 5". Weight: 34 oz. Length: 8-1/2". Grips: Checkered rubber, rosewood, mother-of-pearl. Sights: 3-dot fixed or adjustable; night sights available. Features: Single/double action with three-position safety/decocker. Reintroduced in 2001. Imported by Taurus International.

Price: PT100 .... $602.00 to $664.00

Price: PT101, adjustable rear sight . $617.00 to $633.00

TAURUS MODEL 111 MILLENNIUM PRO AUTO PISTOL

Caliber: 9mm Para., 10- or 12-shot mags. Barrel: 3.25". Weight: 18.7 oz. Length: 6-1/8" overall. Grips: Checkered polymer. Sights: 3-dot fixed; night sights available. Low profile, 3-dot combat. Features: Double action only, polymer frame, matte stainless or blue steel slide, manual safety, integral key-lock. Deluxe models with wood grip inserts.

Price: .... $406.00 to $422.00

TAURUS 140 MILLENNIUM PRO AUTO PISTOL

Caliber: 40 S&W, 10-shot mag. Barrel: 3.25". Weight: 18.7 oz. Grips: Checkered polymer. Sights: 3-dot fixed; night sights available. Features: Double action only; matte stainless or blue steel slide, black polymer frame, manual safety, integral key-lock action. From Taurus International.

Price: .... $422.00 to $439.00

TAURUS 145 MILLENNIUM AUTO PISTOL

Caliber: 45 ACP, 10-shot mag. Barrel: 3.27". Weight: 23 oz. Stock: Checkered polymer. Sights: 3-dot fixed; night sights available. Features: Double-action only, matte stainless or blue steel slide, black polymer frame, manual safety, integral key-lock. Compact model is 6+1 with a 3.25" barrel, weighs 20.8 oz. From Taurus International.

Price: 145, blued or stainless .... $422.00 to $439.00

Price: 745 Compact, blued or stainless,
intr. 2005 .... $410.00 to $425.00

TAURUS MODEL 911 AUTO PISTOL

Caliber: 9mm Para., 10-shot mag. Barrel: 4". Weight: 28.2 oz. Length: 7" overall. Grips: Checkered rubber, rosewood, mother-of-pearl. Sights: Fixed, 3-dot blue or stainless; night sights optional. Features: Double action, semi-auto ambidextrous 3-way hammer drop safety, allows cocked & locked carry. Blue, stainless steel, blue with gold highlights, or stainless steel with gold highlights, forged aluminum frame, integral key-lock.

Price: $569.00

TAURUS MODEL 940 AUTO PISTOL

Caliber: 40 S&W, 10-shot mag. Barrel: 3-5/8". Weight: 28.2 oz. Length: 7" overall. Grips: Checkered rubber, rosewood or mother-of-pearl. Sights: Fixed, 3-dot blue or stainless; night sights optional. Features: Double action, semi-

TAURUS MODEL 945 SERIES

WALTHER P99 AUTO PISTOL

auto ambidextrous 3-way hammer drop safety, allows cocked & locked carry. Blue, stainless steel, blue with gold highlights, or stainless steel with gold hightlights, forged aluminum frame, integral key-lock.

Price: From **$569.00**

TAURUS MODEL 945/38S SERIES

Caliber: 45 ACP, 8-shot mag. Barrel: 4.25". Weight: 28.2/29.5 oz. Length: 7.48" overall. Grips: Checkered rubber, rosewood or mother-of-pearl. Sights: Fixed, 3-dot; night sights optional. Features: Double-action with ambidextrous 3-way hammer drop safety allows cocked & locked carry. Forged aluminum frame, 945C has ported barrel/slide. Blue, stainless, blue with gold highlights, stainless with gold highlights, integral key-lock. Introduced 1995. 38 Super line based on 945 frame introduced 2005. 38S series is 10+1, 30 oz., 7.5" overall. Imported by Taurus International.

Price: From **$609.00**

WALTHER P99 AUTO PISTOL

Caliber: 9mm Para., 9x21, 40 S&W,10-shot magazine. Barrel: 4". Weight: 25 oz. Length: 7" overall. Grips: Textured polymer. Sights: Blade front (comes with three interchangeable blades for elevation adjustment), micrometer rear adjustable for windage. Features: Double-action mechanism with trigger safety, decock safety, internal striker safety; chamber loaded indicator; ambidextrous magazine release levers; polymer frame with interchangeable backstrap inserts. Comes with two magazines. Introduced 1997. Imported from Germany by Smith & Wesson U.S.A.

Price: **$665.00**

Armalite's Super S.A.S.S.

A Semi-Auto Sniper System that Rocks

BY DAVE MORELLI

The bolt-action rifle has traditionally been the base for the sniper rifle. The locking of the bolt with enlarged lugs perfectly fitted by a skilled craftsman and the rugged simplicity of the repeating system has made the bolt-action favored by weekend sportsmen and professional tactical operator. The semi auto, while offering a higher magazine capacity and faster rate of fire, has always suffered because of the tuning of all the moving parts and springs that have to be kept functioning in match-grade condition. There also is the temptation to fall back on the fact that there are additional rounds available and not take each shot with the same precision as if it was the only bullet.

Yet the semi-auto has a place in the modern world and the U.S. military is actively seeking to deploy a semi-auto sniper rifle. That military interest has prompted many manufacturers to get in the game and produce sniper-grade quality like the Armalite S.A.S.S. (Semi-Auto Sniper System). I tested one of Armalite's AR-10 .308 rifles several months ago and really liked the rifle. The SASS is based on the AR-10 lower with flat-top upper and many modifications. The fore grip is a four-rail picatinny

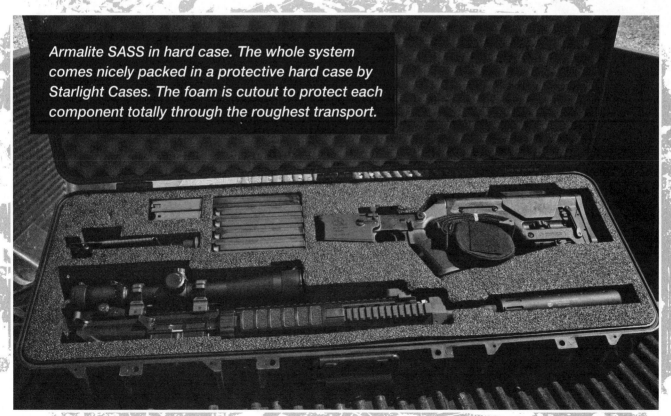

Armalite SASS in hard case. The whole system comes nicely packed in a protective hard case by Starlight Cases. The foam is cutout to protect each component totally through the roughest transport.

type system for adding necessities and allows the 20-inch stainless match-grade barrel to float free. The barrel on he model I fired is fitted with a mock Advanced Armament Corporation suppressor type apparatus that wasn't sound restricting but would hold down muzzle flash. In a police of military environment or where legal it could be fitted with a sound suppressor for quiet shooting and improved velocity and reduced recoil. The unused sections of the rails are covered with rubberized tops that protect the hands and the rails. The lower rail of the fore grip was used for an A.R.M.S. quick-detach

Putting together the SASS Armalite. The gun is based off of the AR frame and quickly assembles out of the hard case. Although the hard case would be preferable for travel a soft case or drag bag with the rifle ready for action would be more convenient on duty.

bipod attachment that was affixed to a Harris bipod. I really like the Harris bipod. It is a quality pod at an economic price.

The Super SASS has an adjustable gas block for precisely adjusting gas flow for consistency and reliable operation. This is an important adjustment to regulate the recoil gasses and is helpful adjusting the gas when shooting the SASS with a suppressor.

The Magpul Precision Rifle Stock adds adjustment to the Super SASS stock. It adjusts for cheek height and length of pull with calibrated dial knobs that are easy to get to and readjust in the field if necessary. I really like the easy adjustment because sometimes I would have to get into a shooting position dictated by the environment that would be more comfortable with some slight readjustment. Adjustments that involve screws and moving parts that need a screwdriver don't offer this advantage.

The lower end of the buttstock also has a rail for accessories like a sling swivel or other leveling attachment that certain shooting situations might dictate.

The already accurate SASS was fitted with a Leupold Mark LR/T 3.5-10x40mm scope. This scope was equipped with M3 dials which have ½ minute windage adjustments and 1 minute elevation. It also was equipped with .308 Win drop compensation numbers on the elevation dial. The 30mm main tube gives better light transmission and increased elevation and windage adjustments. Your average scope usually offers enough windage adjustment but on a long-range rifle, those elevation adjustment can become mighty dear as the distance increases. I have never run out but extras are always appreciated.

The scope has an illuminated reticule that lights the MilDot portion. It also disappears in bright light when it is not needed and lights up when aiming at darker areas. The scope, like all Leupold's prod-

TRU Group I shot a ¾-minute group with the SASS using Federal TRU (Tactical Rifle, Urban) the Federal Police Tactical shot just over a minute group. Both are acceptable groups and with some practice with the system tighter groups should be possible.

ucts, has great clarity and light transmission and is a quality rugged optic. The scope is attached with A.R.M.S. quick-detach rings so that the flip up rear sight and optional front sight could be used to meet the circumstances that might require peep sight shooting. Even though this gun is designed to be a long-range semi auto it is still a semi auto capable of laying down sustained fire when needed. Being able to quickly take the restricting scope off for close-quarter defense should the need arise is a great feature.

The improved magazines for the SASS were improvised designs from the M-14 style sniper weapon. They are rugged and less likely to malfunction.

rifles at 3 pounds so it took some getting used to but it was a smooth, crisp trigger. The action was smooth and the extended handle made the gun easier to charge with the scope on. Shouldering the 13-pound package had a familiar feel as it is based on an AR design. I packed up some Federal Police Tactical and TRU (Tactical Rifle Urban) and headed out.

I assembled the rifle at the range. Again, being based on the AR the upper and lower popped together quickly and the rifle was ready for action. The A.R.M.S. quick detach accessory on the bipod jumped on the lower rail. The scope in stored in the case attached to the upper. It was a great day, 0-3 mph wind at my back and about 79 degrees F. I shot off of a bench using the Harris bipod and a sandbag under the butt. The rifle was rock solid.

I would have preferred a fatter pistol grip on the gun but that's just a personal thing as I have become accustomed to the fat pistol grips on bolt rifle stocks. Anyone working with a rifle in a sniper position would get accustomed to the grip. The fatter grip makes my hand fit better and helps me to place only the tip of my finger on the trigger. As this is a modification that would tailored to each individual I could see Armalite's wisdom in letting the sniper change the pistol grip to fit his hand.

The first couple groups I shot with the Federal Police Tactical ammo. This is a 168-grain soft-nose bullet of match quality. The ammo functioned flawlessly in the semi-auto action and the bolt cycled with a positive feel to it. I didn't fiddle with the adjustable gas block as the rifle functioned great and the recoil seemed a bit milder than a bolt .308. I think it is a valued modification though as adjustments could be made if there was a problem with the addition of suppressor or if the sniper was using subsonic loads.

The groups with this ammo were just a bit larger than one minute. I shot five-shot groups instead of three because that is what my department required and I have adopted that way. I thought that was acceptable for not having worked with the rifle for a training period. I shot up a box of the Tactical ammo giving the barrel time to cool in between

They are also short enough to shoot comfortably from a prone position and still have 20 rounds. The improved ruggedness would be my primary concern so they would survive and function in the toughest of circumstances. The SASS system comes with six 20-round magazines and a 10-rounder. Also included are a sling and cleaning kit all wrapped up in a Starlight Cases hard case. The rifle has to be taken down to fit in the cutout foam lining but that is the best way to transport the system. I would recommend a soft tactical bag from Blackhawk or a similar outfit for a drag system to carry the gun to duty location.

I couldn't wait to take the Super SASS out and heat up the barrel. When I put the trigger scale on the trigger and it weighed in at a crisp 4.5 pounds. The two-stage match trigger had some light take up then it was ready to drop. I keep my precision

Leupold Mark Scope on Armalite SASS The Leupold Mark Scope has half- minute windage and one-minute elevation adjustments with easy-to-read numbers. The A.R.M.S. quick detachable rings allow the scope to be easily removed to access peep sight system and replaced to zero.

shots so every shot was more like a cold shot the police sniper strives for.

The Federal TRU ammo is a hollow point bullet also 168 grains and designed to break up quicker in an urban environment, minimizing over-penetration problems. Both of these bullets have a boat-tail design. I think the best performance that can be achieved in the .308 is with a 165- or 168-grain boat-tail bullet. The 175 bullet is gaining popularity for longer range as its extra weight will help it make the long journey, but my department used Federal Match ammo exclusively in the sniper rifles and our five-shot weekly qualification groups were in the half minute category. For the military sniper where the distances are longer the heavier bullet may be a better choice, but in the police environment shots would be much shorter. The TRU ammo produced a ¾ minute group. That's perfectly acceptable for a police sniper rifle and that group most likely could be shrunk down a bit more with constant practice.

The semi auto sniper system is definitely accurate enough to be an addition to the modern police tactical unit. With the additional threat that the police may encounter terrorist activity in the course of their duties, having a sniper system with additional firepower is an advantage. The semi auto has come a long way and is proving itself in battle and on the street. The Armalite Super SASS is definitely a system to look into if a police tactical unit wants to add a semi auto sniper system to the team.

RIFLES PRODUCT DIRECTORY

Armalite M15A2 Carbine

Armalite AR-180B

Armalite AR-10A4 Special Purpose Rifle

ARMALITE M15A2 CARBINE

Caliber: 223, 30-round magazine. Barrel: 16" heavy chrome lined; 1:9" twist. Weight: 7 lbs. Length: 35-11/16" overall. Stock: Green or black composition. Sights: Standard A2. Features: Upper and lower receivers have push-type pivot pin; hard coat anodized; A2-style forward assist; M16A2-type raised fence around magazine release button. Made in U.S.A. by ArmaLite, Inc.

Price: Green	....	$1,100.00
Price: Black	....	$1,100.00

ARMALITE AR-10A4 SPECIAL PURPOSE RIFLE

Caliber: 308 Win., 10- and 20-round magazine. Barrel: 20" chrome-lined, 1:11.25" twist. Weight: 9.6 lbs. Length: 41" overall. Stock: Green or black composition. Sights: Detachable handle, front sight, or scope mount available; comes with international style flattop receiver with Picatinny rail. Features: Forged upper receiver with case deflector. Receivers are hard-coat anodized. Introduced 1995. Made in U.S.A. by ArmaLite, Inc.

Price: Green	....	$1,506.00
Price: Black	....	$1,506.00

ARMALITE AR-10A2

Utilizing the same 20" double-lapped, heavy barrel as the ArmaLite AR-10A4 Special Purpose Rifle. Offered in 308 caliber only. Made in U.S.A. by ArmaLite, Inc.

Price: $1,506.00

ARMALITE AR-180B RIFLE

Caliber: 223, 10-shot magazine. Barrel: 19.8". Weight: 6 lbs. Length: 38". Stock: Synthetic. Sights: Rear sight adjustable for windage, small and large apertures. Features: Lower receiver made of polymer, upper formed of sheet metal. Uses standard AR-15 magazines. Made in U.S.A. by Armalite.

Price: $750.00

ARMALITE AR-50 RIFLE

Caliber: 50 BMG Barrel: 31". Weight: 33.2 lbs. Length: 59.5" Stock: Synthetic. Sights: None furnished. Features: A single-shot bolt action rifle designed for long range shooting. Available in left-hand model. Made in U.S.A. by Armalite.

Price: $2,999.00

ARMALITE AR-10(T) RIFLE

Caliber: 308, 10-shot magazine. Barrel: 24" target-weight Rock 5R custom. Weight: 10.4 lbs. Length: 43.5" overall. Stock: Green or black compostion; N.M. fiberglass handguard tube. Sights: Detachable handle, front sight, or scope mount available. Comes with international-style flattop receiver with Picatinny rail. Features: National Match two-stage trigger. Forged upper receiver. Receivers hard-

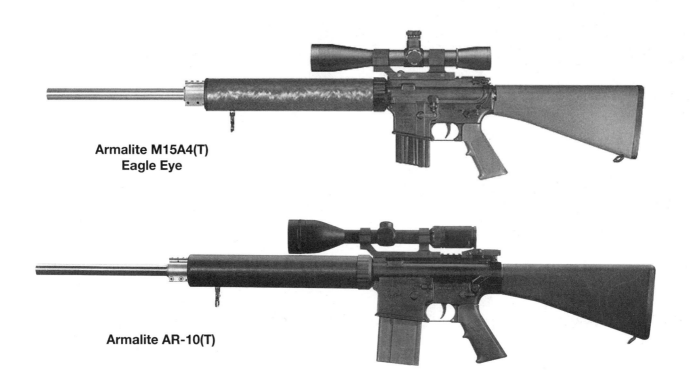

**Armalite M15A4(T)
Eagle Eye**

Armalite AR-10(T)

coat anodized. Introduced 1995. Made in U.S.A. by ArmaLite, Inc.

Price: Green	$2,126.00
Price: Black	$2,126.00

ARMALITE M15A4(T) EAGLE EYE RIFLE

Caliber: 223, 10-round magazine. Barrel: 24" heavy stainless; 1:8" twist. Weight: 9.2 lbs. Length: 42-3/8" overall. Stock: Green or black butt, N.M. fiberglass handguard tube. Sights: One-piece international-style flattop receiver with Weaver-type rail, including case deflector. Features: Detachable carry handle, front sight and scope mount (30mm or 1") available. Upper and lower receivers have push-type pivot pin, hard coat anodized. Made in U.S.A. by ArmaLite, Inc.

Price: Green	$1,378.00
Price: Black	$1,504.00

ARSENAL USA SSR-56

Caliber: 7.62x39mm. Barrel: 16.25". Weight: 7.4 lbs. Length: 35.5" Stock: Black polymer. Sights: Adjustable rear. Features: An AK-47-style rifle built on a hardened Hungarian FEG receiver with the required six U.S.-made parts to make it legal for use with all extra-capacity magazines. From Arsenal I, LLC.

Price:	$565.00

ARSENAL USA SSR-74-2

Caliber: 5.45x39mm Barrel: 16.25" Weight: 7 lbs. Length: 36.75" Stock: Polymer or wood. Sights: Adjustable. Features: Built with parts from an unissued Bulgarian AK-47 rifle, it has a Buffer Technologies recoil buffer, enough U.S.-made parts to allow pistol grip stock and use with all extra-capacity magazines. Assembled in U.S.A. From Arsenal I, LLC.

Price:	$499.00

ARSENAL USA SSR-85C-2

Caliber: 7.62x39mm. Barrel: 16.25". Weight: 7.1 lbs. Length: 35.5". Stock: Polymer or wood. Sights: Adjustable rear calibrated to 800 meters. Features: Built from parts obtained from unissued Polish AK-47 rifles, the gas tube is vented and the receiver cover is plain. Rifle contains enough U.S.-sourced parts to allow pistol grip stock and use with all extra-capacity magazines. Assembled in U.S.A. by Arsenal I, LLC.

Price:	$499.00

BARRETT MODEL 95 BOLT-ACTION RIFLE

Caliber: 50 BMG, 5-shot magazine. Barrel: 29". Weight: 22 lbs. Length: 45" overall. Stock: Energy-absorbing recoil pad. Sights: Scope optional. Features: Bolt-action, bullpup design. Disassembles without tools; extendable bipod legs; match-grade barrel; muzzle brake. Introduced 1995. Made

Barrett Model 82A-1
Semi-Automatic Rifle

Barrett Model 95
Bolt-Action Rifle

Beretta CX4/PX4
Storm Carbine

in U.S.A. by Barrett Firearms Mfg., Inc.

Price: From $4,950.00

BARRETT MODEL 82A-1 SEMI-AUTOMATIC RIFLE

Caliber: 50 BMG, 10-shot detachable box magazine. Barrel: 29". Weight: 28.5 lbs. Length: 57" overall. Stock: Composition with energy-absorbing recoil pad. Sights: Scope optional. Features: Semi-automatic, recoil operated with recoiling barrel. Three-lug locking bolt; muzzle brake. Adjustable bipod. Introduced 1985. Made in U.S.A. by Barrett Firearms.

Price: From $7,200.00

BARRETT MODEL 99 SINGLE SHOT RIFLE

Caliber: 50 BMG. Barrel: 33". Weight: 25 lbs. Length: 50.4" overall. Stock: Anodized aluminum with energy-absorbing recoil pad. Sights: None furnished; integral M1913 scope rail. Features: Bolt action; detachable bipod; match-grade barrel with high-efficiency muzzle brake. Introduced 1999. Made in U.S.A. by Barrett Firearms.

Price: From $3,000.00

Price: Left-hand, blue barrel, no sights,
           walnut stock $1,584.60

BERETTA CX4/PX4 STORM CARBINE

Caliber: 9mm Para, 40 S&W, 45 ACP. Weight: 5.75 lbs.

Barrel Length: 16.6", chrome lined, rate of twist 1:16 (40 S&W) or 1:10 (9mm). Length: NA. Stock: Black synthetic. Sights: NA. Features: Introduced 2005. Imported from Italy by Beretta USA.

Price: Cx4 Carbine, 40 S&W, 10+1 $800.00

Price: Cx4 Carbine, 8000 Series, 9mm, 10+1 ..... $775.00

Price: Cx4 Carbine, 8045 Series,45 ACP, 8+1 ..... $800.00

Price: Cx4 Px4 Carbine, 40 S&W, 14+1 .... $850.00

Price: Cx4 Px4 Carbine, 9mm, 17+1 .... $850.00

BLASER R93 LONG RANGE RIFLE

Caliber: 308 Win., 10-shot detachable box magazine. Barrel: 24". Weight: 10.4 lbs. Length: 44" overall. Stock: Aluminum with synthetic lining. Sights: None furnished; accepts detachable scope mount. Features: Straight-pull bolt action with adjustable trigger; fully adjustable stock; quick takedown; corrosion resistant finish. Introduced 1998. Imported from Germany by SIGARMS.

Price: $2,360.00

BUSHMASTER M17S BULLPUP RIFLE

Caliber: 223, 10-shot magazine. Barrel: 21.5", chrome lined; 1:9" twist. Weight: 8.2 lbs. Length: 30" overall. Stock: Fiberglass-filled nylon. Sights: Designed for optics-carrying handle incorporates scope mount rail for Weaver-type rings; also includes 25-meter open iron sights. Features: Gas-operated, short-stroke piston

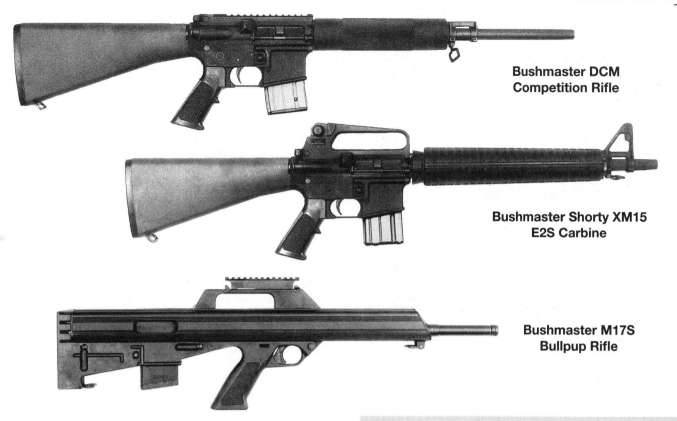

Bushmaster DCM Competition Rifle

Bushmaster Shorty XM15 E2S Carbine

Bushmaster M17S Bullpup Rifle

system; ambidextrous magazine release. Introduced 1993. Made in U.S.A. by Bushmaster Firearms, Inc./ Quality Parts Co.

Price: $765.00

BUSHMASTER DCM COMPETITION RIFLE

Caliber: 223. Barrel: 20" extra-heavy (1" diameter) barrel with 1.8" twist for heavier competition bullets. Weight: Appx. 12 lbs. with balance weights. Length: NA. Stock: NA. Sights: A2 rear sight. Features: Has special competition rear sight with interchangeable apertures, extra-fine 1/2- or 1/4-MOA windage and elevation adjustments; specially ground front sight post in choice of three widths. Full-length handguards over free-floater barrel tube. Introduced 1998. Made in U.S.A. by Bushmaster Firearms, Inc.

Price: $1,395.00

BUSHMASTER SHORTY XM15 E2S CARBINE

Caliber: 223,10-shot magazine. Barrel: 16", heavy; 1:9" twist. Weight: 7.2 lbs. Length: 34.75" overall. Stock: A2 type; fixed black composition. Sights: Fully adjustable M16A2 sight system. Features: Patterned after Colt M-16A2. Chrome-lined barrel with manganese phosphate finish. "Shorty" handguards. Has forged aluminum receivers with pushpin. Made in U.S.A. by Bushmaster Firearms, Inc.

Price: (A2) $985.00

Price: (A3) $1,085.00

BUSHMASTER XM15 E2S DISSIPATOR CARBINE

Similar to the XM15 E2S Shorty carbine except has full-length "Dissipator" handguards. Weighs 7.6 lbs.; 34.75" overall; forged aluminum receivers with push-pin style takedown. Made in U.S.A. by Bushmaster Firearms, Inc.

Price: (A2 type) $995.00

Price: (A3 type) $1,095.00

BUSHMASTER XM15 E25 AK SHORTY CARBINE

Similar to the XM15 E2S Shorty except has 14.5" barrel with an AK muzzle brake permanently attached giving 16" barrel length. Weighs 7.3 lbs. Introduced 1999. Made in U.S.A. by Bushmaster Firearms, Inc.

Price: (A2 type) $1,005.00

Price: (A3 type) $1,105.00

BUSHMASTER M4/M4A3 POST-BAN CARBINE

Similar to the XM15 E2S except has 14.5" barrel with Mini Y compensator, and fixed telestock. MR configuration has fixed carry handle; M4A3 has removeable carry handle.

Price: (M4) $1,065.00

Price: (M4A3) $1,165.00

Bushmaster M4/M4A3 Post-Ban Carbine

Bushmaster A2 Rifle

Century International AES-10 Hi-Cap Rifle

BUSHMASTER A2 RIFLE

Caliber: 308, 5.56mm. Barrel: 16", 20". Weight: 8.3 lbs. Length: 38.25" overall (20" barrel). Stock: Black composition; A2 type. Sights: Adjustable post front, adjustable aperture rear. Features: Patterned after Colt M-16A2. Chrome-lined barrel with manganese phosphate exterior. Forged aluminum receivers with push-pin takedown. Available in stainless barrel and camo stock versions. Made in U.S.A. by Bushmaster Firearms Co.

Price: 20" match heavy barrel
(A2 type) .... $1,025.00 to $1,185.00
Price: (A3 type) $1,135.00

CENTURY INTERNATIONAL AES-10 HI-CAP RIFLE

Caliber: 7.62x39mm. 30-shot magazine. Barrel: 23.2". Weight: NA. Length: 41.5" overall. Stock: Wood grip, forend. Sights: Fixed-notch rear, windage-adjustable post front. Features: RPK-style, accepts standard double-stack AK-type mags. Side-mounted scope mount, integral carry handle, bipod. Imported by Century Arms Int'l.

Price: AES-10, from $450.00

CENTURY INTERNATIONAL GP WASR-10 HI-CAP RIFLE

Caliber: 7.62x39mm. 30-shot magazine. Barrel: 16.25", 1:10 rh twist. Weight: 7.2 lbs. Length: 34.25" overall. Stock: Wood laminate or composite, grip, forend. Sights: Fixed-notch rear, windage-adjustable post front. Features: Two 30-rd. detachable box magazines, cleaning kit, bayonet. Version of AKM rifle; U.S.-parts added for BATFE compliance. Threaded muzzle, folding stock, bayonet lug, compensator, Dragunov stock available. Made in Romania by Cugir Arsenal. Imported by Century Arms Int'l.

Price: GP WASR-10, from $350.00

CENTURY INTERNATIONAL WASR-2 HI-CAP RIFLE

Caliber: 5.45x39mm. 30-shot magazine. Barrel: 16.25". Weight: 7.5 lbs. Length: 34.25" overall. Stocks: Wood laminate. Sights: Fixed-notch rear, windage-adjustable post front. Features: 1 30-rd. detachable box magazine, cleaning kit, sling. WASR-3 HI-CAP chambered in 223 Rem. Imported by Century Arms Int'l.

Price: GP WASR-2/3, from $250.00

CENTURY INTERNATIONAL M70AB2 SPORTER RIFLE

Caliber: 7.62x39mm. 30-shot magazine. Barrel: 16.25". Weight: 7.5 lbs. Length: 34.25" overall. Stocks: Metal grip, wood forend. Sights: Fixed-notch rear, windage-adjustable post front. Features: 2 30-rd. double-stack magazine, cleaning kit, compensator, bayonet lug and bayonet. Paratrooper-style Kalashnikov with under-folding stock. Import-

**Century International GP
WASR-10 Hi-Cap Rifle**

**Century International
M70AB2 Sporter Rifle**

Colt Accurized Rifle

ed by Century Arms Int'l.

Price: M70AB2, from.. $480.00

CHEYTAC M-200

Caliber: 408 CheyTac, 7-round mag. Barrel: 30". Length: 55", stock extended. Weight: 27 lbs. (steel barrel); 24 lbs. (carbon fiber barrel). Stock: Retractable. Sights: None, scope rail provided. Features: CNC-machined receiver, attachable Picatinny rail M-1913, detachable barrel, integral bipod, 3.5-lb. trigger pull, muzzle brake. Made in U.S. A. by CheyTac, LLC.

Price: $13,795.00

COLT MATCH TARGET MODEL RIFLE

Caliber: 223 Rem., 5-shot magazine. Barrel: 16.1" or 20". Weight: 7.1 to 8-1/2 lbs. Length: 34-1/2" to 39" overall. Stock: Composition stock, grip, forend. Sights: Post front, rear adjustable for windage and elevation. Features: 5-round detachable box magazine, flash suppressor, sling swivels. Forward bolt assist included. Introduced 1991. Made in U.S.A. by Colt's Mfg. Co., Inc.

Price: Match Target HBAR, from $1,172.00

COLT MATCH TARGET HBAR RIFLE

Caliber: 223 Rem. Barrel: 20". Weight: 8 lbs. Length: 39" overall. Stock: Synthetic. Sights: Front: elevation adj. post; rear: 800-meter, aperture adj. for windage and eleva-

tion. Features: Heavy barrel, rate of rifling twist 1:7. Introduced 1991. Made in U.S.A. by Colt.

Price: Model MT6601, MT6601C $1,183.00

COLT MATCH TARGET COMPETITION HBAR RIFLE

Similar to the Match Target except has removeable carry handle for scope mounting, 1:9" rifling twist, 9-round magazine. Weighs 8.5 lbs. Introduced 1991.

Price: Model MT6700, MT6700C $1,250.00

COLT MATCH TARGET COMPETITION HBAR II RIFLE

Similar to the Match Target Competition HBAR except has 16:1" barrel, overall length 34.5", and weighs 7.1 lbs. Introduced 1995.

Price: Model MT6731 .... $1,172.00

COLT ACCURIZED RIFLE

Similar to the Match Target Model except has 24" barrel. Features flat-top receiver for scope mounting, stainless steel heavy barrel, tubular handguard, and free-floating barrel. Matte black finish. Weighs 9.25 lbs. Made in U.S.A. by Colt's Mfg. Co., Inc.

Price: Model CR6724.................................... $1,334.00

CZ 700 M1 SNIPER RIFLE

Caliber: 308 Winchester, 10-shot magazine. Barrel:

Colt Match Target HBAR Rifle

Colt Match Target Competition HBAR II Rifle

25.6". Weight: 11.9 lbs. Length: 45" overall. Stock: Laminated wood thumbhole with adjustable buttplate and cheekpiece. Sights: None furnished; permanently attached Weaver rail for scope mounting. Features: 60-degree bolt throw; oversized trigger guard and bolt handle for use with gloves; full-length equipment rail on forend; fully adjustable trigger. Introduced 2001. Imported from the Czech Republic by CZ-USA.

> **Price:** $2,097.00

DPMS PANTHER ARMS AR-15 RIFLES

Caliber: 223 Rem., 7.62x39. Barrel: 16" to 24". Weight: 7-3/4 to 11-3/4 lbs. Length: 34-1/2" to 42-1/4" overall. Stock: Black Zytel® composite. Sights: Square front post, adjustable A2 rear. Features: Steel or stainless steel heavy or bull barrel; hardcoat anodized receiver; aluminum free-float tube handguard; many options. From DPMS Panther Arms.

> **Price:** Panther Bull A-15 (20" stainless bull bbl.)..... $915.00
>
> **Price:** Panther Bull Twenty-Four
> (24" stainless bull bbl.) $945.00
>
> **Price:** Bulldog (20" stainless fluted bbl.,
> flattop receiver) $1,219.00
>
> **Price:** Panther Bull Sweet Sixteen
> (16" stainless bull bbl.) $885.00
>
> **Price:** DCM Panther (20" stainless heavy bbl.,
> n.m. sights) $1,099.00
>
> **Price:** Panther 7.62x39 (20" steel heavy bbl.) $849.00

DSA Z4 GTC CARBINE WITH C.R.O.S.

Caliber: 5.56 NATO Barrel: 16" 1:9 twist M4 profile fluted chrome lined heavy barrel with threaded Vortec flash hider. Weight: 7.6 lbs. Stock: 6 position collapsible M4 stock, Predator P4X free float tactical rail. Sights: Chrome lined Picatinny gas block w/removable front sight. Features: The Corrosion Resistant Operating System incorporates the new P.O.F. Gas Trap System with removable gas plug eliminates problematic features of standard AR gas system, Forged 7075T6 DSA lower receiver. Introduced 2006. Made in U.S.A. by DSA, Inc.

> **Price:** $1,700.00

DSA CQB MRP, STANDARD MRP

Caliber: 5.56 NATO Barrel: 16" or 18" 1:7 twist chrome-lined or stainless steel barrel with A2 flash hider Stock: 6 position collapsible M4 stock. Features: LMT_1/2" MRP upper receiver with 20-1/2" Standard quad rail or 16-1/2" CQB quad rail, LMT_enhanced bolt with dual extractor springs, free float barrel, quick change barrel system, forged 7075T6 DSA lower receiver. EOTech and vertical grip additional. Introduced 2006. Made in U.S.A. by DSA, Inc.

> **Price:** CQB MRP w/16" chrome lined barrel $2,420.00
>
> **Price:** CQB MRP w/16" stainless steel barrel $2,540.00
>
> **Price:** Standard MRP w/16" chrome lined barrel . $2,620.00
>
> **Price:** Standard MRP w/16" or 18" stainless
> steel barrel $2,720.00

DSA SA58 Carbine

DSA SA58 Carbine

DSA SA58 CARBINE

Caliber: 308 Win. Barrel: 16.25" bipod cut w/threaded flash hider. Weight: 8.35 lbs. Length: 37.5". Stock: Synthetic, X-Series or optional folding para stock. Sights: Elevation-adjustable post front, windage-adjustable rear peep. Features: Fully adjustable short gas system, high grade steel or 416 stainless upper receiver. Made in U.S.A. by DSA, Inc.

Price: High-grade steel.................................... $1,595.00

DSA 1R CARBINE

Caliber: 5.56 NATO. Barrel: 16" 1:9 twist D4 w/A2 flash hider. Weight: 6.25 lbs. Length: Variable. Stock: 6 position collapsible M4 stock, D4 handguard w/heatshield. Sights: Forged A2 front sight with lug. Features: Forged 7075T6 DSA lower receiver, forged A2 or flattop upper receiver. Introduced 2006. Made in U.S.A. by DSA, Inc.

Price: A2 or Flattop 1R Carbine $1,055.00

Price: With VLTOR ModStock $1,175.00

DSA XM CARBINE

Caliber: 5.56 NATO. Barrel: 11-1/2" 1:9 twist D4 with 5-1/2" permanently attached flash hider. Weight: 6.25 lbs. Length: Variable. Stock: Collapsible, Handguard w/heatshield. Sights: Forged A2 front sight with lug. Features: Forged 7075T6 DSA lower receiver, forged A2 upper receiver. Introduced 2006. Made in U.S.A. by DSA, Inc.

Price: $1,055.00

DSA STANDARD

Caliber: 5.56 NATO. Barrel: 20" 1:9 twist heavy barrel w/A2 flash hider. Weight: 6.25 lbs. Length: 38-7/16". Stock: A2 buttstock, A2 handguard w/heatshield. Sights: Forged A2 front sight with lug. Features: Forged 7075T6 DSA lower receiver, forged A2 or flattop upper receiver. Introduced 2006. Made in U.S.A. by DSA, Inc.

Price: A2 or Flattop Standard $1,025.00

DSA DCM RIFLE

Caliber: .223 Wylde Chamber. Barrel: 20" 1:8 twist chrome moly match grade Badger Barrel. Weight: 10 lbs. Length: 39.5". Stock: DCM freefloat handguard system, A2 buttstock. Sights: Forged A2 front sight with lug. Features: NM two stage trigger, NM rear sight, forged 7075T6 DSA lower receiver, forged A2 upper receiver. Introduced 2006. Made in U.S.A. by DSA, Inc.

Price: $1,520.00

DSA S1

Caliber: .223 Match Chamber. Barrel: 16", 20" or 24" 1:8 twist stainless steel bull barrel. Weight: 8.0, 9.5 and 10 lbs. Length: 34.25", 38.25" and 42.25". Stock: A2 buttstock with free float aluminum handguard. Sights: Picatinny gas block sight base. Features: Forged 7075T6 DSA lower receiver, Match two stage trigger, forged flattop upper receiver, fluted barrel optional. Introduced 2006. Made in U.S.A. by DSA, Inc.

Price: $1,155.00

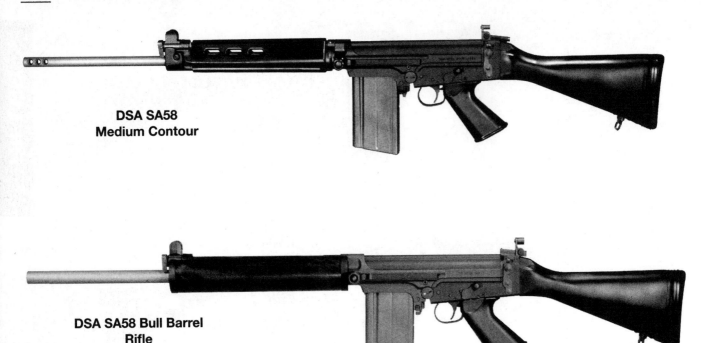

**DSA SA58
Medium Contour**

**DSA SA58 Bull Barrel
Rifle**

DSA SA58 CONGO, PARA CONGO

Caliber: 308 Win. Barrel: 18" w/short Belgian short flash hider. Weight: 8.6 lbs. (Congo); 9.85 lbs. (Para Congo). Length: 39.75" Stock: Synthetic w/military grade furniture (Congo); Synthetic with non-folding steel para stock (Para Congo). Sights: Elevation adjustable protected post front sight, windage adjustable rear peep (Congo); Belgian type Para Flip Rear (Para Congo). Features: Fully-adjustable gas system, high-grade steel upper receiver with carry handle. Made in U.S.A. by DSA, Inc.

Price: Congo $1,695.00
Price: Para Congo $1,995.00

DSA SA58 GRAY WOLF

Caliber: 308 Win. Barrel: 21" match-grade bull w/ target crown. Weight: 13 lbs. Length: 41.75". Stock: Synthetic. Sights: Elevation-adjustable post front sight, windage-adjustable match rear peep. Features: Fully-adjustable gas system, high-grade steel upper receiver, Picatinny scope mount, DuraCoat finish. Made in U.S.A. by DSA, Inc.

Price: $2,120.00

DSA SA58 PREDATOR

Caliber: 243 Win., 260 Rem., 308 Win. Barrel: 16" and 19" w/target crown. Weight: 9 to 9.3 lbs. Length: 36.25" to 39.25". Stock: Green synthetic. Sights: Elevation-adjust-able post front; windage-adjustable match rear peep. Features: Fully-adjustable gas system, high-grade steel upper receiver, Picatinny scope mount, DuraCoat solid and camo finishes. Made in U.S.A. by DSA, Inc.

Price: 243 Win., 260 Rem. $1,695.00
Price: 308 Win. $1,640.00

DSA SA58 T48

Caliber: 308 Win. Barrel: 21" with Browning long flash hider. Weight: 9.3 lbs. Length: 44.5". Stock: European walnut. Sights: Elevation-adjustable post front, windage adjustable rear peep. Features: Gas-operated semi-auto with fully adjustable gas system, high grade steel upper receiver with carry handle. DuraCoat finishes. Made in U.S.A. by DSA, Inc.

Price: $1,995.00

DSA SA58 G1

Caliber: 308 Win. Barrel: 21" with quick-detach flash hider. Weight: 10.65 lbs. Length: 44". Stock: Steel bipod cut handguard with hardwood stock and synthetic pistol grip. Sights: Elevation-adjustable post front, windage adjustable rear peep. Features: Gas-operated semi-auto with fully adjustable gas system, high grade steel upper receiver with carry handle, original GI steel lower receiver with GI bipod. DuraCoat finishes. Made in U.S.A. by DSA, Inc.

Price: $1,850.00

DSA SA58 Congo, Para Congo

DSA SA58 Gray Wolf

DSA SA58 STANDARD

Caliber: 308 Win. Barrel: 21" bipod cut w/threaded flash hider. Weight: 8.75 lbs. Length: 43". Stock: Synthetic, X-Series or optional folding para stock. Sights: Elevation-adjustable post front, windage-adjustable rear peep. Features: Fully adjustable short gas system, high grade steel or 416 stainless upper receiver. Made in U.S.A. by DSA, Inc.

Price: High-grade steel	$1,595.00
Price: Folding para stock	$1,845.00

DSA SA58 TACTICAL CARBINE

Caliber: 308 Win. Barrel: 16.25" fluted with A2 flash hider. Weight: 8.25 lbs. Length: 36.5". Stock: Synthetic, X-Series or optional folding para stock. Sights: Elevation-adjustable post front, windage-adjustable match rear peep. Features: Shortened fully adjustable short gas system, high grade steel or 416 stainless upper receiver. Made in U.S.A. by DSA, Inc.

Price: High-grade steel	$1,595.00
Price: Stainless steel	$1,850.00

DSA SA58 MEDIUM CONTOUR

Caliber: 308 Win. Barrel: 21" w/threaded flash hider. Weight: 9.75 lbs. Length: 43". Stock: Synthetic military grade. Sights: Elevation-adjustable post front, windage-adjustable match rear peep. Features: Gas-operated semi-auto with fully adjustable gas system, high grade steel re-

ceiver. Made in U.S.A. by DSA, Inc.

Price:	$1,595.00

DSA SA58 BULL BARREL RIFLE

Caliber: 308 Win. Barrel: 21". Weight: 11.1 lbs. Length: 41.5". Stock: Synthetic, free floating handguard. Sights: Elevation-adjustable windage-adjustable post front, match rear peep. Features: Gas-operated semi-auto with fully adjustable gas system, high grade steel or stainless upper receiver. Made in U.S.A. by DSA, Inc.

Price:	$1,745.00
Price: Stainless steel	$1,995.00

DSA SA58 MINI OSW

Caliber: 308 Win. Barrel: 11" or 13" w/A2 flash hider. Weight: 9 to 9.35 lbs. Length: 32.75" to 35". Stock: Fiberglass reinforced short synthetic handguard, para folding stock and synthetic pistol grip. Sights: Adjustable post front, para rear sight. Features: Semi-auto or select fire with fully adjustable short gas system, optional FAL rail handguard, SureFire Vertical Foregrip System, EOTech HOLOgraphic Sight and ITC cheekrest. Made in U.S.A. by DSA, Inc.

Price:	$1,845.00

DSA DS-MP1

Caliber: 308 Win. match chamber. Barrel: 22", 1:10 twist, hand-lapped stainless-steel match-grade Badger Bar-

DSA SA58 G1

DSA SA58 Predator

rel with recessed target crown. Weight: 11.5 lbs. Length: 41.75". Stock: Black McMillan A5 pillar bedded in Marine-Tex with 13.5" length of pull. Sights: Tactical Picatinny rail. Features: Action, action threads and action bolt locking shoulder completely trued, Badger Ordnance precision ground heavy recoil lug, machined steel Picatinny rail sight mount, trued action threads, action bolt locking shoulder, bolt face and lugs, 2.5-lb. trigger pull, barrel and action finished in Black DuraCoat, guaranteed to shoot 1/2 MOA at 100 yards with match-grade ammo. Introduced 2006. Made in U.S.A. by DSA, Inc.

Price: $2,800.00

EAA/SAIGA SEMI-AUTO RIFLE

Caliber: 7.62x39, 308, 223. Barrel: 20.5", 22", 16.3". Weight: 7 to 8-1/2 lbs. Length: 43". Stock: Synthetic or wood. Sights: Adjustable, sight base. Features: Based on AK Combat rifle by Kalashnikov. Imported from Russia by EAA Corp.

Price: 7.62x39 (syn.) $239.00

Price: 308 (syn. or wood) $429.00

Price: 223 (syn.) $389.00

ED BROWN SAVANNA RIFLE

Caliber: 30-06, 300 Win. Mag., 300 Weatherby, 338 Win. Mag. Barrel: 22", 23", 24". Weight: 8 to 8-1/2 lbs. Stock: Fully glass-bedded McMillan fiberglass sporter.

Sights: None furnished. Talley scope mounts utilizing heavy duty 8-40 screws. Features: Custom action with machined steel trigger guard and hinged floor plate.

Price: $3,195.00

ED BROWN MODEL 704 TACTICAL

Caliber: 308, 300 Win. Mag. Barrel: 26". SS with GEN III Coating. Weight: 11.25 lbs. Stock: Hand bedded McMillan A-3 fiberglass tactical stock with recoil pad. Sights: None furnished. Leupold Mark 4 30mm scope mounts utilizing heavy-duty screws. Features: Custom short or long action, steel trigger guard, hinged floor plate, additional calibers available.

Price: From $2,995.00

ED BROWN MODEL 704, M40A2 MARINE SNIPER

Caliber: 308 Win., 30-06 Springfield. Barrel: Match-grade 24". Weight: 9.25 lbs. Stock: Hand bedded McMillan GP fiberglass tactical stock with recoil pad in special Woodland Camo molded-in colors. Sights: None furnished. Leupold Mark 4 30mm scope mounts with heavy-duty screws. Features: Steel trigger guard, hinged floor plate, three position safety. Left-hand model available.

Price: From $2,995.00

HECKLER & KOCH USC CARBINE

Caliber: 45 ACP, 10-shot magazine. Barrel: 16". Weight:

DSA DS-MP1

**EAA/SAIGA
Semi-Auto Rifle**

**Ed Brown Model 704
Tactical**

**Ed Brown Model 704,
M40A2
Marine Sniper**

**Heckler & Koch USC
Carbine**

8.6 lb. Length: 35.4" overall. Stock: Skeletonized polymer thumbhole. Sights: Blade front with integral hood, fully adjustable diopter. Features: Based on German UMP submachine gun. Blowback operation; almost entirely constructed of carbon fiber-reinforced polymer. Free-floating heavy target barrel. Introduced 2000. From H&K.

Price: $1,249.00

HI-POINT 9MM CARBINE

Caliber: 9mm Para., 40 S&W, 10-shot magazine. Barrel: 16-1/2" (17-1/2" for 40 S&W). Weight: 4-1/2 lbs. Length: 31-1/2" overall. Stock: Black polymer, camouflage. Sights: Protected post front, aperture rear. Integral scope mount. Features: Grip-mounted magazine release. Black or chrome finish. Sling swivels. Available with laser or red dot sights.

Introduced 1996. Made in U.S.A. by MKS Supply, Inc.

Price: Black or chrome, 9mm.............................. $199.00
Price: 40 S&W $225.00

IAI-65 RIFLE

A civilian-legal version of the original HKM rifle manufactured in Hungary. Manufactured by Gordon Technologies using an original AMD-65 matching parts kit built on an AKM receiver. The original wire stock is present, but it is welded in the open position as per BATF regulations. Furnished with a 12.6" barrel with large weld-in-place muzzle brake to bring its length over the 16" federal minimum. This rifle accepts all 7.62x39mm magazines and drums. Introduced 2002. From Intrac Arms International, Inc.

Price: $799.00

Hi-Point 9MM Carbine

L.A.R. Grizzly 50 Big Boar Rifle

Les Baer Super Varmint Ultimate AR 223

Les Baer IPSC Ultimate AR 223

L.A.R. GRIZZLY 50 BIG BOAR RIFLE

Caliber: 50 BMG, single shot. Barrel: 36". Weight: 30.4 lbs. Length: 45.5" overall. Stock: Integral. Ventilated rubber recoil pad. Sights: None furnished; scope mount. Features: Bolt-action bullpup design, thumb and bolt stop safety. All-steel construction. Introduced 1994. Made in U.S.A. by L.A.R. Mfg., Inc.

Price: $2,350.00

LES BAER CUSTOM ULTIMATE AR 223 RIFLES

Caliber: 223. Barrel: 18", 20", 22", 24". Weight: 7-3/4 to 9-3/4 lb. Length: NA. Stock: Black synthetic. Sights: None furnished; Picatinny-style flattop rail for scope mounting. Features: Forged receiver; Ultra single-stage trigger (Jewell two-stage trigger optional); titanium firing pin; Versa-Pod bipod; chromed National Match carrier; stainless steel, hand-lapped and cryo-treated barrel; guaranteed to shoot 1/2 or 3/4 MOA, depending on model. Made in U.S.A. by Les Baer Custom Inc.

Price: Super Varmint Model............................ $1,989.00

Price: Super Match Model (introduced 2006) $2,144.00
Price: M4 flattop model $2,195.00
Price: IPSC action model $2,310.00

LR 300 SR LIGHT SPORT RIFLE

Caliber: 223. Barrel: 16-1/4"; 1:9" twist. Weight: 7.2 lbs. Length: 36" overall (extended stock), 26-1/4" (stock folded). Stock: Folding, tubular steel, with thumbhole-type grip. Sights: Trijicon post front, Trijicon rear. Features: Uses AR-15 type upper and lower receivers; flattop receiver with weaver base. Accepts all AR-15/M-16 magazines. Introduced 1996. Made in U.S.A. from Z-M Weapons.

Price: $2,550.00

MAGNUM RESEARCH MAGNUM LITE RIFLES

Caliber: 22-250, 223, 280, 7mm WSM, 30-06, 308, 300 WSM, 300 Win. Mag., 3-shot magazine. Barrel: 24" sport taper graphite; 26" bull barrel graphite. Weight: 7.1-9.2 lbs. Length: 44.5-48.25" overall (adjustable on Tactical model). Stock: Hogue OverMolded synthetic, H-S Precision

Olympic Arms K9 Carbine

Olympic Arms K3B Series AR15 Carbines

Olympic Arms K9, K10, K40, K45 Pistol-Caliber AR15 Carbines

Tactical synthetic, H-S Precision Varmint synthetic. Sights: None. Features: Remington Model 700 receiver. Introduced: 2001. From Magnum Research, Inc.

Price: MLR3006B26 H-S Tactical stock $2,295.00

Price: MLR7MMBST24 Hogue stock $2,295.00

Price: MLRT22250 H-S Tactical stock, 26"
bull barrel.. $2,400.00

OLYMPIC ARMS K9, K10, K40, K45 PISTOL-CALIBER AR15 CARBINES

Caliber: 9mm, 10mm, 40 S&W, 45 ACP; 32/10-shot modified magazines. Barrel: 16" button rifled stainless steel, 1x16 twist rate. Weight: 6.73 lbs. Length: 31.625" overall. Stock: A2 grip, M4 6-point collapsible stock. Features: A2 upper with adjustable rear sight, elevation adjustable front post, bayonet lug, sling swivel, threaded muzzle, flash suppressor, carbine length handguards. Made in U.S.A. by Olympic Arms, Inc.

Price: K9, 9mm, modified 32-round
Sten magazine.. $834.00

Price: K10, 10mm, modified 10-round Uzi
magazine.. $834.00

Price: K40, 40 S&W, modified 10-round Uzi
magazine.. $834.00

Price: K45, 45 ACP, modified 10-round Uzi
magazine.. $834.00

OLYMPIC ARMS K3B SERIES AR15 CARBINES

Caliber: 5.56 NATO, 30-shot magazines. Barrel: 16" button rifled chromemoly steel, 1x9 twist rate. Weight: 5-7 lbs. Length: 31.75" overall. Stock: A2 grip, M4 6-point collapsible buttstock. Features: A2 upper with adjustable rear sight, elevation adjustable front post, bayonet lug, sling swivel, threaded muzzle, flash suppressor, carbine length handguards. Made in U.S.A. by Olympic Arms, Inc.

Price: K3B base model, A2 upper...................... $780.00

Price: K3B-A3 flat-top upper, detachable
carry handle $875.00

Price: K3B-M4 M4 contoured barrel & handguards $839.00

Price: K3B-M4-A3-TC A3 upper, M4 barrel, FIRSH rail ....
handguard $1,012.00

Price: K3B-CAR 11.5" barrel with 5.5" permanent flash
suppressor... $810.00

Price: K3B-FAR 16" featherweight contoured barrel $822.00

OLYMPIC ARMS PLINKER PLUS AR15 MODELS

Caliber: 5.56 NATO, 30-shot magazine. Barrel 16" or 20" button-rifled chrome-moly steel, 1x9 twist. Weight: 7.5-8.5 lbs. Length: 35.5"-39.5" overall. Stock: A2 grip, A2 buttstock with trapdoor. Sights: A1 windage rear, elevation-adjustable front post. Features: A1 upper, fiberite handguards, bayonet lug, threaded muzzle and flash sup-

Olympic Arms SM Servicematch AR15 Rifle

Olympic Arms Plinker Plus AR15 Models

Olympic Arms K8 Targetmatch AR15 Rifle

Olympic Arms UM Ultramatch AR15 Rifle

pressor. Made in U.S.A. by Olympic Arms, Inc.

Price: Plinker Plus	$595.00
Price: Plinker Plus 20	$749.00
Price: 30-378, 338-378 with accubrake	$2,861.00

OLYMPIC ARMS SM SERVICEMATCH AR15 RIFLES

Caliber: 223 Rem. minimum SAAMI spec, 30-shot magazine. Barrel: 20" broach-cut Ultramatch stainless steel 1x8 twist rate. Weight: 10 lbs. Length: 39.5" overall. Stock: A2 grip, A2 buttstock with trapdoor. Sights: A2 NM rear, elevation adjustable front post. Features: DCM-ready AR15, free-floating handguard looks standard, A2 upper, threaded muzzle, flash suppressor. Premium model adds pneumatic recoil buffer, Bob Jones interchangeable sights, two-stage trigger and Turner Saddlery sling. Made in U.S.A. by Olympic Arms, Inc.

| **Price:** SM-1, 20" DCM ready | $1,099.00 |
| **Price:** SM-1P, Premium 20" DCM ready | $1,493.00 |

OLYMPIC ARMS UM ULTRAMATCH AR15 RIFLES

Caliber: 223 Rem. minimum SAAMI spec, 30-shot mag-

azine. Barrel: 20"or 24" bull broach-cut Ultramatch stainless steel 1x10 twist rate. Weight: 8-10 lbs. Length: 38.25" overall. Stock: A2 grip, A2 buttstock with trapdoor. Sights: None, flat-top upper and gas block with rails. Features: Flat top upper, free floating tubular match handguard, picatinny gas block, crowned muzzle, factory trigger job and "Ultramatch" pantograph. Premium model adds pneumatic recoil buffer, Harris S-series bipod, hand selected premium receivers and William Set Trigger. Made in U.S.A. by Olympic Arms, Inc.

| **Price:** UM-1, 20" Ultramatch | $1,074.00 |
| **Price:** UM-1P, Premium 24" Ultramatch | $1,559.00 |

OLYMPIC ARMS ML-1/ML-2 MULTIMATCH AR15 CARBINES

Caliber: 223 Rem. minimum SAAMI spec, 30-shot magazine. Barrel: 16" broach-cut Ultramatch stainless steel 1x10 twist rate. Weight: 7-8 lbs. Length: 34-36" overall. Stock: A2 grip and varying buttstock. Sights: None. Features: The ML-1 includes A2 upper with adjustable rear sight, elevation adjustable front post, free floating tubular match handguard, bayonet lug, threaded muzzle, flash suppressor and M4 6-point collapsible buttstock. The ML-2 includes bull diameter barrel, flat top upper, free floating

Olympic Arms K9 Carbine AR15 Rifle

Olympic Arms ML-1/ ML-2 Multimatch AR15 Carbine

Olympic Arms SM Servicematch AR15 Rifle

tubular match handguard, picatinny gas block, crowned muzzle and A2 buttstock with trapdoor. Made in U.S.A. by Olympic Arms, Inc.

Price: ML-1 or ML-2 .... $957.00

OLYMPIC ARMS K8 TARGETMATCH AR15 RIFLES

Caliber: 5.56 NATO, .223 WSSM, .243 WSSM, .25 WSSM 30/7-shot magazine. Barrel: 20", 24" bull button-rifled stainless/chrome-moly steel 1x9/1x10 twist rate. Weight: 8-10 lbs. Length: 38"-42" overall. Stock: A2 grip, A2 buttstock with trapdoor. Sights: None. Features: Barrel has satin bead-blast finish; flat-top upper, free-floating tubular match handguard, Picatinny gas block, crowned muzzle and "Targetmatch" pantograph on lower receiver. K8-MAG model uses Winchester Super Short Magnum cartridges. Includes 24" bull chrome-moly barrel, flat-top upper, free-floating tubular match handguard, Picatinny gas block, crowned muzzle and 7-shot magazine. Made in U.S.A. by Olympic Arms, Inc.

Price: K8 .... $803.00
Price: K8-MAG $1,074.00

PANTHER ARMS CLASSIC AUTO RIFLE

Caliber: 5.56x45mm. Barrel: Heavy 16" to 20" w/flash hider. Weight: 7 to 9 lbs. Length: 34-11/16" to 38-7/16". Sights: Adj. rear and front. Stock: Black Zytel w/trap door assembly. Features: Gas operated rotating bolt, mil spec or Teflon black finish.

Price: $809.00
Price: Stainless, match sights $1,099.00
Price: Southpaw $875.00
Price: 16" bbl. $799.00
Price: Panther Lite, 16" bbl. $720.00
Price: Panther carbine .... $799.00 to $989.00
Price: Panther bull bbl .... $885.00 to $1,199.00

REMINGTON MODEL 700 XCR RIFLE

Caliber: 25-06 Rem., 270 Win., 270 WSM, 7mm-08 Rem., 7mm Rem. Mag., 7mm Rem Ultra Mag, 30-06, 300 WSM, 300 Win. Mag., 300 Rem. Ultra Mag., 338 Rem. Ultra Mag., 338 Win. Mag., 375 H&H Mag., 375 Rem. Ultra Mag. Barrel: 24" standard caliber; 26" magnum. Weight: 7.4 to 7.6 lbs. Length: 43.6" to 46.5" overall. Stock: Black synthetic, R3 recoil pad, rubber overmolded grip and forend. Sights: None. Features: XCR (Xtreme Conditions Rifle) includes TriNyte Corrosion Control System; drilled and tapped for scope mounts. 375 H&H Mag., 375 Rem. Ultra Mag. chamberings come with iron sights. Introduced

Remington Model 700 XCR Rifle

Remington 40-XB Rangemaster Target Centerfire

Remington 40-XC KS Target Rifle

2005. XCR Tactical model introduced 2007. Features: Bell & Carlson OD green tactical stock, beavertail forend, recessed thumbhook behind pistol grip, TriNyte coating over stainless steel barrel, LTR fluting. Chambered in 223 Rem., 300 Win. Mag., 308 Win. Made in U.S. by Remington Arms Co., Inc.

Price: 25-06 Rem., 24" barrel (2007) $1,029.00
Price: 270 WSM, 24" barrel $1,103.00
Price: 7mm Rem. Mag., 26" barrel $1,056.00
Price: XCR Tactical (2007) $1,332.00

REMINGTON 40-XB RANGEMASTER TARGET CENTERFIRE

Caliber: 15 calibers from 220 Swift to 300 Win. Mag. Barrel: 27-1/4". Weight: 11-1/4 lbs. Length: 47" overall. Stock: American walnut, laminated thumbhole or Kevlar with high comb and beavertail forend stop. Rubber non-slip buttplate. Sights: None. Scope blocks installed. Features: Adjustable trigger. Stainless barrel and action. Receiver drilled and tapped for sights.

Price: Standard single shot (right-hand) $1,636.00
(left-hand) $1,761.00
Price: Repeater $1,734.00

REMINGTON 40-XBBR KS

Caliber: Five calibers from 22 BR to 308 Win. Barrel: 20" (light varmint class), 24" (heavy varmint class). Weight: 7-1/4 lbs. (light varmint class); 12 lbs. (heavy varmint class). Length: 38" (20" bbl.), 42" (24" bbl.). Stock: Aramid fiber. Sights: None. Supplied with scope blocks. Features: Unblued benchrest with stainless steel barrel, trigger adjustable from 1-1/2 lbs. to 3-1/2 lbs. Special two-oz. trigger extra cost. Scope and mounts extra.

Price: Single shot $1,876.00

REMINGTON 40-XC KS TARGET RIFLE

Caliber: 7.62 NATO, 5-shot. Barrel: 24", stainless steel. Weight: 11 lbs. without sights. Length: 43-1/2" overall. Stock: Aramid fiber. Sights: None furnished. Features: Designed to meet the needs of competitive shooters. Stainless steel barrel and action.

Price: $1,821.00

RUGER MINI 14 RANCH RIFLE AUTOLOADING RIFLE

Caliber: 223 Rem., 5-shot detachable box magazine. Barrel: 18-1/2". Rifling twist 1:9". Weight: 6.4 lbs. Length: 37-1/4" overall. Stock: American hardwood, steel reinforced. Sights: Protected blade front, fully adjustable Ghost Ring rear. Features: Fixed piston gas-operated, positive primary extraction. New buffer system, redesigned ejector system. Ruger S100RM scope rings included on Ranch Rifle.

Price: Mini-14/5, Ranch Rifle, blued, scope rings $775.00

Ruger Mini 14 Autoloading Ranch Rifle

Sabre Defence XR15A3 Flattop Carbine

Sabre Defence XR15A3 SPR

Price: K-Mini-14/5, Ranch Rifle, stainless,
scope rings **$835.00**

Price: K-Mini-14/5P, Ranch Rifle, stainless,
synthetic stock **$835.00**

Price: K-Mini-14/5T, laminate stock, adjustable
harmonic barrel weight (2007) **$995.00**

RUGER MINI THIRTY RIFLE

Similar to the Mini-14 Ranch Rifle except modified to chamber the 7.62x39 Russian service round. Weight is about 6-7/8 lbs. Has 6-groove barrel with 1:10" twist, Ruger Integral Scope Mount bases and protected blade front, fully adjustable Ghost Ring rear. Detachable 5-shot staggered box magazine. Stainless w/synthetic stock. Introduced 1987.

Price: Stainless, scope rings **$809.00**

SABRE DEFENCE XR15A3 SPR

Caliber: 5.56 NATO, 6.5 Grendel, 30-shot magazines. Barrel: 20" 410 stainless steel, 1x8 twist rate; or 18" vanadium alloy, chrome lined barrel with Sabre Gill-Brake. Weight: 6.77 lbs. Length: 31.75" overall. Stock: SOCOM 3-position stock with Samson M-EX handguards. Sights: Flip-up front and rear sights. Features: Fluted barrel, Harris bipod, and two-stage match trigger, Ergo Grips; upper and matched lower CNC machined from 7075-T6 forgings. SOCOM adjustable stock, Samson tactical handguards, M4 contour barrels available in 14.5" and 16" are made of MIL-B-11595 vanadium alloy and chrome lined. Introduced 2002. From Sabre Defence Industries.

Price: 6.5 Grendel (2007) **$2,699.00**

Price: XR15A3 Competition Deluxe, 6.5 Grendel,
20" barrel **$2,499.00**

Price: XR15A3 Competition Standard, 5.56mm,
18" barrel **$1,899.00**

Price: Massad Ayoob Professional **$1,999.00**

Price: SPR Carbine **$2,499.00**

Price: M4 Carbine, 14.5" barrel **$1,429.00**

Price: M4 Flat-top Carbine, 16" barrel **$1,349.00**

SAKO TRG-42 BOLT-ACTION RIFLE

Caliber: 338 Lapua Mag. and 300 Win. Mag. Barrel: 27-1/8". Weight: 11-1/4 lbs. Length: NA. Stock: NA. Sights: NA. Features: 5-shot magazine, fully adjustable stock and competition trigger. Imported from Finland by Beretta USA.

Price: $3,525.00

Sabre Defence XR15A3 Grendel

Sabre Defence Elite Rifle

Sako TRG-42 Bolt-Action Rifle

SAKO TRG-22/TRG-42 BOLT-ACTION RIFLE

Caliber: 308 Win., 10-shot magazine. Barrel: 26". Weight: 10-1/4 lbs. Length: 45-1/4" overall. Stock: Reinforced polyurethane with fully adjustable cheekpiece and buttplate. Sights: None furnished. Optional quick-detachable, one-piece scope mount base, 1" or 30mm rings. Features: Resistance-free bolt, free-floating heavy stainless barrel, 60-degree bolt lift. Two-stage trigger is adjustable for length, pull, horizontal or vertical pitch. Introduced 2000. Imported from Finland by Beretta USA.

> **Price:** TRG-22 Green Folding Stock $4,525.00
>
> **Price:** TRG-22 Green or black stock $2,825.00
>
> **Price:** TRG-42 300 Win Mag.,
>   green stock .... $2,825.00 to $3,525.00
>
> **Price:** TRG-42 338 Lapua Mag.,
>   green stock .... $2,825.00 to $3,525.00

SAVAGE MODEL 10/110FP LONG RANGE RIFLE

Caliber: 223, 25-06, 308, 30-06, 300 Win. Mag., 7mm Rem. Mag., 4-shot magazine. Barrel: 24", heavy; recessed target muzzle. Weight: 8-1/2 lbs. Length: 45.5" overall. Stock: Black graphite/fiberglass composition; positive checkering. Sights: None furnished. Receiver drilled and tapped for scope mounting. Features: Pillar-bedded stock. Black matte finish on all metal parts. Double swivel studs on the forend for sling and/or bipod mount. Right- or left-

hand. Introduced 1990. From Savage Arms, Inc.

> **Price:** Right- or left-hand $601.00

SAVAGE MODEL 10FP TACTICAL RIFLE

Similar to the Model 110FP except has true short action, chambered for 223, 308; black synthetic stock with "Dual Pillar" bedding. Introduced 1998. Made in U.S.A. by Savage Arms, Inc.

> **Price:** $601.00
>
> **Price:** Model 10FLP (left-hand) $601.00
>
> **Price:** Model 10FP-LE1 (20"), 10FPLE2 (26") $601.00
>
> **Price:** Model 10FPXP-LE w/Burris 3.5-10x50 scope,
>   Harris bipod package $1,805.00

SAVAGE MODEL 10FP-LE1A TACTICAL RIFLE

Similar to the Model 110FP except weighs 10.75 lbs. and has overall length of 39.75". Chambered for 223 Rem., 308 Win. Black synthetic Choate™ adjustable stock with accessory rail and swivel studs.

> **Price:** $729.00

SAVAGE MODEL 112 LONG RANGE RIFLES

Caliber: 5-shot magazine. Barrel: 26" heavy. Weight: 8.8 lbs. Length: 47.5" overall. Stock: Black graphite/fiberglass filled composite with positive checkering. Sights: None furnished; drilled and tapped for scope mounting. Features: Pillar-bedded stock. Blued barrel with recessed target-style

**Savage Model 10FP
Tactical Rifle**

**Savage Model 12 FV
Long Range Rifles**

**Savage Model 10FP-LE1A
Tactical Rifle**

Savage Model 16FXP3

Savage Model 116FXP3

muzzle. Double front swivel studs for attaching bipod. Introduced 1991. Made in U.S.A. by Savage Arms, Inc.

Price: Model 112BVSS (heavy-prone laminated
stock with high comb, Wundhammer
swell, fluted stainless barrel, bolt handle,
trigger guard) $675.00

SAVAGE MODEL 12 LONG RANGE RIFLES

Similar to the Model 112 Long Range except with true short action, chambered for 223, 22-250, 308. Models 12FV, 12FVSS have black synthetic stocks with "Dual Pillar" bedding, positive checkering, swivel studs; Model 12BVSS has brown laminated stock with beavertail forend, fluted stainless barrel. Introduced 1998. Made in U.S.A. by Savage Arms, Inc.

Price: Model 12FV (223, 22-250, 243 Win.,
308 Win., blue) $549.00

Price: Model 12FVSS (blue action, fluted
stainless barrel) $667.00

Price: Model 12FLV (as above, left-hand) $549.00

Price: Model 12FVS (blue action, fluted
stainless barrel, single shot) $667.00

Price: Model 12BVSS (laminated stock) $721.00

Price: Model 12BVSS-S (as above, single shot) $721.00

SAVAGE MODEL 116 WEATHER WARRIORS

Caliber: 375 H&H, 300 Rem. Ultra Mag., 308 Win., 300 Rem. Ultra Mag., 300 WSM, 7mm Rem. Ultra Mag., 7mm Rem. Short Ultra Mag., 7mm S&W, 7mm-08 Rem. Barrel: 22", 24" for 7mm Rem. Mag., 300 Win. Mag., 338 Win. Mag. (M116FSS only). Weight: 6.25 to 6.5 lbs. Length: 41" to 47". Stock: Graphite/fiberglass filled composite. Sights: None furnished; drilled and tapped for scope mounting. Features: Stainless steel with matte finish; free-floated barrel; quick-detachable swivel studs; laser-etched bolt; scope bases and rings. Left-hand models available in all models, calibers at same price. Model 116FSS introduced 1991; 116FSAK introduced 1994. Made in U.S.A. by Savage Arms, Inc.

Savage Model 116FSS
Weather Warrior

SMITH & WESSON
M&P15T RIFLES

SMITH & WESSON
M&P15PC RIFLES

Price: Model 116FSS (top-loading magazine) **$520.00**

Price: Model 116FSAK (top-loading magazine,
Savage adjustable muzzle brake system) **$601.00**

Price: Model 116BSS (brown laminate, 24") **$668.00**

Price: Model 116BSS (brown laminate, 26") **$668.00**

SAVAGE MODEL 16FCSS RIFLE

Similar to Model 116FSS except true short action, chambered for 223, 243, 22" free-floated barrel; black graphite/fiberglass stock, "Dual Pillar" bedding. Also left-hand version available. Introduced 1998. Made in U.S.A. by Savage Arms, Inc.

Price: **$552.00**

SIG 556 AUTOLOADING RIFLE

Caliber: 223 Rem., 30-shot detachable box magazine. Barrel: 16". Rifling twist 1:9". Weight: 6.8 lbs. Length: 36.5" overall. Stock: Polymer, folding style. Sights: Flip-up front combat sight, adjustable for windage and elevation. Features: Based on SG 550 series rifle. Two-position adjustable gas piston operating rod system, accepts standard AR magazines. Polymer forearm, three integrated Picatinny rails, forward mount for right- or left-side sling attachment. Aircraft-grade aluminum alloy trigger housing, hard-coat anodized finish; two-stage trigger, ambidextrous safety, 30-round polymer magazine, battery compartments, pistol-grip rubber-padded watertight adjustable butt stock with

sling-attachment points. SIG 556 SWAT model has flat-top Picatinny railed receiver, tactical quad rail. Imported by SIGARMS, Inc.

Price: SIG 556... **$1,300.00**

SIGARMS SHR 970 SYNTHETIC RIFLE

Caliber: 270, 30-06. Barrel: 22". Weight: 7.2 lbs. Length: 41.9" overall. Stock: Textured black fiberglass or walnut. Sights: None furnished; drilled and tapped for scope mounting. Features: Quick takedown; interchangeable barrels; removable box magazine; cocking indicator; three-position safety. Introduced 1998. Imported by SIGARMS, Inc.

Price: Synthetic stock....................................... **$499.00**

Price: Walnut stock **$550.00**

SMITH & WESSON M&P15 RIFLES

Caliber: 5.56mm NATO/223, 30-shot steel magazine. Barrel: 16", 1:9 Weight: 6.74 lbs., w/o magazine. Length: 32-35" overall. Stock: Black synthetic. Sights: Adjustable post front sight, adjustable dual aperture rear sight. Features: 6-position telescopic stock, thermo-set M4 handguard. 14.75" sight radius. 7-lbs. (approx.) trigger pull. 7075 T6 aluminum upper, 4140 steel barrel. Chromed barrel bore, gas key, bolt carrier. Hard-coat black-anodized receiver and barrel finish. Introduced 2006. Made in U.S.A. by Smith & Wesson.

Price: M&P15 No. 811000 .... **$1,200.00**

Springfield Armory M1A Rifle

Springfield Armory M1A Super Match

Steyr Scout Bolt-Action Rifle

Price: M&P15T No. 811001, free float modular rail forend $1,700.00

Price: M&P15A No. 811002, folding battle rear sight $1,300.00

Price: M&P15PC, no sights with Picatinny rail for optics $1,600.00

SPRINGFIELD ARMORY M1A RIFLE

Caliber: 7.62mm NATO (308), 5- or 10-shot box magazine. Barrel: 25-1/16" with flash suppressor, 22" without suppressor. Weight: 9-3/4 lbs. Length: 44-1/4" overall. Stock: American walnut with walnut-colored heat-resistant fiberglass handguard. Matching walnut handguard available. Also available with fiberglass stock. Sights: Military, square blade front, full click-adjustable aperture rear. Features: Commercial equivalent of the U.S. M-14 service rifle with no provision for automatic firing. From Springfield Armory

Price: Standard M1A, black fiberglass stock $1,498.00

Price: Standard M1A, black fiberglass stock, stainless $1,727.00

Price: Standard M1A, black stock, carbon barrel $1,379.00

Price: Standard M1A, Mossy Oak stock, carbon barrel $1,507.00

Price: Scout Squad M1A .... $1,653.00 to $1,727.00

Price: National Match .... $2,049.00 to $2,098.00

Price: Super Match (heavy premium barrel) about $3,149.00

Price: M1A SOCOM II rifle $1,948.00

Price: M25 White Feather Tactical rifle $4,648.00

SPRINGFIELD ARMORY M1A SUPER MATCH

Caliber: 308 Win. Barrel: 22", heavy Douglas Premium. Weight: About 11 lbs. Length: 44.31" overall. Stock: Heavy walnut competition stock with longer pistol grip, contoured area behind the rear sight, thicker butt and forend, glass bedded. Sights: National Match front and rear. Features: Has figure-eight-style operating rod guide. Introduced 1987. From Springfield Armory.

Price: About... $2,479.00

SPRINGFIELD ARMORY M1A/M-21 TACTICAL MODEL RIFLE

Similar to M1A Super Match except special sniper stock with adjustable cheekpiece and rubber recoil pad. Weighs 11.6 lbs. From Springfield Armory.

Price: $2,975.00

STEYR SCOUT BOLT-ACTION RIFLE

Caliber: 308 Win., 5-shot magazine. Barrel: 19", fluted. Weight: NA. Length: NA. Stock: Gray Zytel. Sights: Pop-up front & rear, Leupold M8 2.5x28 IER scope on Picatinny optic rail with Steyr mounts. Features: luggage case, scout sling, two stock spacers, two magazines. Introduced 1998. From GSI.

Price: From $1,969.00

SIG 556 AUTOLOADING RIFLE

WEATHERBY THREAT RESPONSE RIFLES (TRR)

STEYR SSG BOLT-ACTION RIFLE

Caliber: 308 Win., detachable 5-shot rotary magazine. Barrel: 26". Weight: 8.5 lbs. Length: 44.5" overall. Stock: Black ABS Cycolac with spacers for length of pull adjustment. Sights: Hooded ramp front adjustable for elevation, V-notch rear adjustable for windage. Features: Sliding safety; NATO rail for bipod; 1" swivels; Parkerized finish; single or double-set triggers. Imported from Austria by GSI, Inc.

Price: SSG-PI, iron sights	$1,699.00
Price: SSG-PII, heavy barrel, no sights	$1,699.00
Price: SSG-PIIK, 20" heavy barrel, no sights	$1,699.00
Price: SSG-PIV, 16.75" threaded heavy barrel with flash hider	$2,659.00

STONER SR-15 M-5 RIFLE

Caliber: 223. Barrel: 20". Weight: 7.6 lbs. Length: 38" overall. Stock: Black synthetic. Sights: Post front, fully adjustable rear (300-meter sight). Features: Modular weapon system; two-stage trigger. Black finish. Introduced 1998. Made in U.S.A. by Knight's Mfg.

Price:	$1,650.00
Price: M-4 Carbine (16" barrel, 6.8 lbs)	$1,555.00

STONER SR-25 CARBINE

Caliber: 7.62 NATO, 10-shot steel magazine. Barrel: 16" free-floating Weight: 7-3/4 lbs. Length: 35.75" over-all. Stock: Black synthetic. Sights: Integral Weaver-style rail. Scope rings, iron sights optional. Features: Shortened, non-slip handguard; removable carrying handle. Matte black finish. Introduced 1995. Made in U.S.A. by Knight's Mfg. Co.

Price:	$3,345.00

STONER SR-15 MATCH RIFLE

Caliber: 223. Barrel: 20". Weight: 7.9 lbs. Length: 38" overall. Stock: Black synthetic. Sights: None furnished; flat-top upper receiver for scope mounting. Features: Short Picatinny rail, two-stage match trigger. Introduced 1998. Made in U.S.A. by Knight's Mfg.Co.

Price:	$1,650.00

WEATHERBY THREAT RESPONSE RIFLES (TRR) SERIES

Caliber: TRR 223 Rem., 300 Win. TRR Magnum and Magnum Custom 300 Win. Mag., 300 Wby. Mag., 30-378 Wby. Mag., 328-378 Wby. Mag. Barrel: 22", 26", target crown. Stock: Hand-laminated composite. TTR & TRR Magnum have raised comb Monte Carlo style. TRR Magnum Custom adjustable ergonomic stock. Features: Adjustable trigger, aluminum bedding block, beavertail forearms dual tapered, flat-bottomed. "Rocker Arm" lockdown scope mounting. 54 degree bolt. Pachmayr decelerator pad. Made in U.S.A.

Price: TRR Magnum Custom 300	$2,699.00

Vang Comp System Improves the 870

BY RICH GRASSI

The Remington Model 870 is by far the most common police/defense pump shotgun still in use today. While it's not new technology, it has its advantages.

The problem with using the shotgun for tactical applications is precisely what we – earlier in my career -- thought the advantage was. That is the ammunition. If you use buckshot, it's likely a pellet will blow free from the pattern even at distances less than 15 yards. That pellet is a "miss" on the range. On the street, in a house, in a school, that "miss" becomes an "unintentional hit." As we're account-

able for every projectile that leaves the muzzle of the gun, that unintended hit becomes a personal tragedy and the highway to liability.

FIXING THE PROBLEM

We can horse around with ammunition. If the stray pellet bothers you, it's said, go to a slug.

This single 1-ounce projectile will perforate many things, making it a nice ammunition item to have when the bad guy takes cover. Unfortunately, it can also penetrate things to hit innocents we can't see. The 12-gauge slug may also perforate the human

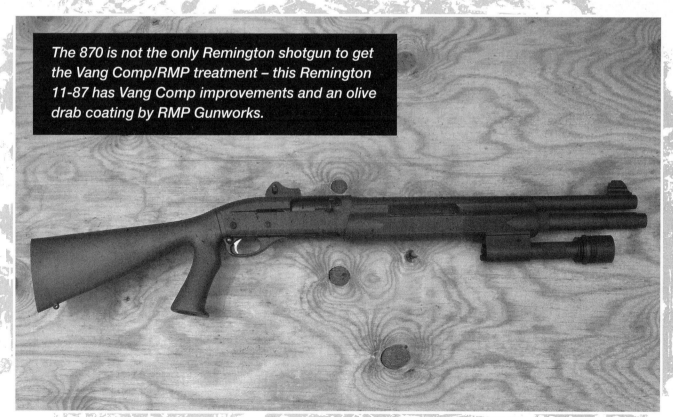

The 870 is not the only Remington shotgun to get the Vang Comp/RMP treatment – this Remington 11-87 has Vang Comp improvements and an olive drab coating by RMP Gunworks.

adversary and continue on with enough power to hurt someone downrange.

There are better loads for tactical use. These include the Remington Low Recoil line of slugs and buckshot as well as the Federal Tactical line and the CCI-Lawman brand of slugs and buckshot.

Out of most cylinder bore barrels, the low-recoil stuff throws better patterns. There is still some concern if the barrel isn't properly cleaned. What's the solution?

VANG COMP SYSTEMS

The Vang Comp barrel treatment is a product of years of gunsmithing experience. Hans Vang developed a system of lengthening the shotgun barrel's forcing cone and back-boring the barrel to give buckshot a smooth trip to the muzzle. In addition, he cuts compensating ports through the barrel. The porting is optimized for barrel length and prevents expanding gasses from blowing through the shot column, spoiling the pattern. Not only that, the Vang Comp ports reduce the more abusive aspects of shotgun recoil. It also tends to lessen muzzle flash.

Now, that's tactical! While there is no black ballistic nylon fabric or hook-and-loop fastener fabric

This newly finished (in DuraCoat) Remington 870 has LPA Precision Ghostring night sights, the Vang Comp System barrel treatment, a SureFire Weapon Light forend, and the Advanced Technology Six-Position stock.

in the Vang Comp barrel system, it's as tactical as you can get. I've had experience with the system since the late 1990s. I've never seen a bad job come out of that shop.

Apparently the Vang Comp System is finding favor among turkey hunters as well. It's about time they found out about it! Tight patterns are essential in that endeavor as well, along with the lessened kick of those long magnum turkey loads.

Add to the improved shot patterns the fact that the Vang Comp System reduces muzzle rise and minimizes muzzle flash, and you have an essential component to the defensive shotgun.

Pete Rafferty of RMP Gunworks, a graduate of the Colorado School of Trades, has taken in some Remington 870 shotguns for repair and refurbish. Working with Hans, RMP built a strategic business alliance with Vang Comp Systems. Hans Vang had been seeking shops to act as Vang Comp dealers and Pete Rafferty stepped up to the plate. The shotguns pictured in this piece are products of the gun mechanic's art, a true collaboration between Hans and Pete.

TRANSFORMATION

The silvery colored shotgun featured has a Vang Comp barrel, ghost ring sights, a new Vang 870 safety and the new Vang stainless steel follower. Pete added a DuraCoat finish, Speedfeed stocks and a Tac Star Sidesaddle. Hans also installed the Remington Flexi-tab conversion to prevent the rounds in the magazine from jumping the shell

stops and tying up the gun. An authorized Remington repair station, Vang Comp Systems has years of experience with the design.

The DuraCoat finish Pete selected was the silvery "stainless steel" color. The effect of this coating was striking on a Remington 870. If a defensive situation occurs during hours of diminished light – like most of them do – there will be no doubt in the predator's mind that the "victim" has a fighting shotgun!

The sights, furniture and Sidesaddle securing bolts are left black. The contrast is appealing.

Above: The Vang/RMP 870 has the Vang Comp extended safety (button behind the trigger guard) and Advanced Technology stock. The finish is DuraCoat by RMP Gunworks.

Lower Left: The Advanced Technology Collapsible Buttstock is similar in appearance and design to the collapsing stock of the AR-15 series of carbines.

Lower Right: The Advanced Technology Collapsible Buttstock is similar in appearance and design to the collapsing stock of the AR-15 series of carbines.

Hans Vang – shown at work in his Chino Valley AZ shop.

the magazine spring from kinking.

The other shotgun pictured differs in that Pete installed a Surefire Weaponlight Fore-End, used a different color DuraCoat and put a six-position collapsible stock on it.

SHOTS FIRED

The shotguns were fired at a law enforcement range on a couple of different range trips.

Our "Stainless Steel" colored example was tried out during preparation for a law enforcement agency shotgun qualification course. This course involved firing slugs for accuracy from 40 yards to 20 yards and involved a buckshot course at distances varying from 20 yards down to 10 yards.

The first member of our test team used Remington "Slugger" express 1-ounce slugs. He dropped a slug out, shooting low. He indicated that it was "operator error." On the buckshot course, he used Federal Classic 9-pellet OO buckshot. There was one pellet over the shoulder of the police silhouette. All but two of the remaining 44 pellets went into the scoring rings of the target. This is "tactical" or low-recoil buckshot quality with express buckshot power!

Jack Morgan, an agency range-master, used ammo by CCI-Speer. Using their Lawman 1-ounce slug, Jack put the first two slugs – from 40 yards – almost touching in the chest! All five of the punkin balls went into the maximum scoring (five) ring.

He used Lawman 8-pellet 00B to fire the buckshot course. Thirty-eight of the 40 pellets went into the "Five" ring. The two "flyers" – if they can be called that – stayed inside the four-ring. This was impressive performance.

I selected Winchester Ranger slugs and put all five inside the five-ring, though low in the scoring box. That's why the gun has adjustable sights! Using Winchester buckshot, I had one pellet fly free of the centered pattern, still well within the silhouette.

Since the newly renovated gun had a silvery finish, I examined the burn pattern from the ports. The scorching was even, showing that the ports were smoothly finished and they were working as intended.

The sights, provided by Hans Vang, are the LPA Precision Sights Ghost Ring sights. The large, thin-rimmed aperture is protected by steel 'wings.' Similarly, the post front sight is centered between protective steel. The front sight has a tritium vial to provide the shooter with a muzzle index during adverse light conditions. Both units, front and back, are rugged and built to withstand hard use.

His 870 safety button is a large, round protrusion. For the right-handed shooter, the trigger finger will encounter the safety as it enters the trigger guard to fire. It features a positive release for the well-trained southpaw as well.

The stainless steel magazine follower won't break. The leader is reasonably long to help keep

Above: Rangemaster Jack Morgan finds the recoil mild between the Vang Comp System and the Advanced Technology stock.

Left: John Burghart fires Remington LE Express buckshot from the Vang Comp/RMP 870.

We fed the new-old 870 from the Tac-Star Side-saddle. Out of the shotguns I have and use, nearly all have the Sidesaddle. I've had no trouble with them and they've given me the ability to change ammo or to replenish the magazine as needed. I like them.

The Speedfeed furniture was functional. Pete Rafferty got banged up a little as he was unfamiliar with the short buttstock that we insisted on. The short stock is better for a defensive shotgun for reasons of stance and use of protective armor. Morgan and I had no trouble with the short stock.

The second shotgun is striking in appearance. It features the eminently practical and well-thought out Surefire Weaponlight Fore-end. The six-volt light is controlled by a pressure pad to allow for momentary on-and-off, a rocker switch for constant on and a system disabling off switch.

The high output lamp provides 65 lumens output for an hour. This is quite a bit of light. The package makes lighting available without juggling a shotgun and a separate light.

The RMP DuraCoat finish was a gray color with dark specks. Pete Rafferty even put the speckle coating on the protective wings of the LPA front sight, making for a striking appearance.

The stock was from Advanced Technology, Inc. It's a collapsible, six-position "SHOTFORCE" branded buttstock patterned after the collapsing AR-15 style stock. This version is fabricated from a matte black glass-filled nylon material. The stock changes length of pull from 9-1/4 inches to 13-1/4 inches. The included butt pad offers stability and it fits other makers' collapsing buttstocks. The pad has a checkered non-slip surface and provides air-cushioned recoil reduction.

Test team member John Burghart shot Remington Law Enforcement "Express" buckshot – the full-power stuff – into fist-sized patterns from about 10 yards with the Vang Comp/RMP 870 shotgun. He said, "This Express is good stuff." I took that to

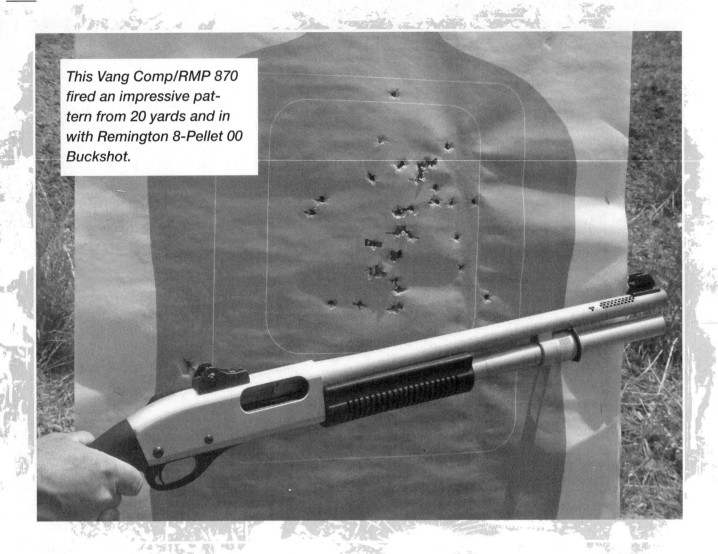

This Vang Comp/RMP 870 fired an impressive pattern from 20 yards and in with Remington 8-Pellet 00 Buckshot.

mean that its power was somewhat more reminiscent of the turkey loads he uses in the game fields than the current law enforcement offerings.

The Vang Comp barrel eats high-velocity ammo like candy, making tight patterns out to 25 or 30 yards.

Morgan also shot the newly refitted 870. He was enamored of the Vang Comp extended safety button, which is a favorite every place it's tried. Likewise, the Advanced Technology Buttstock was appreciated.

Some agency shotguns are fitted with the new stocks to allow for adjustment between users of different statures. The stock is meeting with considerable success.

TOTAL PACKAGE

Hans' Vang Comp System is simply superb. This is the fourth Vang Comp creation I've had the chance to spend some time with. While at Gunsite in October 2003 I got to shoot a few other Vang shotguns and saw others in use at that facility.

If the shotgun is there for your personal defense, Vang Comp is the way to go. I see that as the absolute minimum modification I would perform on a defensive shotgun. The RMP DuraCoat finish prevents corrosion, won't chip or peel and it really looks good, too. The LPA sights, Tac Star "Side-Saddle," SureFire WeaponLight and Advanced Technology stock are handy additions as well. Sights are very important on the defensive shotgun and the light – helping to identify targets – is of huge import. The "Side-Saddle" likewise helps keep spare ammo close to hand, necessary all too often these days.

You can't go wrong with the Vang Comp/RMP Team.

Benelli M4 12 Gauge Tactical Shotgun / Black

Benelli M4 12 Gauge Tactical Shotgun / Desert Camo

Benelli Supernova 12 Gauge Pump Shotgun / Desert Camo

BENELLI M4 TACTICAL SHOTGUN

Gauge: 12 ga., 3" chamber. Barrel: 18.5". Weight: 7.8 lbs. Length: 40" overall. Stock: Synthetic. Sights: Ghost Ring rear, fixed blade front. Features: Auto-regulating gas-operated (ARGO) action, choke tube, Picatinny rail, standard and collapsible stocks available, optional LE tactical gun case. Introduced 2006. Imported from Italy by Benelli USA.

Price: Pistol grip stock, black synthetic	$1,600.00
Price: Desert camo pistol grip (2007)	$1,735.00

BENELLI M3 CONVERTIBLE SHOTGUN

Gauge: 12, 2-3/4", 3" chambers, 5-shot magazine. Barrel: 19-3/4" (Cyl.). Weight: 7 lbs., 4oz. Length: 41" overall. Stock: High-impact polymer with sling loop in side of butt; rubberized pistol grip on stock. Sights: Open rifle, fully adjustable. Ghost ring and rifle type. Features: Combination pump/auto action. Alloy receiver with inertia recoil rotating locking lug bolt; matte finish; automatic shell release lever. Introduced 1989. Imported by Benelli USA. Price with pistol grip, open rifle sights.

Price: With standard stock, open rifle sights	$1,255.00
Price: With ghost ring sight system, standard stock	$1,335.00
Price: With ghost ring sights, pistol grip stock	$1,335.00

BENELLI M2 TACTICAL SHOTGUN

Gauge: 12, 2-3/4", 3" chambers, 5-shot magazine. Barrel: 18.5" IC, M, F choke tubes. Weight: 6.7 lbs. Length: 39.75" overall. Stock: Black polymer. Sights: Rifle type ghost ring system, tritium night sights optional. Features: Semi-auto intertia recoil action. Cross-bolt safety; bolt release button; matte-finish metal. Introduced 1993. Imported from Italy by Benelli USA.

Price: With rifle sights	$1,065.00
Price: With ghost ring sights, standard stock	$1,175.00
Price: With ghost ring sights, pistol grip stock	$1,175.00
Price: With rifle sights, pistol grip stock	$1,065.00
Price: ComforTech stock, rifle sights	$1,175.00
Price: Comfortech Stock, Ghost Ring	$1,280.00

BENELLI SUPERNOVA PUMP SHOTGUNS

Gauge: 12; 3.5" chamber. Barrel: 24", 26", 28". Length: 45.5-49.5". Stock: Synthetic; Max-4 , Timber, APG HD (2007). Sights: Red bar front, metal midbead. Features: 2-3/ 4", 3" chamber (3-1/2" 12 ga. only). Montefeltro rotating bolt design with dual action bars, magazine cutoff, synthetic trigger assembly, adjustable combs, shim kit, choice of buttstocks. 4-shot magazine. Introduced 2006. Imported from Italy by Benelli USA.

Price: Synthetic ComforTech	$455.00
Price: Camo ComforTech	$545.00
Price: SteadyGrip	$465.00 to $560.00
Price: Tactical, Ghost Ring sight	$400.00 to $545.00

Benelli Nova Synthetic 20 Gauge Slug Pump Shotgun

Benelli Nova Synthetic 20 Gauge Short Stock Pump Shotgun

Benelli Nova H2O Synthetic 12 Gauge Tactical Pump Shotgun

Price: Field & Slug combo (2007) $655.00

Price: Rifled Slug ComforTech (2007) $645.00

Price: Tactical desert camo pistol grip, 18" barrel (2007) $545.00

BENELLI NOVA PUMP SHOTGUNS

Gauge: 12, 20. Barrel: 24", 26", 28". Stock: Black synthetic, Max-4, Timber and APG HD. Sights: Red bar. Features: 2-3/ 4", 3" chamber (3-1/2" 12 ga. only). Montefeltro rotating bolt design with dual action bars, magazine cut-off, synthetic trigger assembly, 4-shot magazine. Introduced 1999. Field & Slug Combo has 24" barrel and rifled bore; open rifle sights; synthetic stock; weighs 8.1 lbs. Imported from Italy by Benelli USA.

Price: Black synthetic stock.................................. $360.00

Price: Timber HD or Max-4 camo stock $455.00

Price: H20 model, black synthetic, matte nickel finish..................................... $535.00

Price: APG HD stock (2007) $455.00

Price: Tactical, 18.5" barrel, Ghost Ring sight $375.00

Price: Black synthetic stock, 20 ga...................... $360.00

Price: Black synthetic youth stock, 20 ga. $375.00

Price: Timber HD stock or APG HD stock (2007), 20 ga.............................. $455.00

CROSSFIRE SHOTGUN/RIFLE

Gauge/Caliber: 12, 2-3/4" Chamber: 4-shot/223 Rem. (5-shot). Barrel: 20" (shotgun), 18" (rifle). Weight: About 8.6 lbs. Length: 40" overall. Stock: Composite. Sights: Meprolight night sights. Integral Weaver-style scope rail. Features: Combination pump-action shotgun, rifle; single selector, single trigger; dual action bars for both upper and lower actions; ambidextrous selector and safety. Introduced 1997. Made in U.S. From Hesco.

Price: About... $1,895.00

Price: With camo finish $1,995.00

ESCORT PUMP SHOTGUNS

Gauge: 12, 20; 3" chamber. Barrel: 18" (AimGuard model); 22" (FH Slug model), 24", 26" and 28" (Field Hunter models), choke tubes (M, IC, F); turkey choke w/24" bbl. Weight: 6.4 to 7 lbs. Stock: Polymer, black chrome or camo finish. Features: Alloy receiver w/ dovetail for sight mounting. Two stock adjusting spacers included. Introduced 2003. From Legacy Sports International.

Price: Field Hunter, black stock $247.00

Price: Camo, 24" bbl. $363.00

Price: AimGuard, 20" bbl., black stock $211.00

Price: MarineGuard, nickel finish $254.00

Price: Combo (2 bbls.) $270.00

Escort AimGuard Pump Shotgun

Escort Field Hunter Pump Shotgun

FABARM FP6 PUMP SHOTGUN

FABARM TACTICAL SEMI-AUTOMATIC SHOTGUN

Gauge: 12, 3" chamber. Barrel: 20". Weight: 6.6 lbs. Length: 41.2" overall. Stock: Polymer or folding. Sights: Ghost ring (tritium night sights optional). Features: Gas operated; matte receiver; twin forged action bars; over-sized bolt handle and safety button; Picatinny rail; includes cylinder bore choke tube. New features include polymer pistol grip stock. Introduced 2001. Imported from Italy by Heckler & Koch Inc.

Price: $999.00

FABARM FP6 PUMP SHOTGUN

Gauge: 12, 3" chamber. Barrel: 20" (Cyl.); accepts choke tubes. Weight: 6.6 lbs. Length: 41.25" overall. Stock: Black polymer with textured grip, grooved slide handle. Sights: Blade front. Features: Twin action bars; anodized finish; free carrier for smooth reloading. Introduced 1998. New features include ghost-ring sighting system, low profile Picatinny rail, and pistol grip stock. Imported from Italy by Heckler & Koch, Inc.

Price: (Carbon fiber finish)................................... $499.00
Price: With flip-up front sight, Picatinny rail with
    rear sight, oversize safety button $499.00

MOSSBERG MODEL 500 SPORTING PUMP SHOTGUNS

Gauge: 12, 20, .410, 3" chamber. Barrel: 18-1/2" to 28" with fixed or Accu-Choke, plain or vent rib. Weight: 6-1/4

lbs. (.410), 7-1/4 lbs. (12). Length: 48" overall (28" barrel). Stock: 14"x1-1/2"x2-1/2". Walnut-stained hardwood. Cut-checkered grip and forend. Sights: White bead front, brass mid-bead; fiber-optic. Features: Ambidextrous thumb safety, twin extractors, disconnecting safety, dual action bars. Quiet Carry forend. Many barrels are ported. From Mossberg.

Price: From about $316.00
Price: Sporting Combos (field barrel and
    Slugster barrel). From $381.00

MOSSBERG MODEL 500 PERSUADER/ CRUISER SHOTGUNS

Similar to Mossberg Model 500 except has 18-1/2" or 20" barrel with cylinder bore choke, synthetic stock and blue or Parkerized finish. Available in 12, 20 and .410 with bead or ghost ring sights, 6- or 8-shot magazines. From Mossberg.

Price: 12 gauge, 20" barrel, 8-shot, bead sight. $357.00
Price: 20 gauge or .410, 18-1/2" barrel, 6-shot,
    bead sight $357.00
Price: Home Security 410 (.410, 18-1/2" barrel
    with spreader choke) $360.00

MOSSBERG MODEL 590 SPECIAL PURPOSE SHOTGUN

Similar to Model 500 except has Parkerized or Marine-cote finish, 9-shot magazine and black synthetic stock (some models feature Speed Feed). Available in 12 gauge

Mossberg Model 500 Mariner Pump Shotgun

Mossberg Model 500 Ghost-Ring Pump Shotgun

Mossberg Model 590 Tactical Pump Shotgun

only with 20", cylinder bore barrel. Weighs 7-1/4 lbs. From Mossberg.

Price: Bead sight, heat shield over barrel $525.00

MOSSBERG MODEL 500 PERSUADER SECURITY SHOTGUNS

Gauge: 12, 20, .410, 3" chamber. Barrel: 18-1/2", 20" (Cyl.). Weight: 7 lbs. Stock: Walnut-finished hardwood or black synthetic. Sights: Metal bead front. Features: Available in 6- or 8-shot models. Top-mounted safety, double action slide bars, swivel studs, rubber recoil pad. Blue, Parkerized, Marinecote finishes. Mossberg Cablelock included. From Mossberg.

Price: 12 ga., 18-1/2", blue, wood or synthetic
stock,6-shot... $353.00

Price: Cruiser, 12 ga., 18-1/2", blue, pistol grip,
heat shield $357.00

Price: As above, 20 ga. or .410 bore $345.00

MOSSBERG MODEL 500, 590 MARINER PUMP SHOTGUN

Similar to the Model 500 or 590 Persuader except all metal parts finished with Marinecote metal finish to resist rust and corrosion. Synthetic field stock; pistol grip kit included. Mossberg Cablelock included.

Price: 6-shot, 18-1/2" barrel $497.00

Price: 9-shot, 20" barrel $513.00

MOSSBERG MODEL 500, 590 GHOST-RING SHOTGUN

Similar to the Model 500 Persuader except has adjustable blade front, adjustable Ghost-Ring rear sight with protective "ears." Model 500 has 18.5" (Cyl.) barrel, 6-shot capacity; Model 590 has 20" (Cyl.) barrel, 9-shot capacity. Both have synthetic field stock. Mossberg Cablelock included. Introduced 1990. From Mossberg.

Price: 500 Parkerized $468.00

Price: 590 Parkerized $543.00

Price: 590 Parkerized Speedfeed stock $586.00

MOSSBERG MODEL 590 SHOTGUN

Gauge: 12, 3" chamber. Barrel: 20" (Cyl.). Weight: 7-1/4 lbs. Stock: Synthetic field or Speedfeed. Sights: Metal bead front. Features: Top-mounted safety, double slide action bars. Comes with heat shield, bayonet lug, swivel studs, rubber recoil pad. Blue, Parkerized or Marinecote finish. Mossberg Cablelock included. From Mossberg.

Price: Blue, synthetic stock................................ $417.00

Price: Parkerized, synthetic stock $476.00

Price: Parkerized, Speedfeed stock $519.00

REMINGTON MODEL 870 MARINE MAGNUM SHOTGUN

Similar to 870 Wingmaster except all metal plated with electroless nickel, black synthetic stock and forend. Has

Remington Model 870 FS-2 Tactical Pump Shotgun

Remington Model 870 FS-3 Tactical Pump Shotgun

Remington Model 870 Tactical Pump Shotgun w/SpeedFeed Stock

18" plain barrel (cyl.), bead front sight, 7-shot magazine. Introduced 1992. XCS version with TriNyte corrosion control introduced 2007.

Price:	$733.00
Price: XCS (intr. 2007)	$848.00

REMINGTON MODEL 870 EXPRESS SHOTGUNS

Similar to Model 870 Wingmaster except walnut-toned hardwood stock with solid, black recoil pad and pressed checkering on grip and forend. Outside metal surfaces have black oxide finish. Comes with 26" or 28" vent rib barrel with mod. RemChoke tube.

Price: 12 ga., 20 ga., 16 ga. (28")	$373.00
Price: Express Combo, 12 ga., 26" vent rib with mod. RemChoke and 20" fully rifled barrel with rifle sights, or RemChoke	$507.00 to $543.00
Price: Express Synthetic, 12-ga., 26" or 28"	$373.00
Price: Express Synthetic, 20 ga., 18" barrel (2007)	$388.00

REMINGTON MODEL 870 AND MODEL 1100 TACTICAL SHOTGUNS

Gauge: 12, 2-3/4 or 3" chamber, 7-shot magazine. Barrel: 18", 20", 22" (Cyl or IC). Weight: 7.5-7.75 lbs. Length: 38.5-42.5" overall. Stock: Black synthetic, synthetic Speed-feed IV full pistol-grip stock, or Knoxx Industries SpecOps stock w/recoil-absorbing spring-loaded cam and adjustable length of pull (12" to 16", 870 only). Sights: Front post w/dot only on 870; rib and front dot on 1100. Features: R3 recoil pads, LimbSaver technology to reduce felt recoil, 2-, 3- or 4-shot extensions based on barrel length; matte-olive-drab barrels and receivers. Model 1100 Tactical is available with Speedfeed IV pistol grip stock or standard black synthetic stock and forend. Speedfeed IV model has an 18" barrel with two-shot extension. Standard synthetic-stocked version is equipped with 22" barrel and four-shot extension. Introduced 2006. From Remington Arms Co.

Price: 870, Speedfeed IV stock, 3" chamber, 38.5" overall	$599.00
Price: 870, SpecOps stock, 3" chamber, 38.5" overall	$625.00
Price: 1100, synthetic stock, 2-3/4" chamber, 42.5" overall	$759.00

SMITH & WESSON 1000/1020/1012 SUPER SEMI-AUTO SHOTGUNS

Gauge: 12, 20; 3" in 1000; 3.5" chamber in Super. Barrel: 24", 26", 28", 30". Stock: Walnut. Synthetic finishes are satin, black, Realtree MAX-4, Realtree APG. Sights: Tru-Glo fiber-optic. Features: 29 configurations. Gas operated, dual-piston action; chrome-lined barrels, five choke tubes, shim kit for adjusting stock. 20-ga. models are Model 1020 or Model 1020SS (short stock). Lifetime warranty. Intro-

Remington Model 870 Marine Magnum Shotgun

Remington Model 870 Tactical Pump Shotgun

Remington Model 870 Tactical Pump Shotgun w/Tac-2 Folding Stock

Smith & Wesson 1012 Super Semi-Auto Shotguns

duced 2007. Imported from Turkey by Smith & Wesson.

Price: Black synthetic stock.. NA

SCATTERGUN TECHNOLOGIES TACTICAL RESPONSE TR-870 STANDARD MODEL SHOTGUNS

Gauge: 12, 3" chamber, 7-shot magazine. Barrel: 18" (Cyl.). Weight: 9 lbs. Length: 38" overall. Stock: Fiberglass-filled polypropolene with non-snag recoil absorbing butt pad. Nylon tactical forend houses flashlight. Sights: Trak-Lock ghost ring sight system. Front sight has Tritium insert. Features: Highly modified Remington 870P with Parkerized finish. Comes with nylon three-way adjustable sling, high visibility non-binding follower, high performance magazine spring, Jumbo Head safety, and Side Saddle extended 6-shot shell carrier on left side of receiver. Introduced 1991. From Scattergun Technologies, Inc.

Price: Standard model..................................... $815.00
Price: FBI model $770.00
Price: Patrol model $595.00
Price: Border Patrol model $605.00
Price: K-9 model (Rem. 11-87 action) $995.00
Price: Urban Sniper, Rem. 11-87 action $1,290.00
Price: Louis Awerbuck model $705.00
Price: Practical Turkey model $725.00
Price: Expert model $1,350.00
Price: Professional model $815.00
Price: Entry model $840.00
Price: Compact model $635.00
Price: SWAT model $1,195.00

INTRODUCTION TO
Tactical Gear

BY EDITORS OF GUN DIGEST

Tactical gear is probably the least glamorous, but the most important, element of tactical gear in general.

Only a few decades ago, tactical gear was limited to leather holsters; khaki, canvas, denim or leather wear; steel body protection plates; an military-styled helmets. Today it's a different pictrure entirely, of course. Today nylon reigns supreme as the material of choice for all sorts of tactical gear. And that perhaps deserves an explanation:

In the following section, you will see references to the term "denier" (pronounced duh-neer). Denier is a metric measurement of the density (in casual terms, the thickness) of the individual nylon fiber that makes up a given woven nylon fabric, and it represents the mass per 9,000 meters of that fiber. Thus a "600 denier" nylon fiber is not as massive (thick) as a "1000-denier" fibre. Sometimes you will see "denier" used as just another term – as in "100% denier" – for what we know as good old nylon.

Another term you will encounter in this section is "MOLLE." MOLLE is a military acronym that stands for "MOdular Lightweight Loading-bearing Equipment." "MOLLE generally refers to any piece of apparel that is designed to carry something else: canteens, ammunition, tools, etc. Many types of modern MOLLE gear incorporate the PALS (Pouch Attachment Ladder System) method of attachment. Invented and patented by United States Army

Photo Courtesy BLACKHAWK!

leading independent testing and evaluation companies.

Note that we have tried to limit the following listings to those items that are commercially available. In the world of tactical gear, many manufacturers choose not to make their products available to the general public, for what we hope are obvious reasons. Body armor and bullet-resistant helmets, for example, are generally not available for retail sale; manufacturers of these items usually choose to make them available only to accredited law enforcement agencies and the branches of the U. S. military. Buying them usually requires a boatload of official paperwork, and prices are often negotiable. For that reason, not all of the items listed in this section show retail pricing.

It may come as a surprise to the casual reader that there is such a thing as tactical underwear, but be assured that there is. In today's red-hot tactical gear market, no item is so humble, so everyday, that it cannot be improved on!

Natick Soldier Research, Development and Engineering Center, PALS consists of webbing sewn onto the load-bearing equipment and corresponding webbing and straps on the attachment itself. The straps are interwoven between the webbing on each of two pieces and finally snapped into place, making for a very secure fit which can be easily detached.

Yet another term you will encounter in this section is "MIL-STD." This term refers to a specific military standard, and its application to a particular item means that that item has been built to, and presumably meets, the military specification for that class of item. In some circles MIL-STD has replaced the earlier term "mil-spec," which is verbal shorthand for "military specification."

Some of the gear included in this section refers to an ANSI standard, such as "ANSI Z87.1." ANSI is an acronym for the American National Standards Institute, an independent standards organization that develops specifications for a variety of products, including eyewear. You will also find references to the H. P. White Laboratories, one of the world's

Photo Courtesy BLACKHAWK!

**BLACKHAWK! Level 2
Serpa Light Bearing Holster
for XIPHOS NT**

**BLACKHAWK! 3-LOOP
REINFORCED
WEB DUTY BELT**

BLACKHAWK! Ballistic MICH Helmet

BLACKHAWK! LEVEL 2 SERPA LIGHT BEARING HOLSTER FOR XIPHOS NT

A weapon light and holster combo that makes it practical to carry a light on a concealed handgun. The slim profile of the Xiphos light means that there is no added bulk away from your body.

Price: $144.99

BLACKHAWK! LAW ENFORCEMENT TROUSER INNERBELT

Molded nylon loop hook. Will not fray belt loops or trousers.

Price: $21.99

BLACKHAWK! 3-LOOP REINFORCED WEB DUTY BELT

- Ergonomically designed Duty Belt with padded edges
- Nylon loop backing mates to Duty Gear trouser belt

Price: $21.99

BLACKHAWK! REINFORCED 3 WEB DUTY BELT

Great performance at a great price. Two layers of nylon web are reinforced with a polymer spine for durability and strength. The nylon binding provides a smoother edge, more comfort and a more professional appearance. Plus the binding reduces the abrasion from the edge of the belt and the triple lock buckle helps prevent accidental opening or someone stripping your belt.

Price: $36.99

BLACKHAWK! BALLISTIC MICH HELMET

Based on the original Special Ops MICH, this design epitomizes our Blackhawk! motto: LIGHTER, STRONGER, FASTER, BETTER. This helmet maintains a large coverage area while providing extreme comfort. This helmet is designed for Military and Police special tactical units where compatibility with all NV and communication systems is of critical importance. No civilian sales.

Specifications:
- Construction: Plain weave aramid in a high tensile elongation resin
- Coating: Epoxy and polyurethane shell coatings
- Weight: 2.7 lbs

32BH01BK-SM-GSA (Small)
- Head Size: 50cm - 56cm
- Circ.: 19in - 22in
- Dia.: 5.5in - 6.5in

32BH01BK-MD-GSA (Medium)
- Head Size: 54cm - 59cm

**BLACKHAWK!
32V301CT S.T.R.I.K.E.
Cutaway Tactical
Armor Vest**

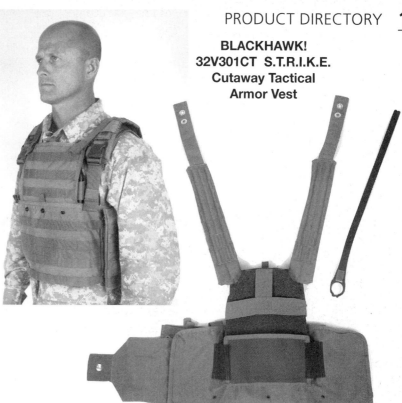

BLACKHAWK! 32HC Head Cover

- Circ.: 21in - 23in
- Dia.: 6.5in - 7.5in

32BH01BK-LG-GSA (Large)
- Head Size: 57cm - 64cm
- Circ.: 22in - 25in
- Dia.: 7in - 8in

32BH01BK-XL-GSA (X-Large)
- Head Size: 61cm - 66cm
- Circ.: 24in - 26in
- Dia.: 7.5in - 8.5in

Price: $599.99

BLACKHAWK! 32HC HEAD COVER

- Helmet cover is designed to fit clean and tight on MICH style helmets
- Built to MIL spec standards
- Designed to mount with suspension and pad style systems
- Made of NYCO nylon cotton rip stop material and NIR compliant
- Features Glint tape mounting locations and covers
- Rear flap with hook and loop opening
- ARPAT color only

Price: $19.99

BLACKHAWK! 32V301CT S.T.R.I.K.E. CUTAWAY TACTICAL ARMOR VEST

- Lightweight: only 3.5 Lbs; lightest cutaway available
- Ambidextrous for high performance
- Fast and easy to put on and take off using side release buckles
- Secure release strap has a round handle that is secured inside a protective band of nylon on the front panel shoulder
- Two-stage release so operator can choose partial cutaway of side panels only
- Cutaway function can be easily disabled if desired
- Simple construction that is very easy to reassemble
- Adjustable waist and shoulder system for girth and torso length for tailored fit
- Full outer vest area usage for any s.T.R.I.K.E./ Molle pouch configurations
- Lined with cool and comfortable soft 3-d mesh to move air around your body
- Armor - holds soft level iiia as well as level iv ballistic armor plates (up to 11x14) in internal adjustable pockets
- Side plates: custom side plate pouch system holds plates up to 6x8
- Accessories: accommodates level 3 collar, groin,

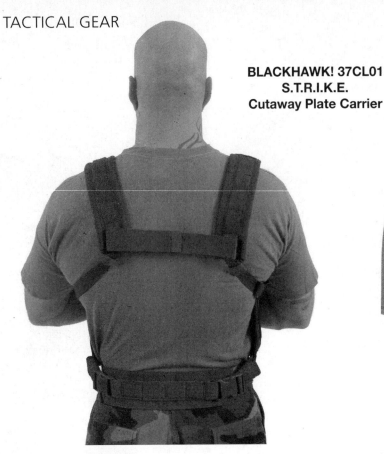

**BLACKHAWK! 37CL01
S.T.R.I.K.E.
Cutaway Plate Carrier**

BLACKHAWK! Battle Bag

and shoulder yokes
- Heavy duty drag handle

Price: $379.00

BLACKHAWK! 37CL01 S.T.R.I.K.E. CUTAWAY PLATE CARRIER

- Takes Level IV ballistic armor plates (up to 11x14) in fully adjustable front and rear pockets
- Front plate pocket with inverted "T" elastic keeper can also accommodate bib when plates are not in use for a lower profile rig
- S.T.R.I.K.E. webbing on inside of front pocket provides the internal platform to mount additional pouches or holsters
- Side plates: custom side plate pouch system holds plates up to 6x8
- Lightweight: only 3.1 lbs; lightest cutaway plate carrier available
- Ambidextrous for high performance
- Fast and easy to put on and take off using side release buckles
- Secure release strap has a round handle that is secured inside a protective band of nylon on the front panel shoulder
- Two-stage release so operator can choose partial cutaway of side panels only
- Cutaway function can be easily disabled if desired

- Simple construction that is very easy to reassemble
- Adjustable waist and shoulder system for girth and torso length for tailored fit
- Fully covered with S.T.R.I.K.E./MOLLE webbing for any pouch configurations
- Heavy Duty Drag Handle

Price: $279.99

BLACKHAWK! BATTLE BAG

"Battle Bag", "Grab-to-Go Bag" - call it what you will, but you need one. Organize all of your warfighting necessities in this over-the-shoulder carry bag. Everything from comms, chem. lights, concealed handgun, spare magazines, maps, GPS - all have a place in this bag to enhance your survivability.

Features Include:
- 1000 denier nylon construction
- YKK® zippers
- Integral shoulder and waist strap (stowable)
- Map pocket (9.5x13-in) inside protective storm flap with side release closure
- Internal pouch for handheld radio with antenna access
- Internal elastic loops for chem. lights
- Internal hook & loop section for handgun and spare pistol magazine (or any modular hook & loop pouches)

BLACKHAWK! ZW5 5" Side Zip Boot

BLACKHAWK! Enhanced Battle Bag

- 2 dividers creating 3 internal sections
- External zippered accessory pocket with elastic securing bands holds 3 magazines
- External (4x5-in) zippered pouches at either end to hold GPS, phones, etc.
- 11" x 5" x 10"

Price: $99.99

BLACKHAWK! ENHANCED BATTLE BAG

Blackhawk! introduces an enhanced modular version of this great selling bag. Designed to be kitted out based on the mission. MOLLE webbing on three sides allows the user to configure it to his needs. Bag is slightly larger than the original and the map case is now detachable.

- Completely configurable version of the popular Battle Bag
- Slightly larger in all dimensions to accommodate a small laptop computer
- Stiffened construction to retain structure
- Flap is also a detachable map case
- Name tag window on flap
- Body of bag is covered by webbing; so operator can mount a variety of pouches
- HawkTex® pad on shoulder strap for comfort
- Carry handle on top of flap and bag when map is detached

Price: $119.99

BLACKHAWK! ZW5 5" SIDE ZIP BOOT

BlackHawk! Warrior Wear™ Side-Zip Boots are fast, light, comfortable, easy to put on, and waterproof. This boot is a 5" tall boot. 7" tall boots are also offered.
Features:

- Durable, easy-to-use molded tooth zipper opening
- Long-wearing, water-friendly polyurethane midsole
- Dri-Lex® inner lining wicks away moisture and dries quickly for maximum comfort
- Vibram® "Multisport" oil resistant TC4+ compound outsole has large, open lugs for traversing debris and provides excellent traction on irregular surfaces
- Waterproof barrier and gusseted tongue
- Water-resistant Cordura® and high-abrasion full-grain leather upper
- Nylon shank
- Washable, Anti-Microbial, Ortholite® custom molded footbed

Price: $164.99

BLACKHAWK! CANTEEN

The new BLACKHAWK! Canteen by Nalgene is made from durable polycarbonate with a one-handed closure system designed to prevent leaks.
Features:

- Military standard 1qt. capacity and design

BLACKHAWK!
Canteen Pouch

BLACKHAWK!
Coupled Magazine
Pouch-Double

BLACKHAWK! Canteen

- Military thread configuration to accommodate issued (NBC) caps
- Sturdy polycarbonate resists unwanted tastes and smells
- Translucent color shows fluid level and cleanliness
- Looped top allows for easy carrying by hand or carabiner
- Sized to military specifications to fit in issued canteen cups and pouches
- Closure prevents leaks and comes apart for easy cleaning
- Color options include Coyote Brown and Foliage Green

NOTE: Pouch sold separately.

Price: $12.99

BLACKHAWK! M16/M4 OLIVE DRAB MAG POUCH

Features:
- Made of 1000 denier nylon for maximum durability
- Fully adjustable 2" shoulder straps, adjustable waist strap
- Four M16/M4 magazine pouches, two adjustable pistol magazine pouches
- Hook & loop lid closures, drainage grommets in bottom of each pouch

- Chest pouches hold M16/M4 or AK-47 mags.

Price: $70.00

BLACKHAWK! COUPLED MAGAZINE POUCH-DOUBLE

Features:
- Designed to accommodate four M4/M16 magazines mounted in two Blackhawk! Magazine Couplers (not included)
- Holds four M-16/M4 30 round magazines (120 ROUNDS TOTAL)
- 6.5" X 9"h X 2.5"d

Price: $44.99

BLACKHAWK! BALLISTIC SIDE PLATE PANEL W/LEVEL IIIA SOFT ARMOR

Blackhawk! Armor products are restricted items to Military, Law Enforcement and Security Personnel only.
- Military / DOD must have copy of military / govt. Id and current command
- Law enforcement / agency / state govt. Must have copy of law enforcement or agency ID or certificate with current department
- Independent security contractor must have copy of drivers license, security certificate and letter on company letterhead approving this purchase
- Civilians: no sale, no exceptions

Price: $84.99

BLACKHAWK! Ballistic
Side Plate Panel
w/Level IIIA Soft Armor

BLACKHAWK!
S.T.R.I.K.E.
Camera Pouch

BLACKHAWK!
S.T.R.I.K.E. GPS
Pouch

BLACKHAWK! S.T.R.I.K.E. SNIPER REST

Provides stability and accuracy as a long-gun shooting platform.

- Attaches to webbing on packs using two #9 speed clips; turns any pack into a sniper pack
- 7.5" square x 2.5" high

Price: $29.99

BLACKHAWK! S.T.R.I.K.E. CAMERA POUCH

Features:

- Small pouch for digital camera, cellphone, PDA, etc.
- Padded throughout for device protection
- Hybrid mounting; belt loop with internal hook and loop or MOLLE mounting using speed clip (included)
- Rounded flap with hook and loop closure for security 3w X 4h X 1.5d

Price: $17.99

BLACKHAWK! S.T.R.I.K.E. GPS POUCH

Specifically designed to fit the Garmin eTrex®; will also hold other GPS units and digital cameras.
Features:

- Padded for device protection
- Attaches using one speed clip; can also be belt-mounted – hook and loop stabilizes pouch on belt

- Interior dimensions 2"w x 3.5"h x 1.25"d

Price: $26.99

BLACKHAWK! TACTICAL HANDBAG

Shoulder carried bag.
Features:

- Waterproof Hawk-tex bottom to protect contents
- Bellowed side pockets to securely carry items (cell phone, small water bottle, PDA, camera, MP3 player, etc.) for quick access
- Main compartment flap secures with a fixed side release buckle
- Pouch for cell phone (or other items) on front secured by hook and loop
- Open pocket on left front, pen channels on right side
- Hook and loop nametag strip at top front of flap for identification
- Sure grip rubberized nylon handle on top
- Adjustable shoulder strap with small non-slip pad
- Zippered exterior compartment on back of bag
- Removable acrylic business card window on back
- Waterproof interior lining
- Back of flap features a mesh zipped pocket and two elastic securing loops for chem-light or small flashlight

J-Tech AEGIS Tactical Vest

**BLACKHAWK!
Tactical Handbag**

- Removable lengthwise zippered pouch secured vertically at both ends using hook and loop as well as snaps
- Interior key ring keeper
- Hook and loop wall on back of bag interior to secure pouches, holsters, etc. (not included)
- 10.5"W x 7"H x 4"D

Price: $59.99

J-TECH AEGIS TACTICAL VEST

Manufactured with military level materials, high strength nylon straps, and structure strengthening stitches. On the front and backside of this vest there are layers to carry any models of bulletproof board and it can also attach any MOLLE gear. On each shoulder there is one buckle for quick release of the vest. On the back it can attach a special backpack to increase the volume of goods carried and on the sides there are 1/2' nylon straps for adjustment.

Price: ....Not available

J-TECH FORCE RECON TACTICAL BACKPACK

100% NYLON 600 Denier). Force recon tacticalbackpack has an extra layer on the main backpack where increases the volume of the backpack. Other functions are the same of U.M.A.B.

Price: ....Not available

J-TECH M7 COVER-TAC TACTICAL VESTS

Carry-all tactical vest made of 100% nylon denier and available in the following configurations:

- Features compass pouch, pistol magazine pouch, shotgun shells pouch, 5.56mm caliber magazine pouch, pistol holster.
- Features compass pouch, pistol magazine pouch, shotgun shells pouch, 9mm submachine gun magazine pouch, pistol holster.
- Features compass pouch, pistol magazine pouch, shotgun shells pouch, fragmentation grenade pouch, pistol holster.
- Features compass pouch, pistol magazine pouch, shotgun shells pouch, fragmentation grenade pouch, 9mm submachine gun magazine pouch.
- Features compass pouch, pistol magazine pouch, shotgun shells pouch, fragmentation grenade pouch, 5.56mm caliber magazines pouch.
- Features compass pouch, pistol magazine pouch, shotgun shells pouch, 2 sets of fragmentation grenade pouch.
- Features compass pouch, pistol magazine pouch, shotgun shells pouch, 5.56mm caliber magazine pouch, 9mm submachine gun magazines pouch.

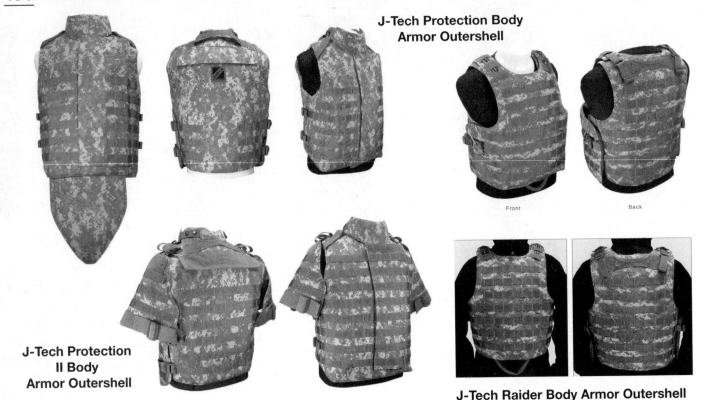

J-Tech Protection Body Armor Outershell

Front Back

J-Tech Protection II Body Armor Outershell

J-Tech Raider Body Armor Outershell

- Features compass pouch, pistol magazine pouch, shotgun shells pouch, 2 sets of 5.56mm caliber magazine pouch.
- Features compass pouch, pistol magazine pouch, shotgun shells pouch, 2 sets of 9mm submachine gun magazine pouch.

  Price: ....Not available

J-TECH PROTECTION BODY ARMOR OUTERSHELL

Vest for MOLLE system tactical gear. Made of heavy-duty 100 nylon denier; adjustable for shoulder width and girth; fits most builds from 36- to 56-inch chests. Nylon web emergency drag handle. Removable collar and protective groin section.

  Price: ....Not available

J-TECH PROTECTION II BODY ARMOR OUTERSHELL

Similar to above but with shoulder protection.

  Price: ....Not available

J-TECH RAIDER BODY ARMOR OUTERSHELL

Vest for MOLLE system tactical gear. Made of heavy-duty 100 nylon denier; adjustable for shoulder width and girth; fits most builds from 36- to 56-inch chests. Quick-release removal feature. Nylon web emergency drag handle.

Removable collar and protective groin section.

  Price: ....Not available

J-TECH TP1E TACTICAL VEST

Velcro-adjustable waist; adjustable for shoulder height. Quick-release removal feature. Nylon web emergency drag handle. Removable collar and protective groin section. Accommodates 3-liter hydration system.

  Price: ....Not available

J-TECH TP4 MOLLE TACTICAL VEST

Similar to above but will accommodate front and back bulletproof panels.

  Price: ....Not available

PAULSON A-TAC TACTICAL GOGGLES

Dual lens configuration goggles have abrasion-resistant outer lens and anti-fog inner lens. Lexan lens is 20 times more impact-resistant than glass. Fits over prescription glasses. Black, with clear lens and adjustable, elastic head strap. Meets ANSI Z87.1 performance standard. Various lens options available.

- Description: A protective goggle designed to specifically address the needs of a tactical operation. Dual lens with a hard coated outer lens and an anti-fog inner lens. Optically correct lens. Baffled top and bottom vents for chemical splash protection. Quick Strap elastic

J-Tech TP1E Tactical Vest   **J-Tech TP4 MOLLE Tactical Vest**

**Paulson A-Tac
Frag Goggles**

adjuxtment and quick release rear strap buckle.

- Material: Silicone frame and strap. Lexan lens, polymer alloy components.
- Hazard Assessment: Impact, splash, smoke, particulate matter, and chemicals.
- Applications: Tactical deployment and other emergency operations. Designed to meet ANSI Z87.1 for use where certain physical hazards are likely to be encountered, such as during forced entry, rescue operations, emergency medical operations, and victim extraction.

Price: $25.00

PAULSON RIOT SHIELDS

A hand held body shield with ergonomic features. The ID label that is supplied must be specified at the time of the order. Example, "POLICIA", "POLICE', "SHERIFF", "CORRECTIONS", etc.

Ergonomic handle allows 2 handed use for extreme circumstances. The handle and break away strap are dielectic to prevent electrical pass through and can be reversed for left or right hand use. The wide nylon arm strap is easily adjustable while in use. The shield has superior optical quality and workmanship.

Models BS-1, BS-2, BS-3, BS-4, BS-5, BS-6, BS-7, BS-8, and BS-9. Features include ergonomic handle, quick release strap, foam cushion at arm placement

Price: ....$59.95 - $129.95

PAULSON DK5/DK6 FACE SHIELDS

Universal fit face shield system that adapts to many helmets to provide face protection in riot conditions. Integral rubber seal provides a liquid barrier at the helmet / shield interface. Shield locks into the stowed or deployed positions and can be released with one hand. Pivot and lock assembly can be transferred to the right or left of the shield for individual preference.

Unparalleled fit and function with existing protective helmets. Attachment is quick, secure and easily removable when necessary. This shield is certified to NIJ 0104.02, and meets MIL-V-43511C.

Price: $35.00

PAULSON A-TAC FRAG GOGGLES

A tactical goggle with optional Nose Shield, silicone frame, V-50 rated triple layer Lexan and anti-fog lens, Quick Strap elastic adjustment and quick release rear strap buckle. Designed to specifically address the needs of a tactical operation that may require fragmentation protection. Triple lens designed with a hard coated outer lens, center fragmentation lens and an anti-fog inner spall lens. Baffled top and bottom vents. Optional nose protection feature.

Material: Silicone frame and strap. Lexan lens, polymer alloy components.

Hazard Assessment: Fragmentation impact, splash, smoke, particulate matter, and chemicals.

Paulson BS-2 (left) & BS-4 (right) Riot Shields

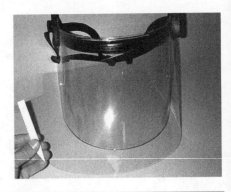

**Paulson DK5
Face Shield**

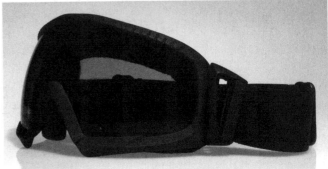

Paulson Repel Goggles

Specification: Designed to meet the performance specifications of ANSI Z87.1 and is V-50 rated.

Price: $45.00

PAULSON REPEL GOGGLES

There is no compromise with the new Paulson Repel goggle. Incredible peripheral vision, a dual layer impact resistant lens, superior anti-fog resistance, 360 degree ventilation and unparalleled face fit answers the questions from Tactical Officers nationwide.

Features and Specifications:
- Aspherical dual lens
- Hard-coated outer lens
- Anti-fog inner lens
- Optically correct lens is baffled, with top and bottom vents for 360° of ventilation and chemical splash protection
- Virtually indestructible Lexan® lens offers outstanding impact resistance

Price: $65.00

REVISION DESERT LOCUST MILITARY GOGGLE KITS

Designed as the ultimate protective eyewear, the Desert Locust Goggle builds upon Revision Eyewear's unmatched ability to protect soldier's eyes. The Desert Locust combines the best ballistic protection with a perfect facial and helmet fit, balancing the soldier's need for comfort with well

sealed eye protection.

Price: ....$59.99 to $119.99

REVISION SAWFLY MILITARY EYEWEAR KITS

Proven to be the top performing impact eyewear available. Designed for fit, function and comfort. The curved lens provides an unrestricted field of view and maximum ventilation, while the adjustable arms and head strap ensure a perfect fit, every time. Two sizes: Large or Regular

Price: ....$44.99 - $149.99

REVISION HELLFLY BALLISTIC SUNGLASSES

Military grade eye protection in a stylish, comfortable and lightweight design that is perfect for people in the line of duty as well as recreational enthusiasts. Hellfly Ballistic Glasses are considered the answer that many soldiers, law enforcement officers, and individuals working or recreating in potentially dangerous situations, have been looking for. The Revision Hellfly Sunglasses provide high-impact fragment protection, excellent optical performance and 100% UV protection packaged in a stylish, comfortable, lightweight design. Hellfly Glasses exceed the U.S. Military's stringent high-impact requirement for spectacles, as well as the ANSI Z87.1 standard for impact and optics.

Price: $94.99

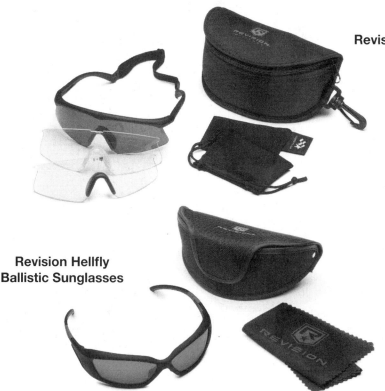

**Revision Sawfly Military
Eyewear Kits**

**Revision Hellfly
Ballistic Sunglasses**

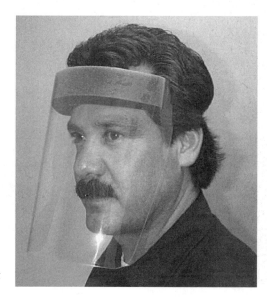

Paulson IDC Spit Shield

PAULSON IDC SPIT SHIELD

This is a complete face shield assembly with elastic attachment and foam cushion. As a complete system, each unit can be disposed after use at minimal expense. The resealable bag keeps the unused product clean and ready for use. Individual units may be rolled into a tube and stowed in a cargo pocket for easy access when needed. One size fits all.

- Description: Infectious disease control shield (Spit Shield) This is a complete face shield assembly with elastic attachment and foam cushion. Packed 5 shields per re-sealable bag.
- Material: Mylar (anti-static)
- Specification: OSHA 1910.1030
- Hazard Assessment: Splash from body fluids.
- Applications: Police, Sheriff, University Police, Jail, Institutional, Medical

Price: $5.00

PAULSON "HAWK" TACTICAL GOGGLES

"The Hawk", a tactical goggle with Nose Shield, silicone frame, dual Lexan and anti-fog lens, Quick Strap elastic adjustment and quick release rear strap buckle.

Description: A protective goggle designed to specifically address the needs of a tactical operation. Dual lens with a hard coated outer lens and an anti-fog inner lens. Optically correct lens. Baffled top and bottom vents for chemical splash protection. Quick Strap elastic adjustment and

quick release rear strap buckle.

Hazard Assessment: Impact, splash, smoke, particulate matter, and chemicals.

Features:

- Urethane cushion at face; contact points allow for snug fit and comfort
- Baffled top and bottom air vents
- Anti-fog inner lens
- Ideal for wear with a helmet or over glasses
- Adjustable elastic strap; quick-release rear snap
- Molded polycarbonate lens
- Built-in nose protection
- Meets ANSI Z87.1 Performance Specs

Price: $29.00

RBR DUTY BAG

The RBR Duty Bag is a durable method of transporting your RBR Vest, rifle plates, accessories and mission specific tactical gear

Features:

- (2) Integrated name tag holders
- Integrated internal radio, multiple magazine and several utility pockets with velcro closure
- Double - Cross Stitched Carry Handle
- 23" L x 23" W x 5 1/2" D
- Dual ambidextrous industrial zip closure
- Color: Black

Price: .... Not available

GEAR

RBR Duty Bag

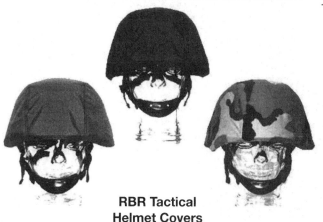

**RBR Tactical
Helmet Covers**

**RBR Tactical
Helmet Bag**

RBR Velcro Identification Tags

RBR TACTICAL HELMET COVERS

RBR Helmet covers are designed for all RBR models of helmet in many different patterns and colors. Solid Cordura Nylon protects your helmet from wear.

Features:

- Velcro secured
- Medium or large
- Reversible available
- Cordura nylon
- Optional night vision compatibility
- Multiple patterns and styles

Price: ....Not available

RBR TACTICAL HELMET BAG

The RBR Helmet Tote Bag is an all purpose carry bag designed for your RBR Ballistic Helmet and Helmet Accessories. Purposely constructed of durable nylon and internal padding, it protects your equipment from scratch and scuff during storage in tactical gear locations such as trunks and lockers.

Features:

- Double layered nylon
- Draw-string closure with spring loaded cinch clip
- Cushioned filler
- Cross-stitched nylon carry straps
- Color: Black

Price: ....Not available

RBR VELCRO IDENTIFICATION TAGS

RBR tactical ID TAGS are designed for all RBR Tactical Vests with ID locations. Manufactured for durability and high visibility.

Features:

- Constructed of highly durable coated nylon
- Specialty ID's are available
- Standard ID's include: SWAT, SPECIAL AGENT, POLICE, SHERIFF

Price: ....Not available

RBR TACTICAL PADDED NECK PROTECTOR, RIOT

The RBR Padded Neck Protector is designed for easy retro-fit to all RBR Helmets and is compatible with most other helmet styles. Providing the wearer with blunt trauma protection to the rear head and neck region in riot control environments, this accessory is an inexpensive FORCE PROTECTION enhancement.

Features:

- Compatible with most standard ballistic helmets
- Durable Cordura Nylon shell
- Available in NIJ IIIA for ballistic protection

Price: ....Not available

RBR TACTICAL PADDED NECK PROTECTOR, IIIA

The RBR Neck Protector offers the wearer added protec-

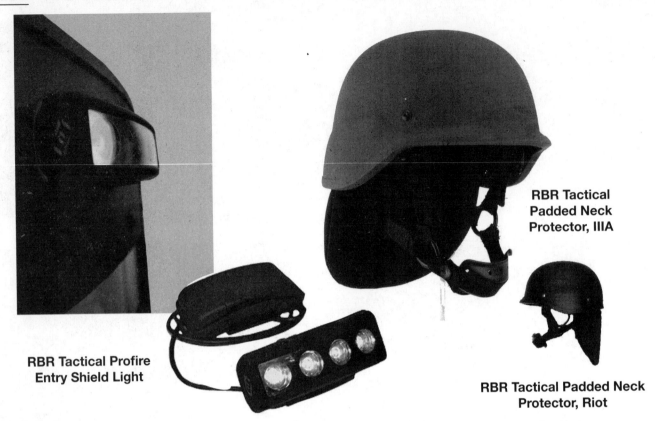

RBR Tactical Profire Entry Shield Light

RBR Tactical Padded Neck Protector, IIIA

RBR Tactical Padded Neck Protector, Riot

tion to the rear head and neck region. Available in both IIIA and riot control protection, it is designed to protect the wearer from blunt force or direct impact trauma to the rear of the neck.

Features:

- Available in all standard colors and patterns
- Firmly attached via suspension system hardware
- Available in Full NIJ IIIA or riot control levels of protection
- Retrofits to RBR Series and most other ballistic helmets

Price: ....Not available

RBR TACTICAL PROFIRE ENTRY SHIELD LIGHT

The Profire-Tac Shield Light provides tactical shield operators with 210 lumens of high intensity ambient light in "constant on" scenarios or "strobe mode" for entries requiring disorientation as a force-multiplier. Highly durable and water resistant to 20 ft, this light system utilizes (4) "C" Cell off-the-shelf batteries and can last from 8 to 16 hours depending upon mode, usage and climate. Also available in 500 lumens that uses 6 lithium CR123 batteries.

This system is the ideal solution for optional carry, retro-fit shield lighting for all styles of dynamic and deliberate entries requiring the use of ballistic entry shields.

Features:

- Operates on (4) "off-the-shelf" C Cell batteries

or (6) CR213 Lithium batteries

- Water resistant to 20'
- 8-16 Hour Battery Life
- Weight = 21.0 oz
- LED operation to 210 Lumens or 500 Lumens
- Multifunction On/Off Pressure Switch
- Peripheral Vision = 80 ft (24 m)
- Strobe mode: 3.5 – 7.0 Hz within 1.5 seconds
- Distance Vision = 250 - 300 ft (76 - 91 m)
- 3M Dual-Lock Industrial Velcro Mount
- 12 Month Warranty

Price: ....Not available

RBR VORTEX DOUBLE PISTOL MAG

The RBR Vortex load-bearing pockets are durably manufactured to withstand the rigors of high-intensity environments. This series of load-bearing pouches compliments the RBR 300, 400, 500, 600 and 700 Series entry vest systems and provides tactical operators with dynamic load-bearing creativity. All RBR Vortex pockets will fit any system which is MOLLE/PALS capable. Constructed exceeding US Government guidelines on stitching and construction, RBR assists the operator by providing securely fitted, combat ready gear. In addition, RBR maintains critical mission focus by NOT utilizing steel snaps in the construction of its pockets or vests ensuring elimination of secondary projectile injuries to the wearer.

**RBR Vortex Double
Pistol Mag**

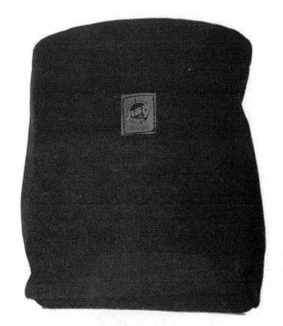

RBR Vortex Drop Leg Utility

**RBR Vortex
Evidence Bag**

Features:
- MOLLE / PALS capable
- Streamlined KYDEX construction holds magazines in place
- Non-Steelsnap construction prevents secondary projectile injuries
- Integrated optional Velcro over-loops for secure storage
- Available in Nomex for tactical operations requiring flame-resistant protection

Price: ....Not available

RBR VORTEX DROP LEG UTILITY

The RBR Vortex load-bearing pockets are durably manufactured to withstand the rigors of high-intensity environments. This series of load-bearing pouches compliments the RBR 300, 400, 500, 600 and 700 Series entry vest systems and provides tactical operators with dynamic load-bearing creativity. All RBR Vortex pockets will fit any system which is MOLLE/PALS capable. Constructed exceeding US Government guidelines on stitching and construction, RBR assists the operator by providing securely fitted, combat ready gear. In addition, RBR maintains critical mission focus by NOT utilizing steel snaps in the construction of its pockets or vests ensuring elimination of secondary projectile injuries to the wearer.

Features:
- Color: Black

- Dual internal elastic loops for medical equipment positioning
- Integrated external pocket
- Size: 8" H x 6.5" W x 3" D
- Ambidextrous industrial zip closure
- MOLLE/PALS Capable
- Available in Nomex for tactical operations requiring flame-resistant protection
- Dual compartments

Price: ....Not available

RBR VORTEX EVIDENCE BAG

The RBR Vortex load-bearing pockets are durably manufactured to withstand the rigors of high-intensity environments. This series of load-bearing pouches compliments the RBR 300, 400, 500, 600 and 700 Series entry vest systems and provides tactical operators with dynamic load-bearing creativity. All RBR Vortex pockets will fit any system which is MOLLE/PALS capable. Constructed exceeding US Government guidelines on stitching and construction, RBR assists the operator by providing securely fitted, combat ready gear. In addition, RBR maintains critical mission focus by NOT utilizing steel snaps in the construction of its pockets or vests ensuring elimination of secondary projectile injuries to the wearer.

Features:
- Deployed: 6 1/2"L x 3 1/2" W x Full 11" Deep
- Stored: 3 1/2" L x 3 1/2" W x Full 4" Deep

**RBR Vortex
Double M4
Mag Pouch**

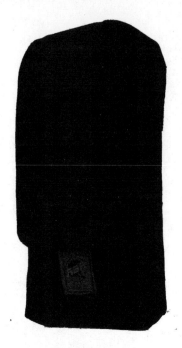

**RBR Vortex Duty
Radio Pouch**

**RBR Vortex Shotgun
Shell Pouch**

- Color: Black
- Available in Nomex for tactical operations requiring flame-resistant protection
- Pull string closure with spring-loaded cinch securement clip
- Can be rolled away during storage or velcro released for deployment
- MOLLE/PALS Capable

Price: ....Not available

RBR VORTEX DOUBLE M4 MAG POUCH

The RBR Vortex load-bearing pockets are durably manufactured to withstand the rigors of high-intensity environments. This series of load-bearing pouches compliments the RBR 300, 400, 500, 600 and 700 Series entry vest systems and provides tactical operators with dynamic load-bearing creativity. All RBR Vortex pockets will fit any system which is MOLLE/PALS capable. Constructed exceeding US Government guidelines on stitching and construction, RBR assists the operator by providing securely fitted, combat ready gear. In addition, RBR maintains critical mission focus by NOT utilizing steel snaps in the construction of its pockets or vests ensuring elimination of secondary projectile injuries to the wearer.

Features:
- Velcro Over-Closure
- Available in Nomex for tactical operations requiring flame-resistant protection

- MOLLE/PALS Capable
- Color: Black

Price: ....Not available

RBR VORTEX DUTY RADIO POUCH

The RBR Vortex Radio Pouch is Molle / PALS compatible and fits 95% of most "brick" style radios.

Features:
- Rear opening for communication cables
- Tapered over-flap for antenna
- Maximum height with velco secured over-flap: 9"
- Deep 6 1/2" Pouch

Price: ....Not available

RBR VORTEX SHOTGUN SHELL POUCH

The RBR Vortex Shotgun Pouch can be dynamically altered to hold six or twelve shells by addition or removal of the internal components.

Features:
- MOLLE/PALS Capable
- Color: Black
- Available in Nomex for tactical operations requiring flame-resistant protection
- (1) or (2) Removable Velcro-backed internal shell platforms

Price: ....Not available

**RBR VORTEX DUTY
UTILITY pouch**

**RBR CERAMIC
RIFLE PLATE
inserts**

RBR VEST CARRY BAG

RBR VORTEX DUTY UTILITY POUCH

The RBR Vortex Duty Utility Pouch is a multi-purpose storage area for tactical gear, ammunition or medical supplies.

Features:

- MOLLE/PALS Capable
- Available in Nomex for tactical operations requiring flame-resistant protection
- Dual ambidextrous zip closure
- External MOLLE Grid
- 9" L x 3 1/2" W x 6 1/2" Deep

Price: ....Not available

RBR VEST CARRY BAG

The RBR Vest Carry Bag is a durable method of transporting your RBR Vest, rifle plates and accessories.

Features:

- Color: Black
- (2) Integrated name tag holders
- Double - Cross Stitched Carry Handle
- 23" L x 23" W x 5 1/2" D

Price: ....Not available

RBR CERAMIC RIFLE PLATE INSERTS

Available in several different sizes and capabilities. RBR has placed protection and comfort as the two highest priorities in plate design. By incorporating both multi-curve and tactical-cut construction, RBR Rifle Plates provide the

operator with the highest achievable level of dynamic rifle protection. The RBR CP (Combination Plate) III/IV has been and continues to be the most commonly selected rifle plate by tactical operators. Specifically designed for weight reduction, the RBR CP III/IV Ballistic Rifle Plate achieves NIJ III/IV protection by deployment with a certified NIJ Level IIIA soft armor system such as RBR Flex IIIA-35. Available in 6X8, 8x10 and 10x12 dimensions in both combination and stand-alone configurations, RBR Ballistic Rifle Plates provide tactical operators with the highest level of personal armor protection today's technology has to offer.

Features:

- Available in multi-curve 10" x 12" (5.6 Lbs.)
- NIJ certified level III, III+ and IV protection
- Multi-hit capability
- Lever III+ capabilities
- Plate weights vary from 2.8 Lbs polyethylene NIJ III+ through 6.2 Lbs steel
- Combination and stand-alone availability
- Ceramic face 99% alumina, backed by kevlar and nylon wrapped

Price: ....Not available

RBR STEEL PLATE INSERTS

For traditional ballistic rifle protection , RBR Steel Plates provide an inexpensive option in obtaining full NIJ III+ protection.

RBR STEEL PLATE inserts

RBR RIOT / FRAGMENTATION CONTROL FACESHIELD

RBR BALLISTIC ENTRY SHIELD

Features:
- Available in 10 x 12 and 5 x 8
- Single Curve
- Tactical cut for long-gun positioning
- Multi-strike capable

Price: ....Not available

RBR BALLISTIC ENTRY SHIELD

Developed over a number of years and through considerable research evolved into the optimum compromise between weight and bullet resistance. It provides the tactical specialist with resistance to ballistic and fragmentation threats. RBR Ballistic Shields incorporate a lightweight design that has protection at NIJ Level IIIA. Our shields have been developed to give unmatched protection while the unique handle design allows for comfortable ambidextrous use and optimum mobility.

Features:
- NIJ level IIIA protection
- Weight: medium(21lbs) large (23 lbs)
- Available in two sizes: medium (22 x 39 inches) or large (22 x 51 inches)
- Medium shield handle can be utilized as a quick step ladder
- Ambidextrous handle
- Neck-retention strap
- Vehicle mounting hooks for downed officer rescue

- 4" X 16" view port to level IIIA

Price: ....Not available

RBR RIOT / FRAGMENTATION CONTROL FACESHIELD

The RBR Riot and Fragmentation Face Shield manufactured by RBR Tactical Armor, Inc is a universal fit face shield that adapts to most tactical helmets including the ACH / MICH. The face shield is designed to protect the face in riot/hazardous conditions and accommodate most gas masks used by both law enforcement and military personal. An integral rubber seal provides a liquid barrier at the helmet/shield interface. The shield locks into two different positions, stowed and deployed, and can be released with one hand.

Features:
- V-50 rated at 250 meters per second against a 17-caliber fragment
- Retro-fit system fits most styles of ballistc helmets
- Durable industrial strength belt-latch attachment system
- Moisture barrier prevents liquids from entering the eyes
- Complies with NIJ 0104.02 and MIL-V-43511C
- Lexan™ (Polycarbonate)
- Anti - fog and hard coated

RBR Ballistic Visor

RBR Patrolman Shield, IIIA

- Designed to protect against impact, splash and fragment hazards

Price: ....Not available

RBR BALLISTIC VISOR

The Ballistic Visor provides protection against multiple hits of NIJ Level II (9mm and .357) and IIIA 9mm rounds. It weighs 2.2 lbs. The visor is securely mounted to the helmet via a form-fitted polymer visor band with adjustable rear lock. The face shield can be locked into 3 positions including fully elevated, mid-level and deployed.

- Weight 2.2 Lbs
- Adjustable grip-lock clamp secures faceshield band in place
- Impact protection against all NIJ level II and IIIA 9mm ballistics
- Fits all RBR and other traditional style helmets except the RBR Mach III
- Durable polymer band construction

Price: ....Not available

RBR PATROLMAN SHIELD, IIIA

The RBR PATROLMAN SHIELD is designed to augment traditional body armor for law enforcement or military use. It is lightweight, versatile, stab-resistant and provides protection from IIIA ballistics. The incorporation of the flashlight as a handle encourages usage and renders this piece of defensive equipment dual purpose, reducing the carry-load of the common law enforcement officer. Its size and shape protect areas not commonly protected by standard body armor alone including the face and under-arm cavity in systems which do not implement the use of IIIA arm guards. In addition and due to the Patrolman's light-weight ambidextrous design, by releasing the flashlight, users can continue to utilize both hands for common purposes. This is the ideal solution for first responders responding to suspicious or minimal threat situations.

Features:

- 16 ¼" H x 12 ¼" W
- Lightweight, rapid up-armor solution at appx. 6.0 lbs
- Ambidextrous Handle
- Durable GERBER® Handle flashlight included
- Industrial grade dense forearm padding
- NIJ Level IIIA Protection
- Durable Nylon and Bungee Sling

Price: ....Not available

RBR U-TAC 600 FULL TACTICAL ENTRY VEST

The RBR 600 U-TAC-MRV marshals series tactical vest is a solid design chosen by federal law enforcement agencies and special operations military. Specifically chosen by the US Marshals Service, this vest includes communications cable channeling and dynamic load-bearing capa-

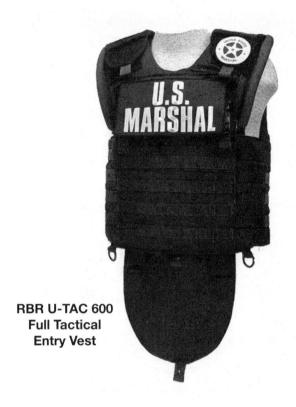

**RBR U-TAC 600
Full Tactical
Entry Vest**

The RBR V-TAPP Assault Panel

bilities. Modular in design, the vest system is available with ballistic arm guards, collar and retractable groin protection. This vest series carries 20% more MOLLE webbing coverage than any tactical vest of its kind allowing users to adapt their pocket and pouch configurations with ease.

Features:

- Internal radio wire channels over right/left shoulder
- 4" Wide elastic waist-band conforms the vest to the body
- Front and back 10" x 12" rifle plate pockets
- Side opening
- Contains NIJ certified aramid fiber protection to nij std 0101.04 And the NIJ 2005 interim body armor requirement; meets usms soft body armor test protocol
- Front to back overlapping side protection
- Integrated long gun retention with side non-slip tubing
- Integrated ballistic arm guard storage
- Overlapping adjustable shoulder protection from overhead threats
- RF welded 100% moisture proof ballistic panels
- Removable ballistic collar, groin and arm guard compatible
- Integrated 50oz hydration system pocket

- Non-steel snap pocket attachment (molle) system prevents
- Integrated d-rings for gas mask carrier retention, and pistol belt attachment

Price: ....Not available

THE RBR V-TAPP ASSAULT PANEL

The RBR V-TAPP Assault Panel was originally designed by RBR to provide law enforcement professionals with light duty assault protection in passive tactical environments where active threats are probable. When up-armored with (1) 10" x 12" Rifle Plate, this system provides the operator with NIJ Level III/IV protection at reduced weight, giving the Law Enforcement First Responder a means of protection to identify and close with a given threat.

Features:

- 10" X 12" pocket for rifle plate up-armor
- Available, standard, in size 20" x 30" and 20" x 36"
- Available in all standard patterns and colors
- Multiple webbing strips and loops for vehicle attachment
- Weight: 7.25 lbs (large)
- Contains NIJ certified armor systems to standard 0101.04 and the NIJ 2005 interim armor standard
- NIJ IIIA and fragmentation tested

**RBR MACH I
Ballistic Helmet**

- Durable webbing grid allows for the attachment of various pouches

Price: ....Not available

RBR COMBAT F6 BALLISTIC HELMET

The RBR COMBAT F6 BALLISTIC HELMET provides a lightweight, compact and streamlined design without any compromise to the ballistic protection. The RBR Combat has been utilized by military, police and tactical teams around the world. The cut of the helmet improves peripheral vision and neck flexibility for the operator. The helmet is fitted with a fully adjustable harness system that can be released, removed and replaced in just a few minutes. RBR Ballistic Helmets are tested at H.P. White Laboratory at Level IIIA. All of the RBR Helmets maintain V-50 performance at over 2100 feet per second, surpassing the Mil Spec of 2000 feet per second.

Features:

- Tested to H.P. White helmet test procedure for IIIA performance (HPW-TP-0401.01B)
- Tested to MIL-STD 662E for fragmentation performance
- Weight: 2.6 lbs - 2.9 lbs
- 3-Point Comfort Plus suspension system
- Tested and certified by H.P. White Labs withstanding multiple impact IIIA ballistics
- Higher cut around the neck for more movement and peripheral vision

- Colors: Black, OD and Tan
- V-50 Performance exceeds 2100 FPS
- Sizes: Medium (Up to 7 1/4") & Large (7 1/4" and above)

Price: ....Not available

RBR MACH I BALLISTIC HELMET

The RBR MACH I BALLISTIC HELMET is based on the original ACH MICH Design with a focus toward reduction in weight while maintaining coverage area and increasing comfort. The MACH I was designed where compatibility with all NOD and communication systems are of critical importance.

Features:

- Weight: 2.7lbs - 3.0 lbs
- Sizes: Medium (Up to 7 1/4") & Large (7 1/4" and above)
- Tested to H.P. White helmet test procedure for IIIA performance (HPW-TP-0401.01B)
- Tested to MIL-STD 662E for fragmentation performance
- 4-Point Comfort Plus suspension system
- Optional Mil-Spec multi-pad suspension system capable
- Full coverage ACH style
- Tested and certified by H.P. White Labs withstanding multiple impact IIIA ballistics
- V-50 Performance exceeds 2100 FPS
- Colors: Black, Olive Drab and Tan

Price: ....Not available

**RBR Military MACH
II Advanced
Combat Helmet**

**RBR MACH III Advanced
Combat Helmet**

RBR MILITARY MACH II ADVANCED COMBAT HELMET

The RBR MILITARY MACH II ADVANCED COMBAT HELMET is based on the original Special Forces MICH Design with a focus toward reduction in size and an elevated cut around the ears. The MACH II was designed for Military and Police special tactical units where compatibility with all NV and communication systems is of critical importance along with wearer comfort.

Features:
- Wider cut around the ears for use with various communications systems
- Colors: Black, OD and Tan
- Tested and certified by H.P. White Labs withstanding multiple impact IIIA ballistics
- V-50 Performance exceeds 2100 FPS
- 4-Point Comfort Plus suspension system
- Weight: 2.6 lbs - 2.9 lbs
- Optional Mil-Spec multi-pad suspension system capable
- Tested to MIL-STD 662E for fragmentation performance
- Tested to H.P. White helmet test procedure for IIIA performance (HPW-TP-0401.01B)
- Sizes: Medium (Up to 7 1/4") & Large (7 1/4" and above)

- Higher cut around the neck for more movement and peripheral vision

Price: ....Not available

RBR MACH III ADVANCED COMBAT HELMET

Based on the original Special Forces MICH Design with a focus toward reduced coverage integrating larger muff-style communications. The MACH III was designed for Military and Police special tactical units where compatibility with all NV and communication systems is of critical importance along with wearer comfort. Helmets provide un-matched Level IIIA protection and include the RBR 4-point suspension system secured with only four bolts to ensure maximum ballistic integrity, comfort and stability. The RBR Mach III Helmet is fitted with a fully adjustable padded head harness, attached via four (4) fastener screws. The head harness includes leather covered front padding, nylon covered rear padding and leather comfort crown pad.

Features:
- Ideal for long range operators including snipers and agents requiring stealth as an operational requirement
- V-50 Performance exceeds 2100 FPS
- Tested and certified by H.P. White Labs withstanding multiple impact IIIA ballistics
- Tested to H.P. White helmet test procedure for IIIA performance (HPW-TP-0401.01B)

RBR F6 PASGT
Helmet

RBR COMBAT F6
MK-II HELMET

- Special design cut for integrated muff-style communications
- 4-Point Comfort Plus suspension system
- Tested to MIL-STD 662E for fragmentation performance
- Weight: 2.4 Lbs – 2.6 Lbs
- Colors: Black, Olive Drab and Tan
- Sizes: Medium (Up to 7 1/4") & Large (7 1/4" and above)
- Optional Mil-Spec multi-pad suspension system capable

Price: ....Not available

RBR MACH IV ADVANCED COMBAT HELMET

Based on the original Special Forces MICH Design with a focus toward a lightweight, compact and streamlined design without any compromise to the ballistic protection. The MACH IV was designed for Military and Police special tactical units where compatibility with all NV and communication systems is of critical importance along with wearer comfort. Helmets provide un-matched Level IIIA protection and include the RBR 4-point suspension system secured with only four bolts to ensure maximum ballistic integrity, comfort and stability. The RBR Mach IV Helmet is fitted with a fully adjustable padded head harness, attached via four (4) fastener screws. The head harness includes leather covered front padding, nylon covered rear padding and leather comfort crown pad.

RBR Helmets are fully adjustable in the circumference as well as the wearing height; therefore, two sizes can be adjusted to fit all heads.

Features:

- Tested to H.P. White helmet test procedure for IIIA performance (HPW-TP-0401.01B)
- Weight: 2.6lbs - 2.9lbs
- 4-Point Comfort Plus suspension system
- Tested and certified by H.P. White Labs withstanding multiple impact IIIA ballistics
- Lightweight, streamlined ballistic protection
- Colors: Black, OD and Tan
- Tested to MIL-STD 662E for fragmentation performance
- Sizes: Medium (Up to 7 1/4") & Large (7 1/4" and above)
- Optional Mil-Spec multi-pad suspension system capable
- V-50 Performance exceeds 2100 FPS

Price: ....Not available

RBR COMBAT F6 MK-II HELMET

The RBR MK-II Helmet is the primary Law Enforcement choice of SWAT units. This helmet is also the current issue to the U.S. Drug Enforcement Administration. Originally designed by RBR Tactical Armor, uses RBR unique processing techniques to provide enhanced shell

**RBR Sniper
Capable Or Urban
Tactical (S.C.O.U.T.)
Vest**

**RBR 203
Tactical
Vest**

protection, at lower weight with improved comfort. The helmet shell is trimmed to allow for maximum compatibility with NVG and weapon optics as well as gas masks and long gun retention. The shell provides the wearer with maximum peripheral vision and no impairment from either ballistic material or suspension straps. The helmet is fitted with a fully adjustable harness system that can be released, removed and replaced in just a few minutes.

Features:

- Tested and certified by H.P. White Labs withstanding multiple impact IIIA ballistics
- 3-Point Comfort Plus suspension system
- Colors: Black, OD and Tan
- V-50 Performance exceeds 2100 FPS
- Wider cut around the ears for use with various communications systems
- Sizes: Medium (Up to 7 1/4") & Large (7 1/4" and above)
- Tested to MIL-STD 662E for fragmentation performance
- Weight: 2.7Lbs - 2.9 Lbs
- High tactical cut illeviating ballistic collar interference
- Tested to H.P. White helmet test procedure for IIIA performance (HPW-TP-0401.01B)

Price: ....Not available

RBR F6 PASGT HELMET

Designed adopting the military "Personal Armor System, Ground Troop" style exceeding fragmentation and comfort standards by performing at full IIIA. D esigned based on the widely adopted Personal Armor System Ground Troop (PASGT helmet used by the U.S. Military. This helmet is structured using RBR's unique processing techniques to provide enhanced shell protection, at lower weight, with improved comfort. It is a general-purpose, full-coverage helmet for the modern Combat Soldier or Law Enforcement Officer in an enhanced ballistic armor resin matrix. The level of protection in RBR helmets exceeds standard issue U.S. Military helmets designed for fragmentation protection only. RBR's unique process technology utilizes the excellent performance of aramid Kevlar bound in a thermoplastic resin matrix. This is the key to achieving an excellent performance to weight ratio. The RBR F6 PASGT Helmet can be worn for extensive periods of time, even in adverse conditions, with superior comfort.

Features:

- V-50 Performance exceeds 2100 FPS
- Full Coverage
- Tested and certified by H.P. White Labs withstanding multiple impact IIIA ballistics
- 3-Point Comfort Plus suspension system
- Weight: 2.9lbs to 3.2 lbs
- Colors: Black, OD and Tan

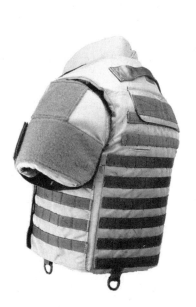
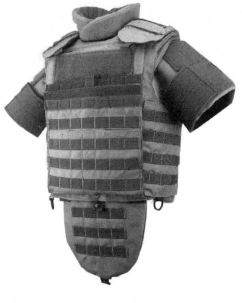

RBR M-TAC 300
Tactical Vest

- Wider cut around the ears for use with various communications systems
- Sizes: Medium (Up to 7 1/4") & Large (7 1/4" and above)
- Tested to H.P. White helmet test procedure for IIIA performance (HPW-TP-0401.01B)
- Tested to MIL-STD 662E for fragmentation performance

Price: ....Not available

RBR SNIPER CAPABLE OR URBAN TACTICAL (S.C.O.U.T.) VEST

The RBR S.C.O.U.T. PLUS Tactical Vest provides maximum protection and tactical diversity in a light duty assault vest posture. Designed to provide tactical protection to operators requiring stealth as an operational consideration. In addition, it provides an excellent level of protection for first responders and stand-off operators such as detail snipers and perimeter security.

Features:
- Available in all standard colors and patterns
- Contains NIJ certified aramid fiber protection to NIJ STD 0101.04 and the NIJ 2005 interim body armor requirement
- Optional groin protection
- Padded return-buckle adjustable shoulder suspension
- ID tag compatible
- Non-steel snap system prevents secondary projectile injuries
- Down-man drag strap
- Weight: 7.5 Lbs (large)

- Hydration system compatible
- Side opening
- Lightweight & versatile for sniper / recon operations
- Front and back 10" x 12" rifle plate pockets
- IIIA over the shoulder protection
- Standard BTS load bearing webbing system
- Optional PALS / MOLLE webbing system for pocket attachment

Price: ....Not available

RBR 203 MEDIA PACKAGE

The RBR Media Package was designed for deployed media staff and includes an NIJ Certified IIIA Vest, IIIA Helmet and cover and ballistic plating. Among independant items purchased by the press from RBR, the RBR Media Vest Package has been purchased and delivered to numerous agencies including Newsweek, Fox News, NBC and ABC.

Features:
- Hydration sytem compatible
- Modeled after the RBR 203 Series Tactical Vest Series for SWAT and Military
- Featured in non-combatant coloring for Geneva Convention Compliance
- Available in all colors and patterns
- Arm guards compatible
- Modular removable collar and groin protection included
- Attachable velcro ID tag locations front and back

Price: ....Not available

**RBR D-TAC 400 MRV
DEA Package**

GEAR

RBR 203 TACTICAL VEST

Modular in design, the RBR 203 Series Vest provides full tactical IIIA protection compatible with Blackhawk! Tactical System load bearing products. Originally designed by RBR to provide law enforcement professionals with full-coverage protection in active shooter environments. Modular in design, this vest system is compatible with ballistic arm guards, collar and retractable groin protection. The system series is in use by some of our nations leading agencies including NYPD, PA State Police and NASA Special Operations. The 203 Vest features a side opening style with front to back overlapping protection, over the shoulder coverage and is compatible with removable ballistic collar, internal groin protector and arm guards. The 203 is equipped with a Velcro backed, 2" wide, nylon webbing pocket attachment system that is compatible with Blackhawk! BTS, Military MOLLE, A.L.I.C.E. and other similar pocket systems, Pistol belt keepers, Officer Rescue Handle, flex-cuff channel on right shoulder and 10" X 12" Plate Pockets on front and rear for up-armoring against rifle attack. Additionally, by not using a Snap Modular Grid system the vest is inherently lighter and the possibility of a steel snap becoming a secondary projectile is eliminated.

Features:
- Manufactured using the Blackhawk! tactical system webbing configuration compatible with all Blackhawk! series pockets
- Non-steel snap system prevents secondary projectile injuries
- Front and back 10" x 12" rifle plate pockets
- 4" Wide elastic waist-band conforms the vest to the body
- Removable ballistic collar, groin and arm guard compatible
- Contains NIJ certified aramid fiber protection to nij std 0101.04 and the NIJ 2005 interim body armor requirement
- Overlapping adjustable shoulder protection from overhead threats
- Integrated ballistic arm guard storage
- Front to back overlapping side protection
- RBR original series in use by thousands of SWAT officers across the U.S.

Price: ....Not available

RBR M-TAC 300 TACTICAL VEST

This armor is the choice of the USAF Security Forces for deployments in Iraq and Afghanistan. It provides full NIJ IIIA protection not commonly offered in military deployment armor. D esigned to meet the needs of high-speed tactical teams and military units with a completely mission adaptable armor system. Chosen by the USAF Security Forces for deployments in Iraq and Afghanistan, this system is capable of enduring rigorous abuse to its construction while maintaining full NIJ IIIA Ballistic Protection not commonly offered in troop deployment armor. Modular in design, the vest system is available with ballistic arm guards, collar and retractable groin protection. This vest series carries 20% more Molle webbing coverage than any tactical vest of its kind allowing users to adapt their pocket and pouch configurations with ease.

**RBR 500
Clan-Lab
Package**

Features:
- Side opening
- Integrated D-rings for gas mask carrier retention
- Overlapping adjustable shoulder protection from overhead threats
- Non-steel snap system prevents secondary projectile injuries
- Left and right 6" x 8" rifle plate pockets
- Front and back 10" x 12" rifle plate pockets
- Front to back overlapping side protection
- Integrated ballistic arm guard storage
- Integrated 50oz hydration system pocket
- Removable ballistic collar, groin and arm guard compatible
- 4" Wide elastic waist-band conforms the vest to the body
- Velcro over-flap load bearing security closure
- Contains NIJ certified aramid fiber protection to NIJ STD 0101.04 and the NIJ 2005 interim body armor requirement

Price: ....Not available

RBR D-TAC 400 MRV DEA PACKAGE

The RBR 400 U.S. Drug Enforcement Administration "BAT" Package is specially certified by the U.S. DEA and is packaged to outfit the needs of Special Agents and trained U.S. DEA personnel on duty nationwide. Package includes: (1) D-TAC 400 MRV Tactical Vest with front to back overlapping side protection and over the shoulder coverage; (2) 10"x12" Steel Rifle Plates with anti-spall sleeves; (1) Navy

Blue concealed vest cover compatible with tactical vest ballistic panels (1) POLICE velcro Identification (1) DEA velcro identification (1) Drug Enforcement Administration Badge.
Features:
- Removable ballistic collar, groin and arm guard compatible
- Integrated long gun retention with side non-slip tubing
- Rf welded 100% moisture proof ballistic panels
- Integrated 6" x 8" side rifle plate pockets
- 4" Wide elastic waist-band conforms the vest to the body
- Side opening tactical vest of choice for military units and federal law enforcement agencies serving in high risk environments
- Non-steel snap system prevents secondary projectile injuries
- Contains NIJ certified aramid fiber protection to NIJ STD 0101.04 and the NIJ 2005 interim body armor standard
- Integrated ballistic arm guard storage
- Integrated D-rings for gas mask carrier retention
- Integrated 50oz hydration system pocket
- Front and back 10" x 12" rifle plate pockets
- Front to back overlapping side protection
- Load bearing over-flap secure vest closure
- Protection from overhead threats
- Interim body armor requirement; meets US DEA soft body armor test protocol

Price: ....Not available

RBR U-TAC 600 U.S. Federal Marshal Package

RBR 500 CLAN-LAB PACKAGE

The RBR 500 Clan-Lab package is certified by the U.S. Drug Enforcement Administration Clan-Lab School and is packaged to outfit the needs of special agents on duty nationwide. RBR D-TAC 500 MRV DEA Package includes: (1) D-TAC 500 MRV Tactical Vest with retractable groin, ballistic collar and yoke assembly; (2) 10 x 12 Steel Rifle Plates with anti-spall sleeves; (1) Navy Blue concealed vest cover compatible with tactical vest ballistic panels (1) POLICE velcro Identification (1) DEA velcro identification (1) Drug Enforcement Administration Badge.

Features:
- Integrated ballistic arm guard storage
- Load-bearing over-flap secure vest closure
- Interim body armor requirement: Meets U.S. DEA soft body armor test protocol
- RF welded 100% moisture-proof ballistic panels
- Removable ballistic yoke, groin and arm guard compatible
- Integrated 50oz hydration system pocket
- 4" Wide elastic waist-band conforms vest to body
- Non-steel snap system prevents secondary projectile injuries
- Integrated D-Rings for gas mask carrier retention
- Integrated long-gun retention with side non-slip tubing
- Front and back 10" x 12: rifle plate pockets
- Integrated 6" x 8" side rifle plate pockets
- Front to back overlapping side protection
- Contains NIJ certified aramid fiber protection

to NIJ Standard 0101.04 and the 2005 Interim Body Armor Standard
- Overlapping adjustable shoulder protection from overhead threats
- Nomex Flame-retardency certified
- Side-opening tactical vest of choice for military units and law enforcement agencies serving in high risk environments.

Price: ....Not available

RBR U-TAC 600 U.S. FEDERAL MARSHAL PACKAGE

The RBR U-TAC 600 U.S. Federal Marshal Package is specially certified by the USMS and is packaged to outfit the needs of U.S. Marshals on duty nationwide. Package includes: (1) RBR U-TAC 600-60 USMS vest w/ groin; (1) concealable cover (black); (2) level III+ (ICW) steel rifle plates w/ spall bags (plate size depend upon vest size); (2) "U. S. MARSHAL" ID tags (front/back) w/ lettering 2.25", Embroidered, silver on black background; (1) USMS badge patch; (1) vest / duty bag.

Features:
- Removable ballistic collar, groin and arm guard compatible
- Integrated 50oz hydration system pocket
- Front and back 10" x 12" rifle plate pockets
- Overlapping adjustable shoulder protection from overhead threats
- Integrated ballistic arm guard storage
- RF welded 100% moisture proof ballistic panels
- Integrated D-rings for gas mask carrier retention, and pistol belt attachment

Tru-Spec GEN-III ECWCS Level-1 Top

Tru-Spec GEN-III ECWCS Level-1 Bottom

- Non-steel snap pocket attachment (molle) system prevents secondary injuries
- Contains NIJ certified aramid fiber protection to NIJ STD 0101.04 and the NIJ 2005
- 4" wide elastic waist-band conforms the vest to the body
- Integrated long gun retention with side non-slip tubing
- Front to back overlapping side protection
- Side opening tactical vest of choice for military units and federal law enforcement agencies serving in high risk environments
- Interim body armor requirement; meets USMS soft body armor test protocol

Price: ....Not available

RBR D-TAC MRV (MULTI-ROLL VEST) SERIES TACTICAL VEST

Tested and chosen by the U.S. Drug Enforcement Administration, the D-TAC Multi-Roll Vest is designed as a complete modular tactical entry package for high-intensity environments. The first true system to integrate 6" x 8" side plate pockets, hydration and long-gun retention, the D-TAC Multi-Roll Vest offers a complete tactical ballistic and load bearing package unsurpassed in the industry. Modular in design, the vest system is available with ballistic arm guards, collar and retractable groin protection. This vest series carries 20% more Molle webbing coverage than any tactical vest of its kind allowing users to adapt their pocket and pouch configurations with ease.

Features:

- Non-steel snap system prevents secondary projectile injuries
- Load bearing over-flap secure vest closure

- 4" wide elastic waist-band conforms the vest to the body
- Integrated 6" x 8" side rifle plate pockets
- Integrated 50oz hydration system pocket
- Overlapping adjustable shoulder protection from overhead threats
- Integrated D-rings for gas mask carrier retention
- Front and back 10" x 12" rifle plate pockets
- Side opening
- Contains NIJ certified aramid fiber protection to NIJ STD 0101.04 and the NIJ 2005 interim body armor requirement
- Integrated ballistic arm guard storage
- Front to back overlapping side protection
- Removable ballistic collar, groin and arm guard compatible
- Integrated long gun retention with side non-slip tubing

Price: ....Not available

TRU-SPEC GEN-III ECWCS LEVEL-1 TOP

- 3.7Oz. Tru-Spec performance plus 100% polyester plaited jersey
- Highly breathable, moisture wicking
- Stretch for easy movement
- Grid fleece aids in breathability and moisture wicking properties
- Thumbholes in the sleeves
- Microban® for anti-microbial and anti-odor defense
- Flat locked construction
- Quick drying
- Extended cold weather system
- Sizes: small - 3xlarge ragular

Price: ....Not available

Tru-Spec GEN-III EC-WCS Level-2 Top

Tru-Spec GEN-III EC-WCS Level-3 Top

Tru-Spec GEN-III ECWCS Level-2 Bottom

TRU-SPEC GEN-III ECWCS LEVEL-1 BOTTOM

- 3.7Oz. Tru-spec performance plus 100% polyester plaited jersey
- Highly breathable, moisture wicking
- Stretch for easy movement
- Grid fleece aids in breathability and moisture wicking properties
- Elastic waistband
- Microban® for anti-microbial and anti-odor defense
- Flat locked construction
- Quick drying
- Extended cold weather system

Price: ....Not available

TRU-SPEC GEN-III ECWCS LEVEL-2 TOP

- 6.6Oz. Tru-Spec performance plus 93% polyester / 7% spandex
- Highly breathable, moisture wicking
- Stretch for easy movement
- Zips up to make turtleneck
- Grid fleece aids in breathability and moisture wicking properties
- Thumbholes in the sleeves
- Microban® for anti-microbial and anti-odor defense
- Flat locked construction
- Quick drying
- Extended cold weather system
- Sizes: small - 3xlarge ragular

Price: ....Not available

TRU-SPEC GEN-III ECWCS LEVEL-2 BOTTOM

- 6.6Oz. Tru-Spec performance plus 93% polyester / 7% spandex
- Highly breathable, moisture wicking
- Stretch for easy movement
- Grid fleece aids in breathability and moisture wicking properties
- Elastic waistband with access fly
- Microban® for anti-microbial and anti-odor defense
- Flat locked construction
- Quick drying
- Extended cold weather system
- Sizes: small - 3xlarge ragular

Price: ....Not available

TRU-SPEC GEN-III ECWCS LEVEL-3 TOP

- 6.4Oz. PolarTec thermal pro 100% polyester high pile velour
- Retains body heat
- Maintains warmth without weight
- Quick drying
- Breathable
- Center front zip opening
- Nylon reinforcements in collar and elbows
- Reglan sleeves
- Grid fleece side panels
- 2-Internal upper chest pockets
- Name and rank loop on right and left chest
- Sizes: small - 3xlarge regular

Price: ....Not available

INTRODUCTION TO
Tactical Electronics

BY EDITORS OF GUN DIGEST

The most rapidly-growing area of tactical gear is, without a doubt, electronics. A book three times this size could have been written on tactical electronics alone.

Advancements in microcircuitry occur almost daily, and many of these have been directed toward tactical law enforcement. Like it or not, we live in the age of Big Brother, and communications and surveillance evices that were unheard-of 20 years ago outside of James Bond novels are now commonplace. Due in part to the 9/11 attacks and the subsequent establishment of the Department of Homeland Security, with its enormous grant-bestowing capacity, even small, local law enforcement agencies can afford sophisticated electronics gear.

Some of this gear, such as the family of Northrop Grummond Remotec tracked robots, have little practical application in the civilian sector. Other products, such as handheld GPS units and walkie-talkies, have been successfully marketed as crossovers that bridge the gap between law enforcement and recreational applications.

Traditionally, procurement at the federal and local levels involved reams of forms, quotations, estimates and all manner of bureaucracy. Today, however, more and more agencies make some allowance for OTS (off the shelf) procurement, which allows the military or law enforcement officer to walk into the nearest discount store with a

Photo Courtesy Shutterstock

hall at the 2008 SHOT Show, we watched as a 300-lb. man accidentally stepped on it. We awaited the inevitable sickening crack – but it never came! The Recon Scout went merrily about its business of impressing showgoers, and we were suitably impressed.

Then there's the Rotomotion SR200 UAV Helicopter System. This is perhaps the ultimate eye in the sky, but it's not that far removed from products that are already available in hobby shops across the country.

charge card and walk out with an armload of radios, headsets or whatever. This uncharacteristically common-sense procurement procedure has given many manufacturers the incentive to cross-market their products to governmental agencies as well as civilians, often with little or no modification to the product itself.

Some of the electronics gear featured in the following pages is just plain cool. Our favorite device may well be the Remington R1 Eyeball Camera, which is a round, grenade-like camera that can be thrown or rolled into a dwelling and gives 360-degree coverage, which it transmits wirelessly back to a video receiver. Such a camera has obvious offensive tactical applications, but it could also come in handy during rescue operations, such as those that took place at Ground Zero.

Another favorite is the Recon Scout Robot. This little remote-video device looks something like a small barbell with an antenna on it, and it operates something like a common remote-controlled race car. But the Recon Scout is no toy! As it scooted around the tactical

In the following pges, we have not included computers, PDAs, digital cameras, and other items that are overwhelmingly commercial in nature. These items have practical applications, of course, but they are not energetically marketed toward the tactical community – a primary requirement for inclusion in this book. Of course, anything from a wristwatch to a toenail clipper – or even a ladder! – can be considered a tactical tool, depending on its application.

Little Giant®

Tactical Ladders and Patriot 3 Ladder Shields: Rising to the Occaision

BY SCOTT W. WAGNER

Editor's Note: Scott Wagner is the commander of the 727-Counter Terrorism Training Unit at Columbus State Community College in Columbus, Ohio. Specializing in aircraft, bus and train assault and drug and bomb interdiction, the 727-CTTU makes its training program available to police and military tactical and specialized teams across the country. For more information go to www.cscc.edu/cttu.

When I was asked to review the Little Giant® Brand Tactical Ladder System, I was somewhat under-whelmed. After all, a ladder can't shoot, blow things up, or be carried readily as a basic part of your "kit" or equipment load. I mean, how exciting can that be? Then I caught myself in mid-error. I was in the final preparation and planning stages for our first Advanced Tubular Assault Class at our 727 Counter Terror Training Unit at Columbus State Community College. We would be training SWAT officers in advanced tubular assault tactics on the platforms of bus, train and aircraft, and we would be needing, guess what, ladders. Plus...I had a couple of Patriot 3's Ballistic Ladder Shields com-

ing in to use for the bus assault anyway. Why not evaluate them together? My error-ridden thought process had been corrected.

In order to begin the process, I contacted Mark Anderton at Little Giant® Ladders. Mark, a former operator himself, developed the tactical version of the Model 17 Little Giant® Ladder System, a brand and style of ladder well known to builders, contractors and the "do-it–your-selfer" across the U.S. This versatile system allows an almost infinite variety of ladder positions: closed, A-frame, staircase, full extension, work platform, and with two ladders, a scaffolding trestle position. The Tactical model we received has a closed or storage position length of

Officers Bart Heslington and Jeff Pledger (In photos on pg 228-229, Heslington is the taller of the two) examine the Little Giant Tactical Ladder on the first day of the 727 CTTU Advanced Tubular Assault Class.

manufacturers is an easy way to market products that may not be up to the task) doesn't make it tactical. In the case of this ladder system, it was ready to go from the start, painting it black was just the final touch. One thing I would suggest, since many teams are moving away from black coloring in their uniforms and gear (since black is visible in Gen 3 night vision as an iridescent sheen), how about a digital camo pattern such as the standard army version, or even a desert tan?

Our combined tactical team of the Union County, Ohio, Sheriff's Office and the Marysville City Police Department has worked with a specialized "tactical" ladder system the city purchased some time ago, and let me tell you, that thing is an abomination to use. While it offers a variety of positions, getting it there is no small feat, and getting it back to its original position is an exercise in frustration, usually requiring a hammer to undo its complicated system of positioning pins. And it

4 feet, 7 inches and an extension length of up to 15 feet.

There are so many potential applications for this ladder system in the tactical world, particularly in the assault training that we are doing at 727-CTTU. The beauty of the Little Giant® system is that it is long proven in the hard-use world of construction. It is not a new design or even a huge variation on another design. It simply works well and works rapidly. In fact the design is so good, it looks like all Little Giant® did to create a tactical model is paint the original black. Don't laugh; that was all it needed, and what did you want to do, leave it in its bright aluminum and orange colors for your operations? The finish, by the way, is not simple paint. It is a hard protective finish. Be that as it may, sometimes, painting something black (which for some

was hugely expensive to boot. The Little Giant® Tactical Ladder moves rapidly through the basic positions simply by pulling out captive spring-loaded "lock tab assemblies" (I called them "hooks") and by unlocking and locking knobbed hinges.

The ladders were given a workout in the first class. We used them in full-extension mode to practice our wing mount positions onto our Boeing 727. The lock tab assemblies, when put into place properly (very easily done) hold the ladders in position as a solid span. Officers quickly and easily used the ladders almost as stair steps to breach the wings. In its storage position, the ladder could be hastily deployed on the side of a school or transit bus for driver's side containment positions. For total stability, the ladder could be opened into their

Officers prepare for Bus Assault with Patriot 3 LadderShield

A-frame position for the bus assault. However, this would require carrying them in that configuration. They can be opened quickly, but not that quickly, which makes them too easy to trip over. But for a long-term elevated cover position, the A-frame provides unsurpassed stability, and because the length of the ladder can be adjusted at both ends unlike your typical extension ladder, one side can be longer than the other, allowing you to position the ladder on surfaces with unequal heights, such as stairways. By using a second ladder and the optional work platforms, an elevated sniper or observation post could be put into place, behind a large wall for example. Anderton told me that they have also developed a quick-release carry strap for the ladders while in their storage position. This strap system would allow the bearer to have at least a handgun available. If you had a team moving in on a bus, train or aircraft, and that team had to retreat quickly, the ladder carrier could quickly drop the ladder, allowing him a quicker exit from the dan-

TRU Group I shot a ¾-minute group with the SASS using Federal TRU (Tactical Rifle, Urban) the Federal Police Tactical shot just over a minute group. Both are acceptable groups and with some practice with the system tighter groups should be possible.

ger zone. The quick-release carry system was not available at the time of this evaluation. The Little Giant® Tactical Ladder received high marks from the operators in the class.

Much more mission specialized is the Patriot 3™ (makers of the RAID and MARS elevated assault systems) ballistic LadderShield. The LadderShield is designed specifically for bus assaults or assaults on buildings where a window has to be covered, but is too high off the ground to cover from a standing position. The ballistic shielding component provides protection for the most vulnerable members of the team, those who have to carry and place ladders. I received a sample, two actually, of the training

Close-up of viewing port on front of LadderShield

WARNING
NON BALLISTIC PANEL
DO NOT SHOOT !

model of their Ladder Shields. The training model is non-ballistic, and so-marked, but replicates the size and weight of the ballistic model. The training model replicated the NIJ-3A model of the ballistic model and is 2 feet by 4 feet, and weighs in at a manageable 31 pounds. Patriot 3™ also makes a NIJ-3 Variant that weighs 75 pounds, and a larger NIJ-3&4 model that weighs in at 110 pounds in NIJ Level 3 and 207 pounds at NIJ Level 4. Both those models have wheels at the base, which is good since you would need your beefiest guy to rapidly sling either of those shields around. The model NIJ-3&4 both feature retractable ladders that can be moved and angled away from the shield. The rungs of the NIJ 3A and 3 shields are fixed as a component ladder on both models and the sample model had 4 rungs evenly spaced inside the shield. They are positioned to also serve as the carry handles. There is the standard Lexan viewing port, rubber capped extensions at the top of the shield for non-slip placement against the surface to be breached,

Close-up detail of Stainless Steel Spike "feet" of Patriot 3 LadderShield

Above: Officers in place on bus with the Patriot 3 LadderShield in containment position.

Right: Close-up of interior rungs of Ladder-Shield.

and pointed anchoring feet (stainless steel spikes actually) for a solid hold on the ground (particularly in dirt or asphalt).

In making a stacked approach to a bus for example, the shield bearer will use the shield for over on approach, place and stabilize the shield, and hold it while the assaulter ascends the rungs. Once up, the ladder holder will brace the assaulter in a stabilizing position from below. This deployment method is very rapid, faster than with a standard ladder, as the carrying position is very natural. Tactical Team members usually are more accustomed to carrying and using shields than ladders. The shields anchor quite firmly. However on a bus assault, their height, which is that of a standard ballistic shield, does not allow solid placement in the bus wheel well. The rubber extensions end up resting against the round surface of the tire, and some stability is lost. This is no problem really, just something to keep in mind when placing the shields. Don't use the wheel wells as your breaching area. The LadderShields can be used in other applications besides bus assault, and could fulfill most standard shield missions, while giving the added bonus of providing an emergency ladder if needed. This is important for team commanders to realize, that the Ladder-Shield, while designed for the bus assault mission,

is more versatile than it appears on its face, and can accomplish the basic shield mission as well as the specialized mission.

I was very happy with the performance of both the Little Giant ® Tactical Ladders and the Patriot 3™ Ladder shield during our training program. While the uses for each system sometimes overlap, there are specific uses where one system will excel over the other. Obviously, the Tactical Ladder is the more versatile of the two. If I worked for an agency with limited funding, and needed a way to breach elevated areas, I would clearly choose the Little Giant® Tactical Ladders as a basic part of my tool kit. If I had the basic ladder needs already covered, and was looking for a ballistic shield system with a high level of versatility, I would go with the Patriot 3 Ladder Shields. In either case, I would be making an excellent choice.

ELECTRONICS
PRODUCT DIRECTORY

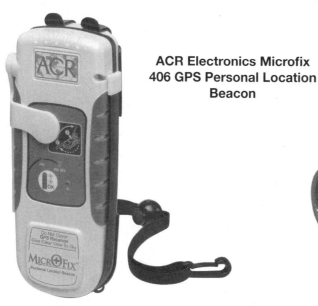

ACR Electronics Microfix
406 GPS Personal Location
Beacon

American Technologies Network
PS14-2 Night Vision Monocular

ACR ELECTRONICS MICROFIX 406 GPS PERSONAL LOCATOR BEACON

Transmits on 406 MHz via the COSPAS-SARSAT satellite system with your registered, unique, digitally coded distress signal and 121.5 MHz (SAR homing frequency); Onboard 12 channel parallel GPS acquires then transmits LAT/LON when the unit is activated, dramatically saving valuable time for your distress message to reach local rescue centers and providing rescue agencies with your exact position to within 110 yards (100 meters); smallest and most functional PLB available; can be easily carried in a pack or pocket; small enough to be worn by skiers, hikers, hunters, kayakers, climbers, pilots, snowmobilers or any other outdoor enthusiast.

Lanyard and removable holster provide functionality and allow for multiple mounting options on backpack, belt, webbing and life vest.

Full functional self test of internal circuitry, battery voltage & power, 406 MHz transmission, and GPS acquisition.

Flat, stainless steel antenna wraps compactly around the unit for easy stowage; and is ready for rapid deployment.

Exceeds RTCM waterproof requirements.

Price: $750.00

AMERICAN TECHNOLOGIES NETWORK PS14-2 NIGHT VISION MONOCULAR

The Multi-use Night Vision monocular is a high per-formance modular, hand-held night vision monocular.

It utilizes a single, Gen.2 intensifier tube to provide crisp, clear images under the darkest conditions. The PS-14 can be hand held or installed in a head-mount. The integrated IR illuminator enhances the ability of the user to read maps, and operate in confined spaces.

The PS-14 is available with a wide range of image intensifier options to meet a wide array of specification requirements.

The PS-14 night vision monocular is a complex opti-coelectronic system for individual use. The device consists of the objective lens assembly, eyepiece and the body. The body contains a image intensifier tube assembly with an integrated high voltage power source and the battery housing.

Objective lens protective cover is intended to protect the objective lens from dust and scratches. It also will act as a daylight filter, allowing you to test the scope in daylight or other bright light situations. The pinhole in the center of the protective cover allows the user to check the operation ability of the device in daylight conditions.

Price: $1768.00

ATN NIGHT STAR GENERATION 1+ NIGHT VISION MONOCULAR

The NightStar provides the user with superior clarity and the highest possible light gain of a first generation night

**ATN Night Star
Generation 1+ Night
Vision Monocular**

**Motorola EM1000
Walkabout Emergency
Two-Way Radio**

vision device at minimal cost. Also the unit comes standard with Total Darkness Technology which will power up a powerful infra-red illuminator with no ambient light. This NightStar is perfect for camping, boating, or home security. Optional camera adapter and headset.

ATN Night Star is the smallest and lightest Night Vision Scope. Gen 1 Night Vision on the budget that fits the palm of your hand.

- Total darkness tech. - Standard
- Diopter adjustment - +/- 5
- Magnification - 1.5X (Optional 3X, 4X, 8X)
- Intensifier tube - High Res. 1st GEN +
- Detection range - 150m
- Recognition range - 100m
- Lens system - 6 (9) Element, F1.2, 35mm
- FOV - 20
- Resolution - 40 lp/mm
- Range of focus - 3' to Infinity
- Controls - Direct
- Power supply - One 3 Volt Litium
- Battery life - 10-20 Hours
- Dimensions 137 X 87 X 43 mm

Price: $229.00

MOTOROLA EM1000 WALKABOUT EMERGENCY TWO-WAY RADIOS

The Motorola Talkabout EM1000 and T9580RSAME radio series are the ideal communication device for emer-

gency kits for outdoor family adventures. Both models feature an emergency checklist and seven National Oceanic and Atmospheric Administration (NOAA) and Environment Canada (EC) weather channels to provide users with continuous broadcasts of local and regional weather updates. In addition, four marine channels are sporadically used (mostly in Canada) for weather broadcasts.

The EM1000R includes an Emergency Alert feature. When the alert button is activated, the radio transmits an alert siren followed by transmission of any spoken or incidental sounds and allows users to send the signal to other radios and warn of impending danger. The T9580RSAME radios also help warn users of emergencies through Specific Area Message Encoding (SAME) technology. SAME technology helps filter out distant warning broadcasts and monitors only programmed localized area, helping reduce the chance of false alarms.The EM1000R features a built-in LED light for peace-of-mind during evening adventures or unexpected emergencies and power outages. The radios also come equipped with both the standard dual drop-in charger, charging adapter, 2 NiMH battery packs and a mini-usb port for convenient charging.

Price: .... $69.95 (pair)

MOTOROLA FV300 TALKABOUT® GMRS/FRS 2-WAY RADIO WITH 10-MILE RANGE

22 channels, 10 mile range, 10 call tones and 16 level digital volume; 18-hour estimated talk time and 12 NiMH;

**Motorola FV300 Talkabout®
GMRS/FRS Two-Way Radio
With 10-Mile Range**

**Motorola Talkabout®
FV700R Two-Way Radio**

time-out timer and priority scan; audible low battery alert and LCD battery meter; plug-in charger and keypad lock; battery save feature and accessory jack; includes 2 radios and runs on 3AAA batteries (not included) and recharge ready. Weight: 0.5 lbs

Price: .... $29.95 (pair)

MOTOROLA TALKABOUT FV700R TWO WAY RADIOS

The Motorola FV700R two way radio is a great family radio, and is perfect for road trips and many types of vacations. The FV700R offers up to a 12 mile range in optimal conditions (typically 1 mile in urban conditions), and privacy will not be a problem as you can choose from 121 privacy codes on each of the 22 FRS and GMRS channels.

The Motorola FV-700R also provides the iVOX feature, offering a built-in hands free system that is perfect for use in the car. The FV700R is also a weather radio, supporting 11 NOAA weather channels. A channel scan feature is also provided, along with 10 call tones.

Features:

- 22 Total Channels
- 12 Mile Range
- 7 FRS Channels
- 8 GMRS Channels
- 7 Shared FRS/GMRS Channels
- 121 Interference Eliminator Codes
- Uses 3 AAA Batteries or Rechargeable Battery Pack

- Rechargeable NiMH Battery Packs Included
- Includeds Dual-Pocket Desktop Charger
- NOAA Weather Channels
- Hands-Free (VOX) Mode
- 10 Call Alert Tones
- Channel Scan
- QT Noise Filter
- Talk Confirmation Tone
- Backlit LCD Display
- Power Boost Option
- Battery Meter Indicator
- Audible Low Battery Alert
- Time Out Timer
- Keypad Lock
- Monitor Channel
- Keystroke Tone Signal
- Drop-In Charge Capable
- Audio Accessory Connector
- One Year Manufacturer Warranty

Price: $49.95

MOTOROLA TALKABOUT FV750R TWO WAY RADIOS

The camouflage-finish Motorola FV750R offers up to a 12 mile range in optimal conditions (typically 1 mile in urban conditions), and interference will not be a problem as you can choose from 121 privacy codes on each of the 22 FRS and GMRS channels.

**Motorola Talkabout®
FV750R Camo
Two Way Radios
(Pair)**

**Motorola Talkabout®
FV750R Camo
Two Way Radios
(Pair)**

The Motorola FV750R is also a weather radio, supporting 11 NOAA weather channels. This is certain to come in handy if you use the radios for hunting, or any other outdoor activity. The FV-750R also provides the iVOX feature, offering a built-in hands free system that is perfect for use in the car! A channel scan feature is also provided, along with 10 call tones.

This value pack includes two Motorola FV750 radios and a dual pocket desk charger with NiMH rechargeable batteries.

Features:
- 22 Total Channels
- 12 Mile Range
- 7 FRS Channels
- 8 GMRS Channels
- 7 Shared FRS/GMRS Channels
- 121 Interference Eliminator Codes
- Uses 3 AAA Batteries or Rechargeable Battery Pack
- Rechargeable NiMH Battery Packs Included
- Includeds Dual-Pocket Desktop Charger
- NOAA Weather Channels
- Hands-Free (VOX) Mode
- 10 Call Alert Tones
- Channel Scan
- QT Noise Filter
- Talk Confirmation Tone
- Backlit LCD Display

- Power Boost Option
- Battery Meter Indicator
- Audible Low Battery Alert
- Time Out Timer
- Keypad Lock
- Monitor Channel
- Keystroke Tone Signal
- Drop-In Charge Capable
- Audio Accessory Connector
- One Year Manufacturer Warranty

Price: .... $59.95 (pair)

MOTOROLA SX600R TALKABOUT GMRS-FRS 2-WAY RADIOS

The compact, rechargeable Motorola SX600R two-way radio is a high powered, feature rich radio that is perfect for the extreme outdoors. Perfect for the outdoor enthusiasts to allow communication in remote locations not covered by cellular phones. While climbing a mountain hands-free communication is possible without removing the SX600R from the belt clip using the iVOX speech activated feature.

The SX600R radios support all 22 FRS and GMRS channels with an amazing 121 privacy codes, there are 2662 combinations for clear uninterrupted connections. This model also offers a channel scan feature, your choice of 10 normal call tone alerts, and a backlit display.

**Motorola Talkabout®
FV750R Camo
Two Way Radios
(Single)**

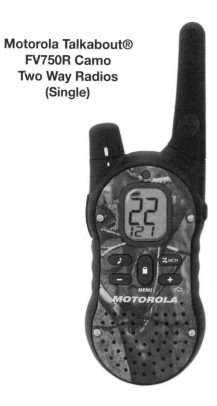

**Motorola Talkabout®
SX900R GMRS-FRS
Two Way Radios
(Single)**

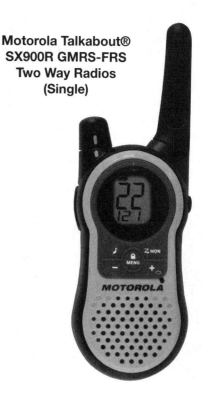

Features:

- 7 GMRS (General Mobile Radio Service) FRS (Family Radio Service) Channels
- 7 FRS Channels
- 8 GMRS Channels
- Mini USB charging and digital signal processing (D.S.P)
- 121 Privacy Codes (that is over 2600 hundred channel combinations)
- 10 Call Tones
- Keypad Lock
- Digital Signal Processing (DSP)
- 11 weather channels
- QT (Quiet Talk) interruption filter
- LCD Meter
- Battery Save Feature
- Audible Low Battery Alert
- Priority Scan
- FCC GMRS License Required
- Includes 2 NiMH Rechargeable Batteries, 2 Belt Clips, Drop in Charger and AC Adapter. Also each radio can run on 3 AAA batteries (Not Included)

Price: .... $43.95 (pair)

MOTOROLA SX900R TALKABOUT GMRS-FRS 2-WAY RADIOS

Similar to above but with following features:

- 7 GMRS (General Mobile Radio Service) FRS (Family Radio Service) Channels
- 7 FRS Channels
- 8 GMRS Channels
- 121 Privacy Codes (that is over 2600 hundred channel combinations)
- 10 Call Tones
- Keypad Lock
- Mini USB charging
- Digital Signal Processing (DSP)
- 11 weather channels
- QT (Quiet Talk) interruption filter
- LCD Meter
- Battery Save Feature
- Audible Low Battery Alert
- Priority Scan
- FCC GMRS License Required
- Includes 2 NiMH Rechargeable Batteries, 2 Belt Clips, Drop in Charger and AC Adapter. Also each radio can run on 3 AAA batteries (Not Included)

Price: $50.00

MOTOROLA TALKABOUT ® T-8500R TWO-WAY RADIO SERIES

The T8500 series of two-way radios feature the ultimate performance in active outdoor communication for today's on-the-go consumer. The T-8500 sold by Crawford Cycle &

**Motorola Talkabout®
T-8500 Two Way
Radios (Single)**

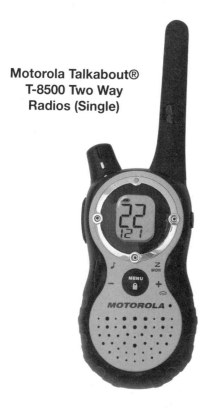

**Motorola Talkabout®
T-8550 Camo
Two Way
Radios (Single)**

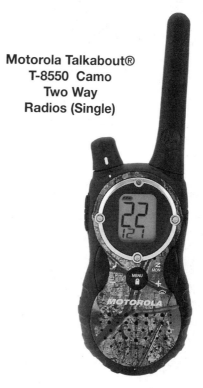

Marine is designed to help deliver the same quality performance Motorola is known for together with a rugged new look, enhanced range and even more features to choose from.

The Motorola Talkabout T9500 radio models are ideally suited for the serious outdoor enthusiast. T8500 models feature 7 National Oceanic and Atmospheric Administration (NOAA) and 4 EC/Canada Marine Weather Channels to provide users with continuous broadcasts of local and regional weather updates. And, in areas where ringing is intrusive, the VibraCall™ feature can be enabled for a silent vibration.

The T8500 series help allow users to maintain clear connections with the convenience and flexibility to fit every adventure. With 22 channels, each with 121 privacy codes, users have 2,662 combinations of communication channels to choose from. For natural sounding communication, the digital audio companding technology helps reduce static hiss between words. Additionally, the radios include Motorola's exclusive Quiet Talk interruption.

Features:
- Delivers A Range Of Up To 18 Miles
- Uses Both Frs And Gmrs Frequencies
- 22 Channels Each With 121 Privacy Codes For 2,622 Combinations
- 27 Hour Alkaline (3 Aa) Or 9 Hour Nimh Estimated Talk Time
- 10 Call Tones

- Vibracall® Vibrating Alert
- Backlit Display
- Noaa Weather Alert Feature
- Qt™ Interruption Feature
- Audible Low Battery Alert
- Keypad Lock
- Time-out Timer
- Priority Scan
- Ivox Hands-free Communication

Price: .... $60.00 (pair)

MOTOROLA T9500XLR TWO-WAY RADIOS

Similar to above but with 25-mile range and additional features.

Features:
- Talk on both FRS (Family Radio Service) and GMRS (General Mobile Radio Service), providing 22 channels each with 121 privacy codes
- Two watts of power allow the radios to transmit and receive signals from up to 25 miles away
- Power is automatically stepped down to a half-watt across FRS-only channels (2-mile range), enabling radios to talk to all existing FRS two-way radios
- Push-To-Talk PowerBoost™ increases transmission range on demand by boosting power output while talking but saves battery power on standby

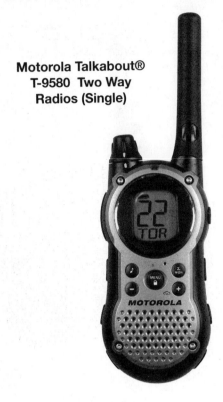

Motorola Talkabout®
T-9580 Two Way
Radios (Single)

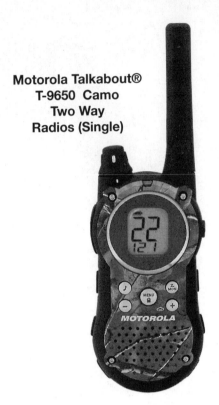

Motorola Talkabout®
T-9650 Camo
Two Way
Radios (Single)

- Companding technology digitally filters out static between words to deliver clearer communications
- Receives NOAA weather channels, offering coverage of all government-operated NOAA weather broadcasts, plus NOAA All Hazard Alert Radio
- Voice activation (iVOX) lets you talk hands-free when used with or without optional accessories
- Ten audible call tones
- LCD backlit display makes the radio easier to read in dark conditions
- Keypad lock prevents your personalized settings from being inadvertently changed
- Audible tone and visual display alert you when batteries are running down; Time Out timer automatically turns off radio
- VibraCall® alert is perfect in hushed or noisy places--vibrates to let you know someone is calling
- Includes NiMH batteries, dual drop-in charger, two quick-release swivel belt-clips and instruction manual

Price: $75.00

MOTOROLA TALKABOUT T9550XLR TWO WAY RADIOS WITH EARBUDS

The Talkabout T9550XLR has the same features and 25

mile maximum range of the T9500XLR, but includes camouflage faceplates and push-to-talk earbuds. The earbuds have a push-to-talk microphone and are a nice addition, giving you the ability to communicate quietly and discretely.

The Motorola T9550XLRCAMO two way radio is Motorola's most powerful consumer two way radio yet. The T9550XLR has a slightly longer antenna than previous Talkabout models, giving it a potential 25 mile maximum range in optimal conditions (typically 2 miles in urban conditions).

In addition to providing great range as a two way radio the Motorola T9550XLR is also a weather radio, supporting 10 NOAA weather channels. With the iVOX hands free feature the T9550-XLR acts as a speaker phone, allowing you to use your hands for other activities. Hands free (VOX) mode on this model works with or without an optional headset. The T-9550XLR also supports Motorola's VibraCall vibrating alert. With VibraCall, you can lower your radio volume and still ensure that you never miss a transmission.

Features:
- 22 Total Channels
- 25 Mile Range
- 7 FRS Channels
- 8 GMRS Channels
- 7 Shared FRS/GMRS Channels
- 121 Interference Eliminator Codes
- Uses 3 AA Batteries or Rechargeable Battery Pack

Newcon Nightwitness Night Vision Monocular

Newcon Phantom 150 Night Vision Monocular

- Rechargeable NiMH Battery Packs Included
- Includeds Dual-Pocket Desktop Charger
- NOAA Weather Channels
- VibraCall® Vibrating Call Alert
- Hands-Free (VOX) Mode
- Companding Feature
- 10 Call Alert Tones
- Interchangeable Face Plates
- Channel Scan
- QT Noise Filter
- Talk Confirmation Tone
- Backlit LCD Display
- Power Boost Option
- Battery Meter Indicator
- Audible Low Battery Alert
- Time Out Timer
- Keypad Lock
- Monitor Channel
- Keystroke Tone Signal
- Drop-In Charge Capable
- Audio Accessory Connector
- One Year Manufacturer Warranty

Price: $79.99

MOTOROLA T9580 SERIES FRS/GMRS RADIO PACK

The T9580 FRS/GMRS includes all the kit components and features of the 9500XLR and adds Same Area Message

Encoding (S.A.M.E.) that filters out weather alerts from distant locations and advises you of weather and emergency information only for the specific area you are in. Range up to 25 miles under good conditions with a PTT power-boost feature. 22 channels and 121 privacy codes for up to 2,662 communication options. It also has 11 NOAA weather radio channels, iVOX hands-free communication, a Quiet Talk™ interruption feature and digital signal processing. Backlit display, battery meter, low battery alert, keypad lock. Vibrating call alert, replacement faceplates, compress and expand audio technology. Comes with two radios, one dual drop-in charger, one charging adapter and two battery packs. Can also be powered by three AA batteries.

Price: $90.00

MOTOROLA T9650 RECHARGEABLE PACK, CAMO

- Similar to above but with following features:
- Up to 25 mile range
- 22 channels, each with 121 privacy codes for 2,662 combinations
- 27 hr. alkaline (3 AA) or 9 hr. NiMH estimated talk time
- iVOX hands-free communication without the need of an audio accessory
- QT (Quiet Talk) interruption feature
- 11 weather channels with alert feature
- Companding technology

Newcon NVS 14 Night Vision Monocular

Newcon Night Vision Goggles NVS7-2

- VibraCall vibrating alert
- Backlit display and LCD battery meter
- PTT Power Boost/Battery save feature
- Digital Signal Processing

Price: $82.00

NEWCON NIGHTWITNESS NIGHT VISION MONOCULAR

Compact lightweight NightWitness monocular is designated for low light observation & photo/video surveillance. It is the most versatile system for law-enforcement and rescue teams, professional photographers, coast guard, etc. Durable water - and corrosion-proof body made from light aluminium and titanium alloys guarantees long trouble-free operation. Replaceable humidity collector filled with desiccant improves its reliability substantially.

NightWitness is distinguished by its handy modular design along with an intelligent control system. It can be supplied in two versions as 1.25x and 5x scope. In addition, it can be equipped with wide variety of accessories like interchangeable professional lenses including Sigma, Canon, Nikon and other brands, and professional optical adapters for coupling with CCTV, photo and video cameras.

Price: ....N/A

NEWCON PHANTOM 150 NIGHT VISION MONOCULAR

This unit is designed to address any military, law enforce-

ment or other professional user requirements. Waterproof, lightweight and compact - this model is the most affordable generation 2+ system on the market. Opposite to many other competing devices, Phantom 150 utilizes only brand new image intensifiers. Camera/video adapter is included in the set, allowing recording of the viewed pictures.

Price: ....N/A

NEWCON NVS 14 NIGHT VISION MONOCULAR

Battle tested NVS 14 goggles can address any Military or Law Enforcement ability to observe the terrain under the darkest conditions. This model is in service with many militaries throughout the world. Extreme durability combined with unprecedented image quality support its impeccable reputation.

Two monoculars can be easily attached together. This quick installation transforms the system into fully operational dual channel goggles / binocular with true stereoscopic vision. Two possible types of standard batteries add flexibility to the device usage in field environment. Large variety of available accessories allows the unit usage with different types of helmets, as a night vision video / camera attachment, as a riflescope or as a 3x magnification night scope with an additional add-on lens.

The device is produced with either Gen. 2+ or Gen.3 Image Intensifier Tubes. It utilizes standard ANVIS size

**Newcon OPTIK 4X100
Night Vision Binoculars
NVS7-2**

Newcon MDN 12X40

tubes, thus allowing to source the tubes from several competing manufacturers.

Price: ....N/A

NEWCON MDN 12X40

World's first integrated Gen. 2+/3 Day/Night monocular makes life easier for those who want to use optics 24 hours a day: from bright sunny daylight through misty twilight to total darkness. Day/night integrated monocular combines a perfect clear daytime optics with advanced night vision image intensified technology.

Large fast lenses, coupled with high quality image intensifier tubes and wide field of view contribute to the best image possible. The built-in infrared illuminator allows observation under extremely dark conditions or even in total darkness. The device is very easy to use: you should just push a single slider to switch between day and night modes.

Ergonomic, lightweight, weather and shock proof, MDN 12x40 is the only compact and robust Day/Night device currently available on the market.

Price: ....N/A

NEWCON OPTIK 4X100 NIGHT VISION BINOCULARS NVS7-2

Battle tested NVS 7 binoculars are based on the popular NVS 7 goggles models. The 1x objective lens of the goggles is easily interchangeable. The personnel can use either goggles or binocular modification according to changing requirements.

All NVS 7 goggles models can be transformed into binoculars in less than a minute. The binoculars are supplied with either 4x or 8x magnification lenses. NVS 7 binoculars are powerful night vision devices suitable for battle, marine or rescue operations under the darkest conditions. NVS 7/4x is the smallest size and weight 4x binocular in its class without compromising the optical quality.

Specifications:
- Generation: 18 mm Gen. 2+
- Image Intensifier Tube modification (IIT) : NC064322
- IIT resolution, Lp/mm : 45-57
- Magnification : 4
- Interpipillary distance, mm : 57-73
- Field of view : 10 degrees
- Objective focal length, mm : 100
- Eye relief, mm : 25
- Focus range, m : .25
- Dioptric correction : +/- 5
- Objective F number : 1.5
- Power supply : 2 standard AA batteries
- Battery life, hours : Over 80 (Without I/R), Over 30 (With I/R)
- Low battery indicator
- I/R ON indicator

**Northrup Gruman
Andros FS6 Robot**

**Northrup Gruman
Andros HD1 Robot**

Northrup Gruman Remotec Wolverine Robot

**Northrup Gruman
Mini Andros II Robot**

**Northrup Gruman
Andros MKV-A1
Robot**

- Automatic shut-off in the up-rise position (optional)
- Waterproof 2 m, 2 hours
- Dimensions mm : 165x120x70

Price: $3500.00

NEWCON OPTIK NVS 14 MONOCULAR

The battle tested NVS 14 night vision goggle can address any military or law enforcement scenario by providing the ability to observe the terrain under the darkest conditions. Features such as extreme durability combined with unprecedented image quality support its impeccable reputation. The heart of this night vision monocular goggle is its high performance second generation plus XT intensifier with a specified resolution of 57-64 lp/mm. This tube ensures that your sight picture will be clear, sharp, and full of detail and contrast. This XT tube boasts a 50 percent longer lifespan over its HD counterpart. The advantages of higher resolution give you tactical supremacy through positive target acquisition.

Price: $3000.00

NORTHROP GRUMMAN REMOTEC ANDROS F6A ROBOT

The Remotec ANDROS F6A is the most versatile, heavy-duty robot on the market. Speed and agility unite to make it your first choice for a wide range of missions.

Features:
- Color surveillance camera with light, zoom, pan/tilt
- Surveillance camera with image stabilization - 216:1 total zoom (26x optical/12x digital)
- Stationary arm camera - 40:1 total zoom (10x optical/4x digital)
- 24-inch camera extender

Price: N/A

NORTHROP GRUMMAN REMOTEC ANDROS HD-1 ROBOT

Similar to above but with following features:
- 210° Shoulder Joint; 180° Wrist
- Color pan/tilt surveillance camera, 216:1 total zoom
- Color drive camera, B/W rear camera, arm mounted light
- 24-inch camera extender
- Up to 4 hours mission dependent
- 72" Max. Gripper Height

Price: .... N/A

NORTHROP GRUMMAN REMOTEC ANDROS MARK V-A1 ROBOT

The Remotec ANDROS Mark V-A1 is your highly stable, tough-as-nails partner for hazardous duty operations. First responders worldwide rely on this larger-than-life robot to

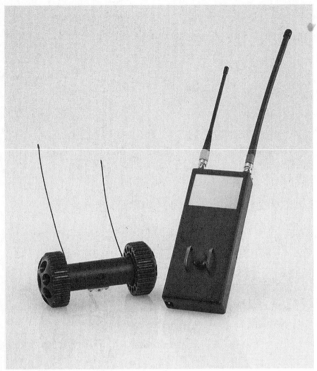

Recon Scout

Remington R1 Eyeball Remote Camera

help assure safe, successful outcome for their most challenging missions.

Features:

- Color surveillance camera with light, zoom, pan/tilt
- Surveillance camera with image stabilization - 216:1 total zoom (26x optical/12x digital)
- Stationary arm camera - 40:1 total zoom (10x optical/4x digital)
- Quick disconnect camera mount
- Multiple-mission tool/sensor mounts with plug-and-play capabilities
- Gripper with continuous rotate

Price: ....N/A

NORTHROP GRUMMAN REMOTEC WOLVERINE ROBOT

The Remotec ANDROS Wolverine is the workhorse robot that won't quit. This heavy-duty, all-terrain robot brings superior strength and manipulator dexterity to the longest, most intense missions.

Features:

- Color surveillance camera with light, zoom, pan/tilt, 216:1 total zoom (26x optical/12x digital)
- Manipulator arm with seven degrees of freedom ensures optional dexterity
- Single-module electronics for quick field replacement

- Switchbox for walk-along control
- Four, 12-volt batteries for extended run-time

Price: Not available

NORTHROP GRUMMAN REMOTEC MINI-ANDROS II ROBOT

The Remotec Mini-ANDROS II is a full-featured, entry-level robot for hazardous duty operations. This small package packs twice the functionality of comparable robots into an easily transportable, low-maintenance body.

Features:

- Two-meter telescoping arm with four degrees of freedom
- Color surveillance camera
- Two-way audio
- Fold-down 18-inch camera extender
- Single-module electronics for quick field replacement
- Quick free-wheel option
- Patented articulating tracks

Price: ....N/A

RECON SCOUT

The Recon Scout is your man on the inside. It's rugged, stealthy, mobile and unfailingly dependable, and it's designed to take whatever abuse the job demands.

Throw it through a window, over a wall, or down the stairs and it lands ready-to-go. You can even drop it from

Rotomotion SR200 UAV Helicopter System

Swatscope Periscope

an unmanned aerial reconnaissance vehicle. Once deployed, you can control its movement at a distance using a hand-held operator control unit. The Recon Scout helps you explore hostile or dangerous environments by providing real-time mission-critical reconnaissance video that enables your teams to act quickly, safely and decisively.

Features:

- Indoor range: 100 ft/30m
- Outdoor range: 300 ft/91m
- Speed: 1 fps/0.3mps
- Drop shock resistance: 30 ft/9.1m vertical
- Throw shock resistance: 120 ft/31.4m horizontal
  Length: 7.375in/187mm
- Shell Diameter: 1.5in/38mm
- Wheel Diameter: 3in/76mm Self-Balancer
- Length: 4in/102mm
- Weight: 1.2lb/544g
- Field of view: 60 degrees
- Framerate: 30 frames per second

Price: $6500.00

REMINGTON R1 EYEBALL REMOTE CAMERA

Remington's Eye Ball R1 is a compact wireless 360° mobile display system, designed to be used in tactical operations where law enforcement personnel need to see the situation before entering a building, floor or room. The Eye Ball R1 is rugged allowing officers to roll, toss, lower or throw it as applications demand.

The Eye Ball R1 transmits streaming video and audio to a Personal Display Unit (PDU). This intelligence is the basis for making the right tactical decision.

Features:

- Omni directional camera
- Near infrared illumination up to 8 meters
- Captures video up to 23 meters and audio up to 5 meters
- Transmits streaming video up to 125 meters from the Eye Ball R1
- Eye Ball R1 rotates 4 RPM and can be directed toward a specific target, capturing a 55° horizontal and 41° vertical field of view
- Eye Ball R1 is battery powered, operating time is 2 hours; standby mode up to 24 hours
- Wireless Transmission operating frequency: Audio & Video: 2.4 GHz; Control: 902-928 MHz

Price: .... N/A

ROTOMOTION SR200 UAV HELICOPTER SYSTEM

Remote-control video surveillance helicopter.

Features:

- 121cc 8.7 HP Gasoline 2-stroke Engine
- Up to 20kg /50 lbs Payload Capacity
- WAAS differential included
- Ready-to-Fly
- Safety/Manual Aircraft Controller & Transmitter

Tactical Electronics BWV1 Body Worn Video System

TAC-CAT Tactical Caterpillar

Tactical Electronics K-9MC Dog-Mounted Camera

- 802.11-based Telemetry System
- Stable hover (Patent Pending)

Price: ....N/A

SWATSCOPE PERISCOPE

The SWATSCOPE is the most economical and versatile surveillance device on the market today. It is is a high-quality, variable power, zoom, hand held periscope, with flashlight attachment capability, allowing the user a surveillance instrument that can also be used in the dark to clear buildings, attics, basements, etc.

The SWATSCOPE can be carried hands free with a belt hook and is stored, ready to use, in an aluminum protective case. The SWATSCOPE will keep you concealed and undetected. Made of a high quality aluminum alloy, highly polished glass prisms and glass lenses. The SWATSCOPE zoom lens has a magnification range of 4X to 9X.

The SWATScope provides a perfect tool to overcome issues with low walls and limited cover and concealment on roof tops and other structures used by Coalition Forces for observation in urban combat (windows, jersey barriers etc.

Price: $169.00

TAC-CAT TACTICAL CATERPILLAR

Protection Development (CA) designed the TAC-CAT for department use by EOD, Narcotics and SWAT teams. Armor upgrade comes with removable rear platform and 'bat' BR

shields which mount on rear left and right sides for sniper protection as unit advances. Roof mounted Haz-mat container (or roof escape hatch). Using the 'Claw' you can go through walls, see & record action on the other side. Roof mounted PTZ (26x optical zoom) camera gives a full 360 degree view of the area around the TAC-CAT. Record the surroundings as the TAC-CAT performs – from all cameras! Numerous tactical accessories available as well as transport trailer and custom storage rack for accessories.

Price: ....N/A

TACTICAL ELECTRONICS BWV1 BODY WORN VIDEO SYSTEM

The BWV2 Body Worn Video System is an officer worn system designed by the officer for the officer. This unit is complete with a belt pack recorder, chest controller / camera, and a head mounted camera; together, the three components are rugged enough to withstand daily punishment yet capable of capturing the high quality video needed for conviction.

When an officer needs to take action, the chest controller has a single push-button to begin recording. As a value-added feature, the chest controller also has a covert camera that automatically activates if the head camera is disconnected. This allows for a continuation of the recording should the officer become involved in a struggle.

The BWV1 belt pack houses the battery pack, recorder, video monitor, and playback controls. The BWV1 comes

Tactical Electronics HTC3
Helmet Camera

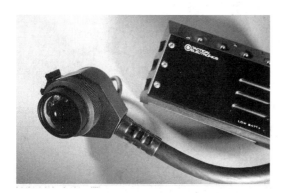

Tactical Electronics PCSS1
Pole Camera

Tactical Electronics HHIT1
Handheld Inspection Unit

with a rechargeable battery that will power the unit for 24+ hours on stand-by and over 8 hours of record time. Each unit includes a 4 GB SD card that will hold approximately 4 hours of high quality video. Each video file is time and date stamped; when the unit is recording, it can only be stopped by holding down two buttons on the belt pack simultaneously — this prevents any chance of an accidental shut-off of the recording.

Price: ....N/A

TACTICAL ELECTRONICS K-9MC DOG-MOUNTED CAMERA

The K-9MC is a compact lightweight camera that mounts to the hind quarters of dogs, thus allowing handlers to accurately see what the dog sees. The camera is an extremely low light, black & white camera that uses enhanced IR illumination to see in areas where most can't. The system was designed to record audio and video directly to the SD card, but the K-9MC1 also incorporates a wireless tranmitter that allows for the transmission of video up to one half mile LOS. The small housing assembly encompasses the wireless transmitter, battery compartment, and on-board DVR.

Price: ....N/A

TACTICAL ELECTRONICS HTC3 HELMET CAMERA

The HCT3 Helmet Camera gives operators a compact and versatile camera system that records and/or transmits exactly what the operator sees and hears, making it perfect for dynamic entry as well as sensitive site operations. The onbarod mini-DVR records video and audio to a 4GB SD card that is included with every unit. The new HCT3 has a combo mounting system which allows the user to choose between rail mount and velcro mount.

Price: ....N/A

TACTICAL ELECTRONICS HHIT1 HANDHELD INSPECTION UNIT

The HHIT1 is a lightweight, highly portable inspection tool that puts an extremely low light black and white camera into a system that is perfect for inspecting containers and rooms or looking around barriers. The HHIT allows the operator to view the picture in the attached eye-piece or transmit to any one of a variety of monitoring options.

Price: ....N/A

TACTICAL ELECTRONICS PCSS1 POLE CAMERA

The PCSS1 Wireless Pole Camera provides ultimate flexibility for tactical teams. The lightweight system has no cumbersome belt packs or external cables. Tactical Electronics Pole Cameras are used all over the world by various EOD and SWAT teams.

Price: ....N/A

Tactical Electronics UDC2 Under Door Camera

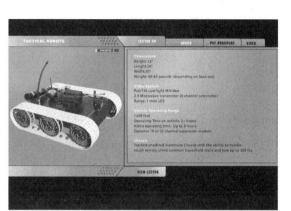

Tactical Systems Lector HD Heavy Duty Robot

Tactical Systems Lector Robot

TACTICAL ELECTRONICS UDC2 UNDER DOOR CAMERA

The UDC2 Wireless Under Door Camera delivers a wide field of view and unmatched light gathering capabilities. Other systems manipulate prisms and mirrors to send a video image through bundled fiber optic cable to an attached camera -- these methods immediately cut the light and the picture quality by 50%. We have mounted our camera chip in the distal tip of the insertion panel, which gives operators a clear view from inside the inspection area. The Under Door Camera is easy to transport weighing only 0.8 lbs.

Price: ....N/A

TACTICAL SYSTEMS LECTOR ROBOT

Tactical Systems announces the Lector robot for law enforcement. Tactical Systems Robotics delivers you the best live, real-time intel available. Our robotic systems are easy to operate, maintain and are affordable. Each system has been 'forged in the field' by use in actual tactical operations. These proven life saving tools are a must for any tactical unit.

Features:
- Dimensions: height: 7"; Length: 12"; Width: 12"
- Weight: 8 pounds
- Video System Pam/Tilt Low light IR Video

- 2.4 Microwave transmitter (4 channel selectable)
- Range: 700+ feet
- Vehicle Operating Range 300-750ft
- Operating time on vehicle: 1+ hour
- Video operating time: Approx. 2 hours
- Chassis Independant 4 wheel drive system
- Split chassis design

Price: ....N/A

TACTICAL SYSTEMS LECTOR HD HEAVY DUTY ROBOT

A heavy-duty, extreme service version of the above.
- Dimensions: height: 12"; Length: 26"; Width: 20"
- Weight: 40-65 lbs., depending on load
- Video System Pam/Tilt Low light IR Video
- 2.4 Microwave transmitter (4 channel selectable)
- Range: 1200 feet
- Vehicle Operating Range 300-750ft
- Operating time on vehicle: 2+ hour
- Video operating time: Approx. 8 hours
- Tracked anodized aluminum chassis
- Optional 16 or 32 channel expansion module
- Can climb household stairs
- Can tow 300 lbs.

Price: ....N/A

Index

TACTICAL LIGHTS

TACTICAL HANDGUNS

TACTICAL RIFLES

TACTICAL ELECTRONICS